AMERICA IN THE PACIFIC

A Century of Expansion

A Da Capo Press Reprint Series

THE AMERICAN SCENE
Comments and Commentators

GENERAL EDITOR: WALLACE D. FARNHAM
University of Illinois

AMERICA IN THE PACIFIC

A Century of Expansion

BY
FOSTER RHEA DULLES

Second Edition

DA CAPO PRESS · NEW YORK · 1969

A Da Capo Press Reprint Edition

This Da Capo Press edition of
America in the Pacific is an
unabridged republication of the second
edition published in Boston and New York
in 1938. It is reprinted by special
arrangement with Houghton Mifflin Company.

Library of Congress Catalog Card Number 73-86595

Published by Da Capo Press
A Division of Plenum Publishing Corporation
227 West 17th Street
New York, N.Y. 10011

Printed in the United States of America

AMERICA IN THE PACIFIC

BOOKS BY FOSTER RHEA DULLES

Harpoon: The Story of a Whaling Voyage

America in the Pacific

Eastward Ho!

The Old China Trade

AMERICA IN THE PACIFIC

A Century of Expansion

BY

FOSTER RHEA DULLES

Second Edition

BOSTON AND NEW YORK
HOUGHTON MIFFLIN COMPANY
The Riverside Press Cambridge
1938

The Riverside Press
CAMBRIDGE · MASSACHUSETTS
PRINTED IN THE U.S.A.

TO

HOWARD C. TAYLOR, Jr.

CONTENTS

INTRODUCTORY CHAPTER

RENEWED conflict between Japan and China has once again focussed world attention on the Far East. Whatever the outcome of this struggle, the international balance of power in the Pacific area as a whole will be profoundly modified. The political and commercial interests of the United States in this part of the world, built up through over a century of overseas expansion, are seriously threatened; the system of collective security whereby it had been hoped they could be peacefully maintained has collapsed. The vital need to re-examine our entire Far Eastern policy cannot be ignored on the specious grounds that the scene of Asiatic war is too distant to concern us directly.

Through its sponsorship of the Open Door in China and its attempts to safeguard Chinese territorial sovereignty, the United States has played an important rôle in Far Eastern affairs during the present century. It has again and again set itself up as the champion of China against the aggressive designs of Japan. Even though we have felt compelled to retreat upon almost every occasion when Japan has swung into action, our persistent opposition to the rising power of Japanese imperialism has been so pronounced that at recurrent intervals there has been widespread talk of the possibility of war between the two nations. But the basic causes for our attitude in respect to the status of China are not to be found in Secretary Stimson's declaration of policy in 1932, in the accords reached at the Washington Conference ten years earlier, or in the pronouncements of Secretary Hay in 1900. The nineteenth century holds the clue to the underlying policy which these declarations and treaties were supposed to implement.

At the close of the period of Pacific expansion traced in this book, a period which began with our first settlements on the western coast and reached a climax with the acquisition of the Philippine Islands in 1898, the United States exerted a commanding influence in the international relations of the Far East. It had established a Pacific Empire. When it formulated a new policy to protect the trade and commerce which had been the primary objective of its overseas advance, its voice was listened to with respect. It was able to take the lead, happily aided by the imperialistic rivalries of the European nations, in a program which it was optimistically believed at that time would solve 'the Chinese problem.'

Actually, the Open-Door policy had its genesis in our earliest relations with the Chinese Empire. The principle of equal privileges and equal opportunities for all nations trading with that country had been consistently upheld throughout our intercourse with the Chinese people. But the threatened partition of China in 1899 seriously endangered the observance of this principle by our commercial rivals. Then it was that, with possession of the Philippines acting as a lever to make our influence in Eastern Asia really felt, the United States specifically proclaimed that doctrine which is now associated with the name of Secretary Hay, and undertook to win for it international recognition.

This move served to avert any actual partition of China or the establishment of additional spheres of foreign influence in the troublous days of the Boxer Rebellion. But since 1900, the efforts of the United States to uphold the principle of the Open Door and Chinese territorial integrity have not succeeded. In the face of the continued assaults upon Chinese sovereignty on the part of Japan, a danger scarcely foreseen at the opening of the century, the Open-Door policy has become increasingly ineffective. The ambition of Japan to dominate China and to establish her political and economic supremacy in the Far East has proved a more potent force than our diplomatic support of Chinese independence.

As early as 1910, Theodore Roosevelt recognized the realities in this situation. In a letter to President Taft, he accepted the implications of what had become a basic conflict between American and Japanese policy in the Far East.

'I do not believe in our taking any position anywhere unless we can make good,' he told his successor; 'and as regards Manchuria, if the Japanese choose to follow a course of conduct to which we are adverse, we cannot stop it unless we are prepared to go to war, and a successful war about Manchuria would require a fleet as good as that of England, plus an army as good as that of Germany. The Open-Door policy in China was an excellent thing, and I hope it will be a good thing for the future, so far as it can be maintained by general diplomatic agreement; but, as has been proved by the whole history of Manchuria, alike under Russia and Japan, the Open-Door policy, as a matter of fact, completely disappears as soon as a powerful nation determines to disregard it, and is willing to run the risk of war rather than forego its intention.'

Some ten years after this pronouncement, growing tension born of Japan's aggressive policy toward China, and intensified by such factors as the proposed renewal of the Anglo-Japanese Alliance and the naval rivalry between the United States and Japan, constituted a new threat to the whole fabric of international relations in the Pacific area. To protect our interests against further Japanese encroachment and yet avoid such a crisis as that feared by Theodore Roosevelt, the Washington Conference was summoned to deal, not only with the immediate question of naval limitation, but with the whole problem of political power in the Pacific.

While it is more popularly known for the reduction of naval armaments which the major Powers agreed upon, its apparent settlement of political issues in the Far East was of the greatest importance. Through the accords signed in 1922, the United States, Great Britain, France, and Japan pledged themselves, in effect, to observe the *status quo* throughout the Pacific. In the Nine-Power Treaty there was definitely written into international law a joint undertaking on the part of the Powers to respect the sovereignty and territorial integrity of China, and to observe the principle of equality of opportunity throughout all Chinese territory for the trade and industry of every nation.

These agreements definitely superseded all previous notes and accords in regard to foreign policy in the Pacific area, and, in so far as the Open Door was concerned, made it finally clear that no special rights in Manchuria or any other part of China were recognized in behalf of Japan because of her geographic relation to China. The success of the Washington Conference appeared to represent the final triumph of American policy in the Pacific, not along the lines of complete supremacy in that ocean as envisaged by so many statesmen of the nineteenth century, but in the form of an international guaranty that the trade routes of the Pacific and the great potentialities of the Chinese market would be free and open to all nations.

In the face of what was thus hoped would prove to be a lasting and peaceful settlement of international rivalries in the Far East, Japan launched an attack upon Manchuria late in 1931. This sudden return to a far more 'positive' policy than that which had characterized Japan's attitude toward China prior to the Washington Conference meant a complete repudiation of the treaties to which Japan was a principal signatory. Imperialism was reborn. For the spirit of international co-operation which had been signalized by the Washington accords, Japan had substituted the sword.

For a time the Powers carefully refrained from any direct intervention in this new situation in the hope that the Japanese militarists responsible for the change of policy would be repudiated by their own people. But such hopes were futile. Japan proceeded to the conquest of all Manchuria. The later protests of the Powers were ignored and public opinion throughout the world was brazenly flouted.

In these circumstances the United States felt called upon to make a more pronounced statement of its position, and in line with our traditional policy in respect to the status of China, Secretary Stimson, early in 1932, addressed identic notes to the Japanese and Chinese Governments. Speaking in behalf of his own Government, he declared:

'That it cannot admit the legality of any situation *de facto*, nor does it intend to recognize any treaty or agreement between those governments, or agents thereof, which may impair the treaty rights of the United States in China, including those which relate to the sovereignty, the independence or the territorial and administrative integrity of the Republic of China, or to the international policy relative to China, commonly known as the open-door policy. . . .'

Secretary Stimson was actuated in this statement of policy by a desire to reaffirm the sanctity of international treaties and to make it abundantly clear that the United States still upheld the principle of respect for Chinese sovereignty. He hoped for such support from Great Britain as would serve to restrain Japan. But no move the United States has ever made in the politics of the Far East has more signally failed. It coincided with the movement in this country to grant the Philippine Islands their independence, and with this practical evidence of the lack of any popular support for aggressive action in the Pacific, Japan was not unduly concerned over any official protests confined to diplomatic notes. There was no faltering upon the course on which she had embarked. Creation of the puppet state of Manchoukuo, with the consequent closing of the Open Door in what had been Manchuria, symbolized Japan's defiance not only of the United States but of the entire Western World.

Our apparent acquiescence in Japan's program to establish paramount authority over North China, and the further breakdown of the Washington accords through Japan's abrogation of the naval treaty, marked the history of the Far East during the next five years. In the face of Japan's determined imperialism, the United States was helpless. For the time being at least, there was no will to protect our interests in Eastern Asia, however gravely they might be jeopardized, because it was recognized that they could be protected only by force. And the American people had no mind to run the risks of war in defense of interests whose importance they could not evaluate.

The renewal of the Japanese offensive against China, in the summer of 1937, consequently found the United States even less prepared than on former occasions to make any effective protest against this further violation of the treaties which had been framed to safeguard China's independence. And passage of the Neutrality Act appeared still further to tie our hands. Even though it had been adopted to meet another situation, and with complete disregard of its possible implications in the event of war in the Far East, it served as a further indication of the reluctance of the American people to become involved in foreign adventures.

However marked the American retreat since Japan first set out to win political and economic control of the Far East, it would nevertheless be foolhardy to conclude that the forces which made for our nineteenth-century advance in the Pacific are entirely spent. We no longer seek new commercial and naval bases. We have forsworn whatever ambitions we may once have harbored for absolute mastery of the Pacific. Our undertaking to grant the Philippines their independence, regardless of opinion as to their strategic value, stands as graphic proof that our nineteenth-century imperialism has run its course. But imperialism may revive in other shapes and forms.

Our failure to apply the Neutrality Act in 1937, upon the pretext that war was not officially declared between Japan and China, and the concurrent move to build up our naval strength in the Pacific, clearly demonstrate that the United States is not prepared to abandon completely its position in the Far East. The factors which led to establishment of that position are not easily dismissed. Even though the demands of trade may not be as insistent as they have been in times past, the strong hold which the markets of China have always had upon the American imagination is still important. The tradition that the United States is the champion of Chinese independence has not been entirely overthrown by our failure to uphold it. And the long record of expansion in the Pacific — Oregon, California, Alaska, Samoa, Hawaii, and the Philippines — reflects a conception of our ultimate destiny in the Pacific which cannot be reconciled with surrender to Japanese imperialism.

New York, *February*, 1938

CHAPTER I

Westward Lies the Course of Empire

IN THE exciting summer of 1898, which found the United States engaged in a war undertaken for Cuban liberty but destined to result in a territorial expansion which carried the American flag to the shores of Asia, an enthusiastic member of Congress took as the text of his imperialistic message the battle of Manila Bay. 'The booming guns of Dewey's battleships,' he proclaimed, 'sounded a new note on the Pacific shores, a note that has echoed and re-echoed around the world, and that note is that we are on the Pacific, that we are there to stay, and that we are there to protect our rights, promote our interests, and get our share of the trade and commerce of the opulent Orient.' [1]*

Subsequent events fully justified this statement, yet it was far from true that we had just arrived upon the Pacific or that we were newly determined to get our share of eastern trade. An ambition to win the mastery of the Pacific and control its rich commerce runs persistently through the entire history of the United States. It was a powerful motivating force in every acquisition of territory on the Pacific from Oregon and California to Hawaii and the Philippines. This is not to say that these instances of territorial growth can be neatly fitted into exactly the same pattern, but there is a thread of consistency in this expansion which draws our possessions together as component parts of a Pacific empire.

---

* All numerical symbols throughout the text refer to source references to be found in the bibliographical notes at the end of the book. They may be ignored by the reader not interested in source material.

The ambition to dominate the Pacific was first awakened by the old China traders whose ships discovered the Western Ocean for the seaports of the Atlantic Coast in the early days of the Federal period, and it was thereafter kept alive by a long line of statesmen who believed that in the Pacific rather than in the Atlantic lay the logical field for the expansion of American power and influence. In many ways our acquisition of the Philippines as an unexpected outgrowth of the war with Spain marked a new and radical departure in American policy, but viewed solely in the light of an extension of our influence in the Pacific it was the natural culmination of a doctrine whose roots were firmly embedded in the tentative advances toward Asia which we had been making for the past half-century.

The idea of actual territory even on the Pacific shore had matured slowly during the period which found the United States taking its place in the world as an independent nation. The western coast of the continent was separated from the Atlantic by so vast an expanse of desert and mountain that it was for long believed absolutely impossible that any settlement Americans might make on the Pacific could have political connections with the United States. Even that great expansionist Thomas Jefferson was convinced that any American colonies on the western coast would remain connected with us only by the ties of blood and interest.

It did not, however, take the development of modern communications to break down this theory. Nor did our interest in political power in the affairs of the Pacific wait upon the settlement of continental America. Just as the potentialities of the trade of the Far East had first awakened our consciousness in the existence of the Pacific, so did they lead us to assert our early claims to territory on the Pacific Coast. Even before the great trek across the plains to Oregon and California which cast such a romantic glamour over the eighteen-forties, a strong feeling developed that we should have to have ports and harbors which would enable us to forestall England's sinister conspiracy 'to fence us out from the Pacific Ocean, to belt us about, yet more closely, with her kingly despotism.'[2]

The propaganda in favor of occupation of the Pacific Coast, the diplomatic attempts to secure both Oregon and California, the first movement of settlers to the Pacific shore, were the answer to a national demand that we should assert our rights in the Pacific. They constituted, in the phrase of Frederick Jackson Turner, the historian of the frontier, 'a call to the lodgment of American power on that ocean, the mastery of which is to determine the future relations of Asiatic and European civilizations.'[3]

In the Congressional debates from 1820 to 1848 we hear again and again a note which was to be echoed half a century later, when it was not a question of controlling Oregon and California, but of winning Hawaii and the Philippines. In order to attain that naval and commercial ascendancy in the Pacific believed vital to our national growth, we had to have the naval bases which would enable us adequately to protect our interests, the ports which would lead to the full development of our trade, and the territorial outposts which in the hands of any other power would be a constant menace to our national security. In 1898 our appetites had grown, but there was a distinct similarity in the motives behind our annexation of the islands of the Pacific and those which first carried us to the Pacific shore.

With the overland movement of the middle of the century there was superimposed upon the desire for a commercial and naval hold upon the Pacific the agitation of the new settlers for the protection of the United States. The feeling grew up that the entire continent was ours by right. It was the era of 'Manifest Destiny.' And that phrase, first used in 1845 in a significant editorial which spoke of 'the right of our manifest destiny to overspread and possess the whole of the continent which Providence has given us for the development of the great experiment of liberty and federated self-government entrusted to us,'[4] symbolized the spirit of the age. Forces were at work which would have carried us to the Pacific had there been no desire to control its commerce.

It is not through oversight of the economic causes which led to settlement of the coast, of the desire for free land, or of the natural restlessness of the frontiersman symbolized by Daniel Boone's complaint against the damned Yankee who had settled down within one hundred miles of him, that so much emphasis is placed in this study upon the part played by our commercial interests in the Pacific. It has been stressed in order to demonstrate how two streams of national interest converged to bring about our expansion to the coast. We are interested in Oregon and California, not as examples of the conquest of the continent, but as the basis and point of departure for Pacific empire. The evidence which would show that this conception of the significance of our expansion to the coast was not foreign to the statesmen of the day has been consciously sought out.

President Polk, that determined expansionist whose aggressive policy won Oregon and California, was fully alive to the importance of the Pacific. His readiness to compromise with Great Britain on our claims in the Northwest provided we were assured of the ports we needed in Oregon, and his intense interest in acquiring San Francisco Bay, are conclusive evidence that a position in which we could dominate the Pacific, as well as the natural extension of our western boundaries, was his conception of 'manifest destiny.' The expansionists of that day seldom dwelt upon what Oregon or California themselves might mean to the United States. It was their reiterated theory that once established on the Pacific Coast, we would command the commerce of the East, and just so in 1898 did their imperialistic heirs contend that, given Hawaii and the Philippines, we would dominate this same trade.

With the triumph of the expansion movement in 1848, our national ambitions were not satiated as they might have been had a natural extension of our boundaries been our sole objective. For a young and aggressive nation a more openly imperialistic policy was perhaps inevitable.

We had a confidence in our powers and a faith in our institutions which admitted no limits. To some the next step seemed to be Canada or Cuba; others clung to the belief that the course of empire still pointed westward. Seward mounted the rostrum of the Senate to give his great panegyric on the future of the Pacific as the 'chief theatre of events in the world's great hereafter,' and proclaimed that our population was destined 'to roll its resistless waves to the icy barriers of the north, and to encounter oriental civilization on the shores of the Pacific.' [5] Commodore Perry, whose expedition to open up Japan was itself a tangible expression of our new ambition, recommended in his dispatches the acquisition of island colonies, and declared that it was self-evident 'that the course of coming events will ere long make it necessary for the United States to extend its territorial jurisdiction beyond the limits of the western continent.' [6]

These two men were far ahead of their time, yet their prophecies might conceivably have been borne out far sooner than they were had not the Civil War intervened to concentrate men's attention upon questions nearer home. And upon the conclusion of this struggle, domestic problems continued for more than thirty years to absorb our national energies. It was not that the idea of further consolidating our power in the Pacific was completely forgotten. Throughout this period the forces which were to be responsible for our second great advance into the Pacific were slowly gathering weight and creating a situation which prepared us to seize eagerly upon the unexpected opportunities presented by the war with Spain.

Nor should the progress actually made in developing our Pacific interests between the war with Mexico and that with Spain be ignored. Seward purchased Alaska to secure one more base on the Pacific, we asserted rights in the Samoan Islands which eventually led to the acquisition of American Samoa, and slowly but surely Hawaii was brought so closely under American domination that, when we finally annexed these islands, President McKinley was able to declare that this was not a change but a consummation.

Public discussion and Congressional debates on these developments indicate how clearly they were considered progressive links in a definite policy, even if it was pursued somewhat erratically and without full consciousness of where it was leading. Certainly the charge that we acquired our colonial possessions, as England has been said to have acquired hers, in a fit of absent-mindedness, is not warranted. Seward's supporters declared that the purchase of Alaska would serve to render our commercial and naval supremacy in the Pacific as complete as that of Great Britain in the Atlantic. The proponents of a naval base in Samoa dwelt upon the increasing importance of our trade in the Pacific and the imperative need for further protection of our interests in that ocean. The friends of Hawaiian annexation reiterated with a growing insistence the absolute necessity of our controlling those islands, and based their arguments on the same grounds as the early expansionists had urged the acquisition of ports in Oregon and California. In each of these instances of expansion there was, furthermore, another decisive motive. If we did not acquire the territory in question, it was urged, some other Power would, to the immediate endangerment of the position in the Pacific which we were slowly building up.

Another aspect of the gradual development of our Pacific empire after 1848 was that the party of expansion, whose imperialism had been somewhat colored by the desire of the 'slavocracy' for new slave states, was now in opposition. It was upon the Republicans, as the dominant political faction, that the responsibility fell for any further extension of our boundaries. With a complete reversal of their traditional rôles, the Democrats consistently resisted each advance which the Republicans, as successors of the Whigs, attempted to make. Whether this opposition to expansion, to entangling alliances, to an aggressive foreign policy, is thus shown to be a matter of political expediency rather than one of political conviction raises an interesting question.

The changed position of the two parties is illustrated both in the case of Hawaii and that of Samoa. Whereas the Democrats had first advocated annexation of the former islands, toward the end of the century they for a time blocked the Republicans' attempt to carry out their own policy. Also, in connection with our attitude toward Samoa, they first suggested a form of tripartite control which involved an alliance with Germany and Great Britain, but, when it was actually put into effect by the Republicans, they vigorously condemned it.

In fact, the advances and retreats in our Samoan policy, the warnings against foreign entanglements and the con- clusion of the tripartite treaty, the avowed determination to protect Samoan independence and the tenacious clinging to our rights in the islands, constitute a striking illustration of a recurrent characteristic of our whole foreign policy. Perhaps it is due even more to what appear fundamental inconsistencies in the American character than to changing party positions prescribed by political requirements. For it has always been difficult for the United States to know just where it stands, with principle ever warring against expediency, protestations of altruism denied by an aggres- sive nationalism. Just as in Hawaii and in Samoa we again and again forswore territorial ambitions and moved steadily toward ultimate control of those parts of the islands which we really coveted, so have we always decried imperialism while creating an empire and honored the ideals of peace while refusing to join the League of Nations or the World Court.

In any event, the slow and halting moves toward Pacific expansion which marked the period from 1865 to 1898 were the prelude to our advance to the very shores of Asia ushered in with the booming of Dewey's guns at Manila Bay. They supplied a precedent; they pointed the way. To any close student of American expansion they might have shown how unlikely it was that once the Philippines were in our hands, we would easily let them go. It was natural that we should hesitate and debate the question, as we had in every previous instance of expansion even though no such grave problems were raised as those in- cidental to the retention of the new colony. But given

Dewey's victory, our eventual action might have been foreseen, as indeed it was in Europe.   The devious path by
which President McKinley arrived at his decision to hold
the islands was an unconscious search for the moral justification with which our every act in international affairs
must be clothed, but whatever path he had followed, the
end would probably have been the same.

This was due not only to our tradition of expansion in
the Pacific, but to circumstances which made the imperialism of 1898 even more natural than that of 1848.   We had
in the former year reached a point in our development
where our energies demanded a new outlet and an aggressive foreign policy appeared the only way of satisfying national aspirations.   Other Powers were expanding, acquiring new territory.   There was a wave of imperialism in
Europe to which we were anything but immune.   Everywhere the proponents of expansion were refurbishing their
doctrine of 'manifest destiny' with far broader implications than would have occurred even to the most aggressive
of the expansionists of 1848.

Furthermore, the Pacific was still the logical field for
such activities.   It was the area to which we had always
looked for the assertion of our maritime power, the nations
of Europe were threatening the position we already held
there by an apparent intention to portion out China
among themselves, and as never before in our history the
markets of Asia seemed to represent the one outlet for a
country hard upon the heels of prosperity, but faced with a
mounting surplus of manufactured goods.   At the close of
the nineteenth century, the Pacific appeared to be in a good
way toward verifying Seward's prophecy that it would become the chief theater of events in the world's great hereafter.

'Within that great area,' wrote an English observer
whose comment is so apt that we cannot refrain from a
lengthy quotation, 'Britain, America, Russia, France, and
Germany are contending for supremacy in trade, if not for
advantages in territory; Japan is establishing her claim to
be ranked as a World Power; and China is awaiting a new

birth that will revolutionize the West as well as the East. Where seven empires meet is the battle-ground on which will be fought out the great racial struggle of the future, as well as the economic struggle of the present. Where Europe and America impinge on Asia, we behold already the beginning of a series of the most interesting problems known to human history....

'When she gathered Hawaii into the Federal fold, the American Republic precipitated herself into the Pacific arena of which she had hitherto held the gate on one side. When she sent her fleet to the Philippines, she committed herself to an international policy "at the gateways of the day," which she had previously only flirted with in Samoa, and had tried to commercialize in Japan. Henceforward, for good or evil, the United States takes her place among the nations as one of the Maritime Powers of the Pacific.'[7]

If there was to be widespread controversy and bitter debate before the United States could make up its mind to accept the full implications of the battle of Manila Bay and confirm the opinion of this British writer, it was because in the case of the Philippines the tradition of Pacific expansion came into conflict with other American traditions. In no other instance of the acquisition of new territory had there been any question of eventual settlement by Americans, or, to any vital extent, the problem of absorbing an alien population. But in addition to their distance from the American coast, the Philippines presented these two problems in the most serious possible form. Their annexation raised a new issue of imperialism and colonialism. Had the islands been sparsely inhabited by a race which definitely had no capabilities for self-government, or by a people anxious for union with the United States, even these hurdles might have been taken more easily, but the Filipinos were not uncivilized and they showed no desire for American rule. So it was that expansion clashed with democracy, and there developed a fundamental conflict between the imperialists and those who placed above the urge for national power the principle that government should depend upon the consent of the governed and believed that foreign colonies had no place in the American system.

It was a bitter conflict. The Democrats were ironically to declare that a nation could not exist half republic and half empire, while the Republicans, with principles no less lofty, called upon the nation to assume the burden of the Philippines for the sake of humanity. The imperialists had the advantage of urging a positive course of action. To our need for a naval and commercial base off the coast of Asia they could as usual add the decisive imperialistic argument that we had to hold on to the islands to prevent their falling into the hands of some national rival. They had on their side the restlessness of the period and the excitement engendered by war. They were able to point to the long record of our previous advance into the Pacific — the settlement of our western coast, the purchase of Alaska, the establishment of our authority in Samoa, the annexation of Hawaii.

They won the day. The defenders of those liberal and democratic principles upon which America itself had grown to greatness were routed. The public endorsed the policy which President McKinley had adopted and Spain's involuntary cession of the Philippines was confirmed. We took our place as an accepted World Power with a position off the Asiatic coast which gave us a new voice in the determination of the policies of the Far East, a new importance in the balance of power in the Pacific, and an even more vital interest than heretofore in any future developments either in the Pacific or in Eastern Asia which might threaten to upset the *status quo.*

To a coastline of over one thousand miles on that ocean's eastern shore, a vast territory in the north, an island possession in mid-ocean, and a naval base in the south, we had added a colony of 114,000 square miles and 7,000,000 inhabitants. Four of the most strategic harbors in the Pacific and two of its most productive island groups were now in our control.[8] Whereas at the opening of the nineteenth century the American flag was to be found in the Pacific only on the vessels of a handful of enterprising Yankee merchants, by its close it waved over a veritable empire.

CHAPTER II

Cape Horn Around

THE forces making for trade in the Pacific and those leading to empire converged on the Northwest Coast. Before
the first appearance of American ships, its rugged shoreline had been explored by several of the European Powers.
Russia had established a colony in what is now Alaska;
Spain, with her possessions in South America, Mexico, and
California, had gone so far as to assert vague claims to the
entire Western Ocean, and England had initiated a fur
trade between Oregon and Canton. The United States
was entering an already crowded field when in 1788 two
little trading vessels from Boston, the *Columbia* and the
Lady Washington, reached Nootka Sound, on Vancouver
Island, as unconscious harbingers of the Pacific empire
which was to come into being a century later.

These two ships were the belated answer to the impor-
tunities of a certain John Ledyard, traveler, visionary, and
enthusiast, who first brought to the United States reports
of the tremendous possibilities of Pacific trade. Although
an American, he had served as a corporal of marines on the
last voyage of the English explorer, Captain James Cook,
and had seen with startled eyes the rapacity with which
the Chinese merchants of Canton bought up the sea-otter
furs which he and his companions had casually collected
from the Indians of the Northwest Coast. 'Skins which
did not cost the purchaser sixpence sterling,' he wrote in
the account of his travels published in America in 1783,
'sold in China for 100 dollars.' ¹ Inspired by the vision of
such profits, he returned to this country as a self-appointed
apostle of a trade between Oregon and Canton in which
furs would be exchanged for China's teas and silks.

This early advocate of American commerce in the Far
East found little response to his schemes for extending our
trade. By every means in his power he tried to persuade

his countrymen to forestall a British monopoly in this new field of activity, but his ideas were everywhere greeted with skepticism. At one time he had Robert Morris, the financier of the Revolution, almost convinced of the importance of the Northwest, and this merchant did indeed send direct to Canton the first ship to carry the American flag to the Pacific, but no one would attempt the fur trade. Whereupon Ledyard left for Europe, still hugging his dream of trade and exploration in the Pacific Northwest, and attempted to find in England or France the support he had failed to win in America.

Disappointment still dogged his trail. A project planned with John Paul Jones, who was then in France, fell through on the eve of success; an expedition from England, on which he actually set out with his complete equipment 'two great dogs, an Indian pipe, and a hatchet,' was called back when his ship was at sea. Yet his trip to Europe had one result which was not without significance in the further development of American interest in the Pacific and particularly in the western coast of the continent whose eastern seaboard still represented the total of our territorial claims. For in Paris he met and discussed his plans with Thomas Jefferson, at this time our minister to France.

This statesman had already shown an interest in the Pacific Coast and in 1783 had suggested to General George Rogers Clark an expedition 'for exploring the country from the Mississippi to California.' [2] But there can be no question that the enthusiasm of Ledyard, who excitedly told Jefferson that he was dying with anxiety 'to be on the back of the American States, after having either come from or penetrated to the Pacific Ocean,' nourished the germ which was subsequently to evolve into the Lewis and Clark expedition.[3]

Even at this time Jefferson, whose comment on Ledyard was that he was 'a person of ingenuity & information,' but 'unfortunately he has too much imagination,' supported this erratic prophet of Pacific trade in a project for exploring the western coast of America by crossing over Siberia and then sailing from Kamchatka.[4] It came to nothing when Ledyard was arrested by the Russian authorities at Yakutsk, on the river Lena, and politely but expeditiously escorted back to the Polish border, but Jefferson never lost interest in the plans he and Ledyard had discussed.

In the meantime the seeds Ledyard had planted in his talks at home with the merchants of New York and Boston began to grow, and when the publication of Captain Cook's journals confirmed everything he had said upon the possibilities of trade between Oregon and Canton, a group of Bostonians at last had a change of heart. They decided to dispatch an expedition to the Pacific Northwest and the *Columbia* and the *Lady Washington* reached Nootka Sound, by one of history's poignant ironies, in the very year in which the original promoter of their voyage was dying a disappointed man on a new exploration in Africa.

It was also a year in which unexpected clouds were gathering in the Pacific which almost precipitated a European war. The rivalry of England and Spain over their rights in this ocean came to a head in 1789, and in the presence of the two little American ships off Vancouver Island there was played the first act in a drama which had immediate repercussions in all the chancelleries of the Old World. A Spanish expedition, finding British ships in territory to which Spain believed its title to be all-inclusive, promptly seized the trespassers and placed the English seamen under arrest.

When word of this outrage reached London, William Pitt prepared for war. England was ready to challenge by force of arms Spain's pretensions to control of the entire Pacific Coast. For a time peace hung in the balance and it was only because Spain could not count upon French support that hostilities were averted. Forced to compromise, the Spanish Government thereupon reached an agreement with England in the Nootka Sound Convention whereby the subjects of both countries were to be allowed free navigation of the Pacific and the right to establish settlements on the coast in places not already occupied by either Power.[5]

No attention was paid to the two American ships in Nootka Sound during this controversy and no one consulted the United States as to rights of navigation, trade, or settlement on the Western Ocean. Nor could the commanders of these two trading vessels, interested only in the commerce which was the objective of their long voyage, have any conception of the rôle their country was one day destined to play in the affairs of the Pacific. They were passive spectators of events beyond their control. Yet there was one Spanish official, the Viceroy of Peru, who saw more clearly the portent in the presence of the *Columbia* and the *Lady Washington* on the Northwest Coast and looked into the future more prophetically than had even Ledyard or Jefferson.

'We should not be surprised,' this official reported to the Spanish Minister of Foreign Affairs, 'that the English colonists of America, republican and independent, are putting into practice the design of discovering a safe port in the South Sea and trying to hold it by traveling across the immense territory of this continent above our possessions in Texas, New Mexico, and California. Much more wandering about may be expected from an active nation, which bases all its hopes on navigation and trade; and in truth it could hold the riches of Great China and of India, if it succeeds in establishing a colony on the western coasts of America.' [6]

It was, nevertheless, to be some time before the United States itself had any such conception of its possible destiny. The merchants of Boston responsible for the voyage of the *Columbia* and the *Lady Washington* were interested solely in the fur trade, and on the success of their venture — for the *Columbia* returned to its home port with a rich cargo of China goods which had been collected in Canton in exchange for sea-otter skins bought from the Indians of the Northwest — they prepared to send out additional vessels without any thought of possible colonies in Oregon. In the next season five ships sailed for the Pacific Coast; within a decade otter furs worth half a million were being taken to Canton every year; but still no move was made to plant the American flag on the Pacific shore.

The Northwest traders were accustomed to spend one or more seasons cruising along the coast, occasionally putting into its many bays and inlets, waiting for the Indians to bring them furs. They would then barter for the rich and glossy pelts of the sea otter, so highly prized by the Chinese, from their stores of miscellaneous goods and trinkets, muskets, blankets, and iron chisels. During the period in which this trade was at its height, immense profits could be garnered by these methods. The value of the articles bartered for the furs was almost infinitesimal in comparison with that of the tea and silks and chinaware for which the skins could be exchanged in Canton, and when a cargo of China goods was in turn sold in the United States many a shrewd Yankee trader found that his voyage had netted him a tidy fortune.

It was not a commerce in which everything was as clear sailing as this might seem to indicate, however. Not always were the Indians willing to trade. They were a cruel and treacherous lot and the Nor'westmen had to be on constant guard against unexpected attack and eternally vigilant to forestall any attempt on the part of the savages to seize their vessels and massacre their crews. Trade was conducted with cannon loaded, the seamen armed with muskets and cutlasses, and boarding-nets strung up to prevent too many of the Indians from getting aboard ship at one time. It was a hazardous business in which the possibility of great profits was counterbalanced by the ever-present danger of total loss of both vessel and cargo.

Many a tale of narrow escape from capture and massacre was brought back to Boston by the Yankee traders; occasionally there were reports from survivors of Indian treachery which gave harrowing accounts of comrades butchered in cold blood. There was, for example, the destruction in 1802 of the ship *Boston*, and the massacre of all but two of her crew. One of these survivors has left a record of his experiences in which he tells of being dragged out from his hiding-place in the hold to find lying on the deck in a grisly row the heads of the vessel's captain and twenty-five of his fellow seamen. There were not many cases of such complete disaster, but the Northwest fur trade never outgrew its hazards.[7]

It was perhaps the character of the Indians, who were churlish and unfriendly when not actually treacherous, which was responsible for the slow growth of the idea of settlement on the coast. But the rocky shore of Oregon was also dour and forbidding, the deep forests stretching back inland somber and uninviting. It is really surprising that the project of an American colony materialized as soon as it did; and even more unexpected to find that one of the earliest traders had some vague idea of Oregon's future.

This was Captain John Kendrick, of the *Lady Washington*, who remained on the coast after the *Columbia* had completed her voyage and returned to Boston. 'The passing two-penny objects of this expedition,' wrote John Hoskins, the young clerk of the *Columbia*, 'were swallowed up in the magnitude of his Gulliverian views. North-East America was on the Lilliputian, but he designed N.W. America to be on the Brobdingnagian scale.'[8]

As proof of his belief that some day Oregon would become an outpost of American civilization on the Pacific, he made extensive purchases of land from the Indian chiefs and endeavored to secure legal title to them. Deeds of sale were carefully drawn up, registered at the American consulate in Canton, and sent home in duplicate to Thomas Jefferson for the archives of the State Department. One tract of land eighteen miles square was bought for 'two muskets, a Boat's sail and a quantity of powder'; another, nine miles round, for 'two muskets and a quantity of powder.'[9] Not overgenerous on Captain Kendrick's part, perhaps, but nevertheless prices which compare very favorably with the beads and trinkets traded for Manhattan Island.

Unfortunately, the sequel to this episode in Northwest history did not have a happy ending. Captain Kendrick was killed long before his dreams of Oregon's development were realized, the deeds to his property disappeared, and, although in later years the question was brought up in Congress, no member of his family ever profited from his phenomenal foresight.

The primary importance of the fur trade was that it forged the first links between the United States and the Pacific Coast. One of these was the discovery in 1792 by Captain Robert Gray, in the *Columbia*, of the great river of the Northwest to which he gave the name of his vessel; another was the establishment of a trading center at that river's mouth by John Jacob Astor some twenty years later. Together with the Lewis and Clark Expedition, these events constituted the basis for our original claim of title to the Oregon country.

From the time of the earliest explorations in the Pacific, the existence of a large river somewhere on the northern coast of America had been known, and in the seventeenth century it was widely believed that it led into the Straits of Anian, a legendary Northwest Passage joining the waters of the Pacific and the Atlantic. But none of the successive voyagers along the coast had been able to discover the mouth of this mysterious river. When, in the years just before the *Columbia's* voyage, Spanish and English explorers were cruising more carefully along the Oregon shore, Nootka Sound, Juan de Fuca Straits, and other bays and inlets were visited, but the Columbia still proved elusive. Several of these navigators sighted the breakers which guarded its mouth, but, never dreaming that navigable waters lay beyond them, did not take the risk of further exploration. In the very year of the *Columbia's* voyage, Captain George Vancouver had such an experience, only to note in his journal that 'not considering this opening worthy of more attention, I continued our pursuit to the N.W.' [10]

Greater daring rather than mere chance consequently led Captain Gray to find the long-sought river leading into the interior of Oregon. Where other seamen had hesitated to risk their vessels, he sailed with that fine disregard of danger which characterized the voyages of the Yankee Nor'westmen.

'At eight, A.M., being a little to windward of the entrance of the Harbor,' reads the memorable entry in the *Columbia's* log for May 12, 1792, 'bore away, and run in east-north-east between the breakers, having from five to seven fathoms of water. When we were over the bar we found this to be a large river of fresh water, up which we steered.'[11] Had Captain Gray not dared to run these breakers, which have since cost the lives of many seamen, or had Captain Vancouver or some other English explorer done so, the whole course of history in the Pacific might have been changed. Discovery of the Columbia gave the nation under whose flag it had been made a first claim upon the territory drained by the river and its tributaries, and in subsequent years, when our rights in Oregon were in dispute with Great Britain, Captain Gray's exploit stood us in good stead.

Belief in the practicality of a trading-post on the Columbia was as old as its discovery — 'this River in my opinion wou'd be a fine place for to set up a *Factory*,' wrote the *Columbia's* fifth mate, John Boit, Jr.[12] — but before Astor's venture in 1811 only two half-hearted attempts seem to have been made to establish one. Our scant knowledge of the first of these settlements has only recently come to light, but it appears that a mysterious Jeremy Finch led a party of Americans overland in 1807, after the return of the Lewis and Clark Expedition, to set up a military post on the Columbia and occupy the surrounding country. Just what happened to these pioneers is not known, but their presence in the Northwest is attested by the reports of the British fur traders who were already resentful of this evidence that the United States might intrude upon a domain which they had hoped to secure for themselves.[13]

The second attempt at settlement is better known, but it had no more permanent results. The Winship brothers of Boston, for long traders on the coast, tried in 1810 to establish a headquarters on the Columbia to which the

Indians would be able to bring their furs. They planned
to build a log fort beside the river and clear enough ground
to raise crops, but they had hardly begun to make any
progress with their venture when the Indians showed un-
mistakable hostility to the white intruders. To the great
disgust of the hopeful settlers, who deeply felt the humilia-
tion of being obliged 'to knuckle to those whom you have
not the least fear of, but whom, from motives of prudence,
you are obliged to treat with forbearance,' it was consequently decided to abandon the undertaking.[14] Friendly
trade could not be promoted if the Indians resented their
presence, and the Winships felt forced to forego their
sanguine hope 'to have planted a Garden of Eden on the
shores of the Pacific, and made that wilderness to blossom
like a rose.' [15]

It was the very next year, however, that the shrewd,
hard-headed New York fur merchant, John Jacob Astor,
whose resources enabled him to undertake settlement on
the Pacific Coast on a far grander scale than could either
Finch or the Winships, succeeded where his predecessors
had failed. He planned, as he was later to write to John
Quincy Adams, to establish a permanent dépôt on the
Columbia for the assembling of furs and then to provide
further facilities 'for conducting a trade across the continent to that river, and from thence, on the range of the
northwest coast, &c., to Canton, in China, and from thence
to the United States...' [16] Thus our first actual settlement
on the western coast, forerunner to the occupation of both
Oregon and California, was directly linked to trade in the
Pacific and the development of the markets of the Far
East.

The establishment of Astoria, as the new settlement was
called, was carefully planned, but it received no official
support from Washington. Even though Lewis and Clark
had by now opened up the overland trail to the coast, Oregon was still too distant from the Atlantic seaboard for it
to seem very real or important to anyone other than the
fur merchants of Boston and New York. The Louisiana
Purchase had left us with an indefinite western boundary,

but it was impossible to believe that the United States could ever actually extend its frontier to the Pacific. We have seen how keen an interest Thomas Jefferson had in every phase of Western exploration and he wrote to Astor enthusiastically about his project, expressing the hope that some day American colonies would be established the length of the Pacific Coast, but it was at this time that he stated his conviction that any such colonies should be 'unconnected with us but by the ties of blood and interest.' [17]

Astor, however, had the broad vision of an empire-builder and went ahead undeterred. After organizing the Pacific Fur Company, he sent out two parties to the Columbia. One group followed the overland trail of Lewis and Clark and succeeded in reaching the coast despite almost incredible hardship and suffering; the other took the more familiar route about Cape Horn, and after their full share of mishaps and misfortunes reached their goal in the ship *Tonquin*. Soon thereafter, on the edge of that impenetrable forest of gigantic pine which lined the Columbia's banks, the settlement of Astoria slowly arose. A log fort, several warehouses for furs, living quarters for the settlers, constituted the first American outpost on the Pacific, significant augury of a future not even Jefferson could foresee.

Affairs at Astoria never went too well. The settlers almost immediately found themselves facing the competition of British fur traders who had come overland from Canada and were endeavoring to monopolize the trade of the interior, while a tragic disaster overwhelmed their attempt to trade along the coast. The *Tonquin* was sent on a northward voyage from which it never returned, and not until some time later did the Astorians learn that it had been attacked by Indians and its entire crew treacherously massacred. Furthermore, there were internal dissensions among the partners in the enterprise which boded no good.

These troubles seemed to reach a climax when a party of Britishers, representing the Northwest Fur Company, brought to Astoria the ominous news of war between

England and the United States. They also reported that Great Britain had dispatched a sloop-of-war to capture Astoria and then proceeded to settle down and wait until the settlement should be delivered into their hands.

The Americans did not know what to do. They felt themselves to be completely isolated, without any possibility of government support and with a strong probability that the war would break off all communications with Astor. Consequently they lent a welcome ear to the suggestion of the British traders that they sell out their interests to the Northwest Company and surrender their post rather than await the arrival of the British sloop and the forcible seizure of Astoria and all their property. More determined leadership in the American colony might have led to the adoption of a bolder course, but it was not forthcoming, and so with rather questionable loyalty to Astor's interests the settlers decided to meet their rivals' terms. In a complete capitulation the Astorians turned over their fort, their trading-station, and their furs to the Northwest Company, and when the British sloop actually arrived at the Columbia, it found its work already done. The Union Jack waved over a post which had been rechristened Fort George and Astor's far-sighted scheme to plant an American outpost on the Pacific had apparently failed.[18]

Fortunately for the United States, this was not the last chapter in Astoria's history. Even though the Government had no direct concern in Astor's project, nothing could so arouse its interest as English interference. It had no intention of allowing a settlement established on American initiative to slip so easily into the control of a rival nation. Consequently the peace negotiated at the close of the War of 1812 provided for the return of the territory England had seized during the hostilities and President Madison specifically instructed the American commissioners at Ghent that Astoria should be included in this category. 'It is not believed,' he wrote, 'that they [the British] have any claim whatever to territory on the Pacific Ocean.' [19]

The British commissioners raised strenuous objections to this demand, but upon American insistence they were forced to grant it. It was agreed that Astoria should be restored, and in 1818 a naval officer was dispatched to the Columbia to accept the fort's formal transfer. Astor did not again take up his project because the Government still refused to grant him military support and all his properties remained in the possession of the Northwest Company. England was returning only the empty shell of a settlement which had once seemed to have such great possibilities. Nevertheless, the American flag still waved on the Pacific shore. A victory in principle had been won; what rights we had on the Columbia had been preserved.

In the negotiations at Ghent no attempt had been made to reach an understanding on the general title to the Oregon country, which was then held to comprise that section of the continent lying west of the Rockies between Russian America on the north and California on the south, but this question was soon definitely raised. Both the United States and Great Britain set forth claims in the ensuing negotiations held in 1818 which were to remain substantially the same for thirty years. England declared its title to Oregon rested upon the voyages of discovery made by Cook and Vancouver and on the overland explorations of Alexander Mackenzie who had discovered the Fraser River in 1793; the United States asserted its rights on the basis of Captain Gray's discovery of the Columbia River, the Lewis and Clark Expedition, and the settlement of Astoria.

Here was a definite conflict of interests in which each nation could make out a good case for its own position and neither country was willing to surrender its rights. But the time had not yet come when they were prepared to press them very insistently. Both England and the United States were thinking of the fur trade rather than territorial possession, and consequently a compromise was adopted. It was agreed that for ten years the two countries would hold jointly all territory between the possessions of Russia and Spain which lay 'westward of the Stony Mountains.' [20]

It was thus as a corollary to our commercial interests in the Pacific and our fur trade with China that we first staked out our claim to Oregon. In reporting on the agreement they had reached in regard to this territory beyond the Rockies, our boundary commissioners definitely reflected the American attitude at that period. 'We did not know with precision what value our Government set on the country to the westward of those mountains,' Rush and Gallatin wrote Adams, 'but we were not authorized to enter into any agreement which would be tantamount to an abandonment of the claim to it.' [21]

While these events were building up a substantial American interest in that section of the Pacific Coast which now includes the States of Oregon and Washington, our trade in the Western Ocean had also drawn attention to territory farther south which constituted the Spanish province of California. This inviting country was not, like the Columbia Valley, open to trade and settlement. Spain's title admitted of no doubt. Yet from the very first the pioneers in the trade of the Pacific looked upon California with hungry and envious eyes.

It was visited and its coastline explored in the hunt for sea-otter furs. As the supply to the north gradually dwindled, the American traders inevitably crept farther south, and, despite all of Spain's strict regulations against her subjects' engaging in foreign commerce, open smuggling was soon under way along the southern shore from Santa Cruz to San Diego. The *Otter*, Captain Ebenezer Dorr, of Boston, is said to have been the first American vessel to visit California, putting into Monterey in 1796.[22] It was soon followed by other Yankee ships, and in the first decade of the next century a profitable if illegal trade was flourishing in which the Americans exchanged specie and manufactured goods for the otter furs which were collected for them by Indians and Spanish settlers.

The usual practice of the Yankee seamen was to corrupt the Spanish guards at whatever ports they visited and thereafter trade perfectly openly. Occasionally this method failed and the result would be an open clash with authority. Captain George Washington Eayrs had his ship confiscated and was himself arrested at Santa Barbara, while Captain Richard Cleveland met a similar threat at San Diego by fighting his way out of the harbor with his contraband cargo intact.   As the latter wrote in the story of his adventurous voyages, the choice with which he was presented 'was that of submission, indignant treatment and plunder; or resistance and hazarding the consequences.' [23] Naturally it did not take a Yankee seaman of this period long to decide which course he should follow.

Away from the ports the Americans found their welcome to be more than hospitable.   For the scattered ranches and mission stations the arrival off the coast of an American vessel was an event to which both *rancheros* and *padres* eagerly looked forward.   It was virtually their one contact with the outside world.   Official regulations in regard to trade were completely ignored and to their mutual profit and pleasure the Spanish and the Americans exchanged furs and fresh supplies of beef, hogs and grain, for such articles as shoes, hardware, crockery, cotton, silk, pepper and spices.

As time went on, this traffic in furs was superseded by the hide trade and the ties binding New England with the distant Spanish province were drawn still more closely. From San Diego north the hills and valleys of California were covered by great herds of cattle, offspring of those brought to the West by the first Spanish explorers, and in selling hides and tallow to the American traders the Californians were able to secure all that they needed in their easy and indolent life.   The skins were stacked in huge piles at certain specified points along the shore, and when an American ship arrived, it was left to its crew to load them while the Californians went aboard the vessel, turned for the time being into a general store, to select from its miscellaneous cargo those articles which they wished in exchange for the skins.   Not until a period considerably later than that with which we are immediately concerned did this hide trade become important, but it falls within the history of our contacts with California by sea rather than by land.   'Through the hide and tallow trade, more than through any other agency,' one historian of California has asserted, 'New England began her expansion to the Pacific Coast.' [24]

To all these American visitors California seemed almost unbelievably attractive and inviting. Especially after the rugged coast and often harsh weather of Oregon, the climate and fertility of the Spanish province gave it the aspect of a promised land. Moreover, these Yankee seamen soon acquired a fine scorn for Spanish authority as they realized how slight a hold Spain held upon her province and saw how lax and easy-going were all the officials. In their eyes California was entirely too pleasant a country to remain indefinitely in the possession of a Power which valued it so lightly, and long before there was any move toward American settlement within its borders, we find these traders vaguely contemplating the action which the United States was eventually to take.

'The conquest of this country would be absolutely nothing,' sighed William Shaler, who traded along the coast in 1810 with Captain Cleveland: 'it would fall without effort to the most inconsiderable force.' [25] Some years later, Richard H. Dana, Jr., whose 'Two Years Before the Mast' gives such a picturesque account of the hide trade, significantly declared: 'In the hands of an enterprising people, what a country this might be!' [26] And even more specific was Benjamin Morrell, Jr., whose observations convinced him that if California were a possession of the United States 'the eastern and middle states would pour into it their thousands of emigrants, until magnificent cities would rise on the shores of every inlet along the coast, while the wilderness of the interior would be made to blossom like the rose.' [27] A pleasing echo of the Winships' dream for Oregon!

If the United States learned of California, as it had learned of Oregon, through the enthusiastic reports of the Pacific traders, so did the threat of aggrandizement by a foreign Power serve to accentuate this interest. In the case of Oregon the seizure of Astoria by Great Britain had

set in motion the Oregon controversy; in California encroachments from quite a different quarter aroused our
first apprehensions. With Spanish control of the province
we had no quarrel, but when it appeared possible that
Russia might establish herself in California, the United
States felt it had to be on guard to protect its own interests.

It was before the establishment of Astoria that the ambitious Russian colonizers in Alaska began to consider
expansion farther south. They had their eyes on Oregon;
they also looked longingly at California. When the
Czar's chamberlain, Nikolai Rezanof, visited the Pacific
Coast in 1805 and endeavored to obtain at some southern
port provisions for the almost starving Russian colony at
Sitka, 'political reasons led to the choice of St. Francisco.'
His romance there with the daughter of the Spanish commandant may have served still further to increase his
interest in California, but in any event he was soon contemplating plans which would allow Russia 'to make use
of any favorable turn in European politics to include the
coast of California in the Russian possessions.'[28]

Six years later, a start was made toward putting his
policy into effect by settlement. With the avowed purpose of developing a source of supplies for their more
northern colony, the Russians established a post near
Bodega Bay, some forty-eight miles north of the present
San Francisco, to which they gave the name of Fort Ross.
Spain protested, but nothing further was done, and the
hundred-odd Russian colonizers built up their settlement
without any interference on the part of the native Californians.

The first official word of this surprising development was
sent to the United States in 1818 by the naval officer, J. B.
Prevost, who had been authorized to accept England's surrender of Astoria. He viewed the Russian activities with
distinct apprehension.

'The port of St. Francis,' he wrote, 'is one of the most
convenient, extensive, and safe in the world, wholly without defence, and in the neighborhood of a feeble, diffused,
and disaffected population. Under all the circumstances,

may we not infer views as to the early possession of this harbor, and ultimately to the sovereignty of all California? Surely the growth of a race on these shores, scarcely emerged from the savage state, guided by a chief who seeks not to emancipate but to enthrall, is an event to be deprecated — an event, the mere apprehension of which ought to excite the jealousies of the United States, so far at least as to induce the cautionary measure of preserving a station which may serve as a barrier to northern aggrandizement.' [29]

For a time his warning was not heeded in Washington. Yet our interest in the Pacific was growing. The agreement with England over Oregon was evidence of our claim to the Northwest, and in 1819 the treaty by which Florida had been ceded by Spain also provided for the extension of the boundary between American and Spanish possessions beyond the Mississippi as far west as the coast. Through this pact the United States fell heir to whatever claims Spain might have asserted to territory north of California, and John Quincy Adams, who as Secretary of State was responsible for this agreement, rightly considered it one of the most important provisions in the treaty. 'The acknowledgement of a definite line of boundary to the South Sea,' he confided to his diary, 'forms a great epocha in our history.' [30]

What finally aroused American determination to check any further Pacific advance upon the part of Russia, however, was an imperial ukase of 1821 which declared that the North Pacific from Bering Straits to the fifty-first parallel was henceforth to be closed to trade or navigation by the vessels of any Power other than Russia. Taken in conjunction with the settlement in California, this seemed to leave no doubt as to Russian ambitions on the Pacific Coast. Adams now acted promptly and energetically. The Russian minister at Washington was told for the information of his Government that 'the United States would contest the right of Russia to any territorial establishment on the American continent, and that they would distinctly assume the principle that the American continents were no longer subjects for any new European colonial establish-ments.' [31]

When, as a result of other developments in regard to possible European intervention in South America, it was decided by President Monroe to make a definite announce-ment of American policy, this warning to Russia on non-colonization was reaffirmed in more general terms. The first part of the Monroe Doctrine, as this clearly shows, was distinctly framed as an answer to Russian encroach-ments in California and possible designs on other parts of the Pacific Coast. It achieved its immediate objective al-most at once. Russia accepted our policy and the next year a treaty was signed fixing the southern limit of Rus-sia's possessions in North America at the present line separating Alaska and British Columbia.

Through three treaties negotiated in the first quarter of the nineteenth century we had thus set up certain rights to the Pacific Coast. The agreement with Russia estopped the Czar from extending his influence beyond what is now Alaska, that with Spain confined her possessions on the coast to Mexico and California, and finally the treaty with England pro-vided that the territory between Russia on the north and Spain on the south should be held jointly by England and the United States for ten years. It was not that we yet actually felt the need for a Pacific shoreline, but that we were determined that no other Power should acquire such influence on the coast that we would be permanently barred from it. If our maritime activity in the Pacific had not altogether persuaded us that we should ever expand to the extreme limits of the continent, it had convinced us that we could not afford to allow any other country to endanger our rights. There was already at work that motive of jealous protection of our political and com-mercial interests which was to prove more responsible than any other single factor for our future expansion.

CHAPTER III

The Overland Trails

BETWEEN the conclusion of the treaties first reserving our rights on the Pacific Coast and those which actually established our ownership of Oregon and California, there intervened little more than two decades. During this comparatively brief period the overland movement — first a thin stream of trappers and fur traders, then an irresistible wave of land-hungry emigrants — advanced our continental frontier to its westernmost limits. To the desire for an outlet upon the Pacific in the interests of trade and commerce were added the imperative demand of the settlers on the coast for American protection and an aroused, nation-wide feeling that our 'manifest destiny' unmistakably pointed to expansion to the coast whatever might be the claims or rights of any other Power.

Even before these new forces came into play, however, possible occupation of the Columbia Valley was presented to Congress. Representative John Floyd of Virginia introduced in 1821 a bill providing for government land grants in this area, the appointment of Indian agents, the establishment of local government, and the designation of an official port of entry. After some four years of periodic debate, the House accepted Floyd's program, but it was defeated in the Senate. The time had not yet come for effective action. Oregon was too distant, the prospect that our territorial claims on the coast would ever receive the substantial support of actual settlement too nebulous, for the most fervid pleas of the early expansionists to convince Congress that Oregon was really important.

In these congressional debates the proponents of settlement of the Columbia Valley repeatedly stressed the question of political and commercial control of the Pacific. They believed that, with an establishment at the mouth of the Columbia, the United States could reap many of the benefits which were going to England and Russia, and that the fisheries on the Pacific Coast, the fur trade with China, and the whaling industry demanded immediate attention. Floyd eloquently declared that America's reward for occupation of Oregon would be that Eastern trade which the West had been seeking ever since Solomon sent his ships in search of the gold of Ophir.   There were references to a future isthmian canal which would open up new and tremendous possibilities for the development of Pacific commerce, and, interestingly enough, one congressman even mentioned trade with the Philippines.[1]

At first none of these advocates of territory on the Pacific contemplated the acquisition of Oregon as the result of a westward sweep across the continent.   The frontier at this time, as the result of the great migration of 1816–21, was roughly marked by the boundaries of Indiana, Illinois, Missouri, Tennessee, Mississippi, and Louisiana.   This was believed to be the extreme limit of possible expansion. Beyond lay the Indian country — a vast expanse of prairie land, so barren and arid that it was not believed possible that the white man could ever wrest a subsistence from its unyielding soil.   Its only importance to the United States, Major H. S. Long reported after an exploratory expedition throughout the country, was that it was 'calculated to prevent too great an extension of our population westward.'[2]

This view was widely accepted.   The West was characterized as the Great American Desert, and the speakers in Congress held that this 'convenient, natural, and everlasting boundary' was a cause for satisfaction and not for regret.   With a complacency which today is hard to understand, Representative Tracy of New York told the House in 1823 that 'Nature has fixed limits for our nation; she has kindly interposed as our Western barrier, mountains almost inaccessible, whose base she has skirted with irreclaimable deserts of sand.'[3]   In time the little band of Oregonists, inspired by a distant vision of their country's future, found the courage to challenge this conception of our national limitations, but at first even they thought of Oregon as a distant colony and were prepared to accept the Jeffersonian thesis that any settlements on the Pacific Coast would in time become independent, related to the United States only by the ties of blood and interest.

It was Floyd's contention, for example, that whatever the future status of the colonies he would have had the United States establish in the Northwest, it was far better to have the coast inhabited by descendants of Americans than by 'English, Russians, or French, with all their disgusting notion of monarchy.' [4] So, too, did Senator Thomas Hart Benton, who was to become one of the most active of Western expansionists, cheerfully face at this time the prospect of Oregon's becoming the nucleus of a free and independent Power which would separate from the mother country as a child separates from its parents.

The latter statesman also had another idea, shared by Floyd, which today makes strange reading. Coupled with a grandiose conception of the effect upon Asia of the establishment of an American Power on the coast whereby 'science, liberal principles in government, and the true religion might cast their lights across the intervening sea,' was the proposal that the Columbia Valley itself might be peopled by Chinese. He saw this territory as 'the granary of China and Japan, and an outlet to their imprisoned and exuberant population.' [5]

It is interesting to speculate on what might have been the future of the Pacific Coast had this advice of the earliest proponents of its occupation been followed. If the wholesale introduction of Chinese labor into the Northwest had been made our official policy more than a century ago, we should have had on our hands a problem toward whose solution our subsequent exclusion acts would have availed us little.

In the light of these theories it is not surprising that the proposed occupation of the Columbia Valley had an air of unreality about it to the Congress of this period. Floyd might declare that we needed Oregon for security in time of war and for the development of our commerce in time of peace.[6] Francis Baylies might expound upon the value of the whale fisheries and state that the occupation of the

Columbia Valley was a measure for their protection, 'not of expediency but of necessity.'⁷   Trimble of Kentucky might paint a glowing picture of the riches of the Pacific and significantly point out that it was an ocean as yet without a master.   Benton might thunder in the Senate that if we did not establish our position in Oregon, England would so dominate the Western Ocean that 'not an American ship will be able to show itself beyond Cape Horn but with the permission of the English.'⁸   Yet so long as overland expansion and permanent control of territory on the coast seemed so impossible, nothing could be done.

Even when the supporters of the Oregon bill advanced their position and in the face of public skepticism debated the possible extension of our frontier to the Rockies; even when Floyd finally dared to ask, 'Why not, then, to the Pacific?' — Congress could not be aroused from its apathy.⁹

It is difficult today to visualize Oregon as so far distant from the Atlantic seaboard that the hazardous overland journey could barely be made between spring and winter, while the long voyage about Cape Horn might take almost a year.   It is hard to imagine the prairie States which now present apparently limitless vistas of wheat and corn, broken by the railroad lines and motor roads leading to their thriving cities, as a trackless waste roamed by great herds of buffalo.   Nor is it any easier to consider the Rockies the insurmountable barrier they appeared to be to a generation which knew none of our modern means of communication.   But Congress interpreted Floyd's suggestion of trans-continental expansion in the light of conditions with which it was familiar.   His conception of America's future won a few far-sighted converts; more generally it aroused open ridicule.

'Not even within the realm of fancy itself,' Mitchell of Tennessee declared, 'can the advocates of this bill [for the occupation of the Columbia Valley] point out the time when Oregon Territory will have to be organized.'¹⁰ Could it ever become a State? asked another opponent, Senator Dickerson of New Jersey.   And then in answer to his own rhetorical question he stated what was then perfectly true: 'A young and able-bodied Senator might travel from Oregon to Washington and back once a year; but he could do nothing else.' [11]

If it was thus too early in the nineteenth century's third decade for active, sustained interest in the expansionists' nebulous dreams and ambitious projects, these early imperialists nevertheless kept alive the idea of our destiny upon the Pacific. They complemented the pioneering work of the Northwest fur traders; they laid the groundwork for our ultimate action.

How prophetic were some of the expansionists' speeches, in fact, even they could hardly have realized. 'Our natural boundary is the Pacific,' Francis Baylies told a House which was laughing out of court the idea that we could ever hold Oregon permanently. 'The swelling tide of our population must and will roll on until that mighty ocean interposes its waters and limits our territorial empire. Then, with two oceans washing our shores, the commercial wealth of the world is ours, and imagination can hardly conceive the greatness, the grandeur, and the power that await us.' [12]

Certainly it would be asking too much of even this prophet of expansion to have expected him to foresee that in the fullness of time not even the waters of the mighty Pacific would serve to limit the territorial empire of a nation as young and aggressive as the United States.

When it is recalled that this Oregon country on which Congress was holding such vigorous debates was in actual fact held jointly by the United States and Great Britain under the agreement of 1818, it would be surprising if England were found accepting with equanimity our proposed occupation of the Columbia Valley. And she by no means did so. The British minister in Washington was aroused to offer an emphatic protest against such action as that contemplated in the bills before the House and Senate.

In Secretary of State Adams, however, any move for the extension of our influence to the Pacific Coast had a warm defender. The position he assumed was that Great Britain's rights in the Oregon country were confined to the territory lying north of the forty-ninth parallel, which would be an extension of the boundary already agreed upon as far west as the Rockies, and that south of that line the United States' claims could not be disputed. If he acknowledged England's title through discovery and exploration to northern Oregon, he determinedly held that Captain Gray's discovery of the Columbia gave the United States an even clearer title to all the country which that river drained up to its intersection with the forty-ninth parallel.

Consequently, his answer to the British minister's protest against Congress's debate upon occupation of the Columbia Valley took the form of a sharp rebuke. 'I do not know what you claim nor what you do not claim,' Adams bluntly told him. 'You claim India; you claim Africa... there is not a spot on *this* habitable globe that I could affirm you do not claim; and there is none which you may not claim with as much color of right as you can have to the Columbia River or its mouth.'[13]

This assertion of our rights to the Columbia Valley was followed in succeeding years — in 1824, 1826, and 1827 — by sustained efforts to settle the issue through negotiation with England. The debates in Congress had shown that it might well become a burning question some time in the future and that an unsettled northwest boundary held the seeds of possible conflict between the two countries concerned. But England clung to its demand that the Columbia River should constitute the boundary; the United States held as firmly that the only possible line was the forty-ninth parallel.

The area in dispute was thus only the narrow strip of territory between the Columbia and the forty-ninth parallel, but by both countries it was felt to be vital to their interests on the Pacific. England wanted to control the Columbia as a St. Lawrence of the West; the United States wanted the harbors of Puget Sound.[14] It was as much rivalry over influence in the Pacific as ownership of the interior which gave such significance to the Oregon controversy.

In 1826, when a formal proposal for making the forty-ninth parallel the boundary was submitted by the United States, Henry Clay instructed our minister in London to let it be known that we would make no further concession. 'This is our ultimatum,' he wrote, 'and you may so announce it; we can consent to no line more favorable to Great Britain.' [15] But England just as summarily rejected our proposals. A deadlock ensued which could not be broken. Under these circumstances a temporary solution was accepted to replace the expiring agreement of 1818. Joint occupation of the entire Oregon country was to be continued until either nation chose to give a year's notice of its termination.

For almost twenty years this agreement was to remain in force, and before further serious attempts were made to revise it, negotiations in another direction had been undertaken with a view toward securing that outlet upon the Pacific which at least temporarily was blocked in Oregon. For California had not been forgotten. Even though Congress had had no occasion to debate our possible expansion to that part of the western coast and the former Spanish province was now an integral part of the Mexican Republic as a result of the revolution of 1821, there were many who felt that somehow or other California as well as Oregon must some day belong to the United States.

It was still our interests in the Pacific rather than territorial expansion which turned men's eyes toward the coast, and there was not yet the force and drive behind the movement to acquire ports in California, any more than there had been behind the effort to secure the ports of Puget Sound, which in later years was to carry it to success. Nevertheless, it is significant that in 1835, some eight years after the second agreement with England on Oregon, President Jackson attempted to purchase San Francisco Bay from Mexico.[16] It shows how strongly the ambition to dominate the Pacific, to restrict the possible extension of British influence in that ocean, served to establish a basis for our future action when the call of the settlers on the coast and the spirit of expansion had fully aroused the country to its destiny.

Needless to say, Mexico promptly rejected Jackson's offer of $500,000 for San Francisco Bay. Her hold upon California was even slighter than that of the Spanish authorities had been, and it was widely believed that the province would some day fall into the hands of a stronger Power, but the Mexican Government itself had no idea of alienating any part of the national domain. The movement for Texan independence was under way and the open evidence of American ambitions in that direction placed Mexico very much on the defensive. No administration could afford to consider a project which seemed to point toward the country's dismemberment and the enrichment of its northern neighbor. For the time being the United States appeared to be no nearer control of the Pacific Coast than it had been when the fur traders first dreamed of the development of the Northwest and reported on how easily California might be conquered.

Nevertheless, the vanguard of the westward pioneers who were to give such a different aspect to our interests on the Pacific by bringing both Oregon and California so immeasurably nearer the eastern seaboard, was by this time actually reaching the coast. A few scattered settlers, taking in their stride both the western plains and the Rocky Mountains, had pointed out the path which was to be followed within a few years by that great wave of emigration which was to sweep everything before it in its progress toward the Pacific.

Lewis and Clark had first traced the overland trail to the shore of the Western Ocean in the expedition they undertook in 1804 under the orders of President Jefferson. It was an epochal day, significant in the history of American expansion, when after eighteen months of weary travel they found themselves in sight of 'this great Pacific Octean which we been so long anxious to see.' [17] Then some six years later, the overland party sent out by John Jacob Astor for the settlement of Astoria made its way to the coast and soon thereafter the Rocky Mountain trappers began to follow the trails which led down, not only into Oregon, but also into California.

From the Snake River to the Colorado, from the Rockies to the Sierras, these indefatigable pioneers blazed new trails and opened up new territory. Their quest for furs led them back and forth along the Pacific slope from Puget Sound to the Mojave Desert. It was they who discovered the passes over which the emigrant trains were later to cross the Rockies; it was they who took the first wagons over the continental divide. Our forefathers' desire for beaver hats was responsible for the opening-up of the overland road to the Pacific, just as their wives' demand for Chinese tea and silks had set the course of the Nor'westmen on the seaward route to Oregon and California.

In the Northwest the trappers were penetrating territory which had become more and more British ever since the withdrawal of Astor from his ventures in the Columbia Valley. Despite the agreement for joint occupation and the debates in Congress relative to American settlement, it was in reality a vast game preserve under the control of the Hudson's Bay Company. In California the Americans had even less reason to expect a welcome reception. The local authorities were openly suspicious of their intrusion and feared their possible influence upon those elements which already showed their discontent with Mexican rule.

But neither England's paramount influence in Oregon nor Mexico's unquestioned title to California had any real effect upon the trappers' activities. They could no more be deflected from their quest for beaver skins by boundary lines than they could be by stretches of desert or by mountain ranges.[18] There grew up among them, born of their Yankee independence and aggressiveness, a feeling that the entire continent was theirs by right whatever might be the claims of either England or Mexico. And through their letters and reports, through the stories they brought back home, they began to communicate this feeling to the people of the Mississippi Valley and even to those of the Eastern States. In Congress timid representatives and senators might still declare that the limits of our national growth were irretrievably fixed by desert and mountains. They might piously thank a kind Providence that this was so.

The pioneers of the Far West thought and spoke otherwise.

The response to the trappers' reports on the great possibilities of the territory on the Pacific Coast was a movement to promote the emigration of settlers who might turn
into American channels the future agriculture, industry,
and commerce of Oregon and California. Its propaganda
emphatically stressed the potentialities of the trade with
the Far East. If it would be absurd to state that the motive
behind the individual emigrant of this period was the development of our commercial and political power in the
Pacific, nevertheless this was the underlying cause for
popular support of the westward movement.

One of the most active propagandists for the settlement
of Oregon and an enthusiastic advocate of the annexation
of California — which he believed 'sure of accomplishment
and earnestly to be desired' — was an erratic Boston school
teacher, Hall J. Kelley. He toured the country making
speeches, wrote innumerable pamphlets, and organized
local Oregon societies in the interests of the cause of which
he had made himself so zealous a spokesman. He actually
started the leaven working and several little groups of prospective settlers made their way to the Northwest, both by
land and sea, under his immediate inspiration.

The undermining of England's hold upon the Far Eastern
trade was one of his declared objectives for settlement on
the coast, and he rhapsodized about a future commercial
alliance between the Chinese Empire and 'a government
the most liberal, refined and free' which would disenthral
American trade 'from the monopolies, the vexations and
the bondage of the East India Company.' In a booklet
published in Boston in 1831 he foretold an extension of our
commerce in the Pacific through occupation of the coast
which 'would provoke the spirit of American enterprize, to
open communications from the Mississippi Valley, and
from the Gulf of Mexico to the Pacific Ocean, and thus
open *new channels*... which opening across the bosom of a
widespread ocean, and intersecting islands, where health
fills the breeze and comforts spread the shores, would con-

duct the full tide of a golden traffic into the reservoir of our national finance.' [19]

Fifteen years later, when settlement of the coast was no longer in question, we find a Senate committee reaffirming Kelley's stand. 'In the occupation of Oregon,' read its report, 'we are about to connect ourselves with the Pacific Ocean, to open our way to a new and indefinite commerce, and bring ourselves in connection with Asia, Polynesia, and Southern America.' The author of this document foresaw a day when American tobacco would replace opium throughout the Orient, while China, Japan, and the Indies would buy our cotton, rice, and other provisions in unlimited quantities. Outlining the manifold products of eastern manufacture, he declared that 'all this mighty laboratory whence the world has supplied itself for fifty centuries with articles of luxury, comfort and common use, will pour itself forth in exchange for the produce of the Mississippi Valley.' [20]

Here was the theory which a far-sighted Spanish viceroy had expressed in 1789 when he declared that with a port on the Pacific Coast the United States might 'hold the riches of Great China and India,' the theory which had led John Jacob Astor to establish his settlement on the Columbia in 1811, and the theory which Floyd and Benton promoted so vigorously in the congressional debates of the early eighteen-twenties. It was to run like a thread through all our activities in the Pacific. It still does. We have won our fair share of the commerce of the East, but even yet its potentialities are not fully realized. The United States still hopes that the influence exerted in China by a government 'the most liberal, refined and free' will continue to return rich profits in the form of an ever-increasing share of China's trade, and that the markets of the Far East will absorb the mounting products of our farms and factories.

Whatever the future of American commerce in the Pacific, however, this propaganda in respect to it played an effective rôle in encouraging emigration to the little American communities which were being founded on the western coast. They at first grew very slowly, but they grew. To those in Oregon, moreover, there was added about 1835 an element which so often enters into the acquisition of new territories and acts as an aid and spur to national expansion. This was the advent of missionaries. They came to the Columbia Valley, in response to a dramatic Indian appeal for the White Man's Book of Heaven, to save the savages of the Northwest from the error of their ways; they stayed, fortunately for American interests on the coast, to help save Oregon from the tightening grip of the British fur companies.

So active were the missionaries in building homes, tilling the land, and promoting colonization that the English came to regret the cordial reception they first gave them. In 1841 we find Sir George Simpson, who was touring the Northwest in the interests of the Hudson's Bay Company, reporting to London that they were 'making more rapid progress in the extension of their establishments and in the improvement of their farms, than in the ostensible objects of their residence in this country.'[21] It was about the missionaries' headquarters in the Willamette Valley that American influence in Oregon centered, and they were no more anxious than the other settlers from the Eastern States to submit to the control which the British attempted to exercise over the country from the Hudson's Bay Company's post at Vancouver. When this community in 1838 boasted some sixty residents, a memorial was sent to Congress praying that the settlement should be placed under American jurisdiction. Five years later, the further step was taken of organizing a provisional government which was to remain in force 'until such a time as the United States extend their protection over us.'[22]

At the same time a somewhat similar development was under way in California which seemed to invite settlement with an even more glowing prospect of future prosperity than that of the Northwest. Scattered along the coast were a number of Americans engaged in the hide trade; at Monterey the American consul, Thomas O. Larkin, had made himself the advance agent of our occupation of a province which was still an integral part of Mexico, and the settlement founded in the Sacramento Valley by the Swiss emi-grant, John A. Sutter, was becoming the focal point for those Americans who sought out California by the overland trails.

To those who could read the handwriting on the wall, it was evident that the Yankees were occupying California as they had occupied Texas and that the end would probably be the same. Again Sir George Simpson bears witness to the process of American expansion which was covertly under way. He would have liked to see California declare its independence of Mexico and fall into British hands, and he reported to London that if England did not promote such a development he was assured 'that some step will very soon be taken, with the like object, in favor of the United States.' [23]

Under the pressure of these developments, Washington again began to bestir itself over possible measures for extending our political control to the Pacific Coast. No-thing had been done under President Jackson's successor, Martin Van Buren, but when President Tyler came into office in 1841 there was at least a halting response to the growing urge for national expansion. Texas, it is true, ab-sorbed most of the Administration's energies, but attempts were also made to settle the Oregon controversy with Great Britain and to purchase California. If they were not at this time pressed more vigorously than they were, it was largely because of a widespread feeling that 'masterly inactivity,' a policy of watchful waiting while American settlers cap-tured Oregon and California as they had captured Texas, would soon carry our borders to the Pacific without involv-ing the risks of any precipitate move.

In view of later developments it is especially interesting that the most persistent diplomatic efforts to reach the coast at this time involved California rather than Oregon. The possible rôle of San Francisco Bay in the future de-velopment of trade on the Pacific seized upon the imagina-tion of many Americans who were skeptical of the value of the Northwest. This was notably true in the case of Daniel Webster, who remained as Tyler's Secretary of

State after Harrison's death in order to complete his negotiations with England on the northeast boundary. He was not an expansionist. His position upon the slavery issue naturally forced him into opposition on the annexation of Texas, and he did not believe that Oregon could ever be held as a permanent possession of either the United States or Great Britain. He saw it rather as the nucleus of 'a great Pacific Republic, a nation where our children may go for a residence, separating themselves from this Government, and forming an integral part of a new government.' [24] Nevertheless, as a representative of New England's mercantile interests, he did favor the purchase of California and declared the port of San Francisco to be 'twenty times as valuable to us as all Texas.' [25]

Another factor which was probably responsible for Webster's interest in California was the general belief, now becoming a firm conviction, that England planned to occupy the province. From our minister in Mexico City, Waddy Thompson, who considered California 'the richest, the most beautiful, and the healthiest country in the world,' came warnings of British designs and also of possible ambitions on the part of France. Only by prompt action could we assure our ascendancy in the Pacific against these Powers, he reported to Washington, and emphatically declared that 'the importance of the acquisition of California cannot be overestimated.' [26]

Nor was he the only American official alarmed at England's supposed threat to our position in the Pacific. In 1842, Commodore Thomas ap Catesby Jones heard reports on the South American coast that England was about to seize California, and when to these rumors was added another that war had broken out between the United States and Mexico, he determined to forestall any move England might make. Steaming north with his squadron, he entered the harbor of Monterey and called upon the surprised and defenseless Mexican officials to surrender the port to the United States. They had no recourse but to submit to superior force and Commodore Jones ran up the American flag.

It was, of course, all a mistake. There was no war. Consequently, when the ambitious naval officer learned that relations between the United States and Mexico were still officially friendly, however strained they might be in actual fact, there was nothing for him to do but withdraw from the field with profuse apologies. An open break with Mexico was avoided, but the incident was not one to increase Mexican confidence in the peaceful or friendly intentions of the United States.[27]

In the meantime Webster's failure to include any agreement on Oregon in his treaty with England on the northeast boundary had aroused such public dissatisfaction that he felt it necessary to make some further attempt to settle the issue. This seemed to offer an opportunity to deal at the same time with the Californian question and Webster proposed a tripartite treaty. Mexico was to cede Upper California to the United States in return for a sum of money which would be used to settle the claims of both American and British citizens against the Mexican Government, and Great Britain was to give its approval to the transaction in return for a settlement of the Oregon controversy which met her demand for the Columbia River as the northwest boundary. Instructing our minister in London to present such a proposal to the British Government, Webster suggested that if London showed itself at all receptive to his ideas he was prepared to head himself a special mission for the negotiation of a new Oregon treaty. 'If I could see a strong probability of effecting *both* objects — California and Oregon,' he wrote Edward Everett in London, 'I should not decline the undertaking.' [28]

There were too many objections to this surprising proposal for it to make much headway. From the American point of view it represented a sacrifice of our interests in the Columbia Valley which the influx of settlers to that region rendered completely unacceptable. President Tyler, who supported Webster's position, was later to defend himself against the charge of being willing to sacrifice so much of Oregon by stating that he would never have dreamed of ceding the northern territory 'unless for the greater equivalent of California, which I fancied Great Britain might be able to obtain for us through her influence in Mexico.' [29] But public opinion would not countenance any bargaining with England over its rights on the Pacific Coast. Webster's fine scheme died a-borning because the Oregon issue had reached a point where the advocates of formal occupation of the disputed territory, in and out of Congress, no longer talked of our right to assert our claims in the Northwest, or of the advisability of such a move, but declared that it was absolutely necessary.

What had chiefly brought this home to the Government, to Congress, and to the public was the increasing emigration to the coast, now in its full stride. The pioneers were pouring across the plains by the thousand. Where there had been only a scattered handful of American residents on the coast in the days when Adams had bluntly told the British minister that England had no rights whatsoever in the Columbia Valley, and when Jackson had attempted to purchase San Francisco Bay, there was now in the closing days of the Tyler Administration a rapidly growing American population which demanded government action and communicated to the people at home their conviction that the time had come when 'manifest destiny' could no longer be denied.

It was in 1841 that the first organized caravan of covered wagons set out from Independence, Missouri, in answer to the call of the trappers, settlers, and missionaries who had already made their way to the Pacific shore. On the way the party of sixty-nine emigrants divided. Half of them followed the more familiar trail to Oregon; half of them turned off in the trackless wilderness toward a destination farther south. 'We knew California lay west,' wrote the leader of the latter group, 'and that was the extent of our knowledge.'

There was no stopping by the way on the part of these pioneers. They crept steadily across the monotonous plains, laboriously made their way over the mountain passes, and at long last descended the river valleys to join their countrymen in Oregon and California. The Pacific was their objective. Settlement of the intervening country was left to the future; the buffalo and the Indian remained in undisturbed possession of the rolling prairies.

Two years later was the year of the 'great emigration,' and almost a thousand men, women, and children heard the cry of 'On to Oregon.' In 1845 three thousand made the long trek across half a continent. Throughout the decade the tide of expansion rose and fell. Like a river which at times flows gently, then again rushes ahead torrentially, but always seeks the sea, so the emigrants made their way to the Pacific. By 1846 there were perhaps five thousand settlers in Oregon clamoring for incorporation into the Union and another thousand in California urging American annexation of the Mexican province.

CHAPTER IV

'Manifest Destiny'

UPON this stage, so clearly set for an extension of American territory to the Pacific Coast, there now appeared the enigmatic figure of James K. Polk. As a compromise candidate suddenly thrust forward to break the deadlock in the Democratic Convention, he was nominated in 1844 as the presidential standard-bearer of the expansionist movement. The time had come for action. The influences leading to the first step in the creation of American power in the Pacific had gathered a momentum which was irresistible. Polk was both an ardent expansionist himself and a keen interpreter of the prevailing temper of his countrymen. The result was his election to the presidency and a series of developments which definitely and finally carried the frontier to the westernmost limits of the continent.

It is difficult to disentangle this movement entirely from that for the annexation of Texas, which reached its final stage in the last days of the Tyler Administration, or to state precisely how much the Democrats were influenced in their expansionist program by the desire for new slave territory. Yet there is no question that Polk, even though he was a representative of the slave power in his capacity as spokesman for the Southern Democracy, keenly appreciated the larger issues involved. He favored settlement of the Oregon controversy and the acquisition of California no less strongly than annexation of Texas. He believed in 'manifest destiny'; he saw the United States as a continental Power with those possessions on the western coast which would enable it to dominate the Pacific.

His campaign for the presidency, with its stirring call for the 're-annexation' of Texas and the 're-occupation' of Oregon, marked a new phase in the development of the popular demand for control of the Northwest. Hitherto the expansionists had been content with the idea of a settlement of the boundary along the forty-ninth parallel, the line advanced in our abortive negotiations with Great Britain ever since the settlement of 1818, but they now declared that the United States could be content with nothing less than the entire Oregon country. They denied England's right to any part of the Northwest, and in a wave of jingoistic enthusiasm the country rang with the cry of 'Fifty-Four Forty or Fight.'

This extreme demand for a territory on the Pacific shore which would extend as far north as the present Alaskan boundary, bearing little relation to either our rights or our needs upon the western coast, was the outgrowth of the congressional debates and public discussion which coincided with the mounting wave of westward emigration. The spectacle of England grimly clinging to a country which American settlers were fast filling up, and attempting to block the United States from any outlet upon the Pacific, had aroused a violent anti-British feeling which the expansionists were quick to capitalize. Their basic arguments for the need of establishing American power in the Northwest remained the same, but they could now add an emotional fervor to their demand for action which had been impossible before the westward emigration got into full stride.

In 1838, Senator Lewis F. Linn of Missouri had introduced a new bill for the occupation of the Columbia Valley, and in the ensuing debates, a more and more aggressive note was sounded. There were still conservatives no more able to foresee their country's future than the opponents of Floyd's bills had been in the eighteen-twenties. Senator Archer of Virginia felt that the Northwest was so distant and the intervening country so difficult of passage that Oregon was more fit to be an Asiatic than an American dependency; Senator McDuffie of South Carolina even more emphatically declared that there never could be practical communications with the Pacific Coast, and that in any event Oregon was so utterly worthless that he would not give a pinch of snuff for the entire territory.[1] But their protests were being drowned out. 'Seat the United States firmly in Oregon,' C. J. Ingersoll declaimed in a speech which much more accurately reflected public opinion, 'and the commercial enterprise and wealth of the world will centralize within our limits.... Europe would seek in our Atlantic ports the products of the tropical gardens of southern Asia. No question has yet arisen in our history so closely connected with the extension of American power and greatness.' [2]

To the independent citizens of the New West, moreover, England's continued hold upon Oregon represented an intrusion of European autocracy upon a continent dedicated to democracy and freedom. They wanted American control firmly established in the Northwest for the sake of American settlers there, and for the sake of our position in the Pacific, but perhaps above all to prevent any further spread of British power and influence.

Senator Benton, still in the forefront of Oregon's champions as he had been twenty years earlier, bitterly assailed Great Britain for taking possession of the Columbia Valley, fortifying it, colonizing it, and monopolizing its fur trade without a shadow of right. Senator Allen of Ohio delivered his trenchant attack upon this arrogant Power which was seeking 'to fence us out from the Pacific Ocean, to belt us about, yet more closely, with her kingly despotism.' Senator McRoberts of Illinois, a still more rabid defender of our rights in the Northwest, was ready for war.[3]

Outside of Congress this feeling, spurred on by newspaper insistence upon our 'manifest destiny,' was reflected in 1843 in a series of mass meetings. Worked up to a high pitch of excitement by the propaganda in favor of Oregon's settlement and the enthusiasm of the emigrants themselves, these meetings in Pittsburgh, Cincinnati, St. Louis, and other cities of the West, adopted resolutions declaring that the Northwest could not be allowed to fall into British hands without a struggle.[4]

It was a popular movement which reached its climax in the Oregon convention held in Cincinnati in the summer of 1843, which was attended by ninety-six delegates from six States of the Mississippi Valley. These expansionists had no patience with any moderate proposal for a settlement with England which would allow that country any access to the Pacific. They demanded for the United States the whole western coast. They urged an official reaffirmation of the Monroe Doctrine declaring that the North American continent was no longer subject to colonization by any European Power. They adopted a series of resolutions for the protection of our rights on the Pacific shore through the construction of a string of forts across the continent and the dispatch of a fleet about Cape Horn.[5]

Swept into office on the tide of this enthusiasm President Polk soon indicated that he had a definite program for attaining the objectives of the expansionist movement. In his inaugural address in March, 1845, he declared it to be his duty 'to assert and maintain by all constitutional means the right of the United States to that portion of our territory which lies beyond the Rocky Mountains,' and in no uncertain terms announced to England that 'our title to the country of Oregon is "clear and unquestionable."' [6] Less widely heralded, but no less important in his own mind, was his firm intention to complement settlement of the Oregon controversy and round out our possessions on the Pacific by acquiring California. He told Senator Benton that the fine bay of San Francisco had to be kept from England, and confided to George Bancroft, whom he made his Secretary of the Navy, that he was determined by one means or another to bring the rich Mexican province under American control.[7] It was with an ambitious program that he entered upon office, but it was to be carried through to success.

Although he had acquiesced in the Democratic campaign slogan of 'Fifty-Four Forty or Fight' and was apparently prepared to claim the entire Oregon country up to Alaska as of right belonging to the United States, it soon developed that Polk was actually willing to reach an agreement with Great Britain on a more moderate basis. He reverted to the position of his presidential predecessors who had consistently sought a settlement along the forty-ninth parallel as representing a fair and equitable division of American and British claims. He was not willing to grant England free navigation of the Columbia, as some of his predecessors had been, but if the United States were assured of full and complete control of the territory which that river drained, he was prepared to concede the northern half of Oregon to Great Britain.

The old proposal for settlement of the Oregon boundary first suggested by John Quincy Adams was consequently again made to Richard Pakenham, the British envoy in Washington. But without even consulting his own Government and with a complete disregard of popular feeling in this country as brought out in the campaign of 1844, Pakenham bluntly rejected Polk's suggestion and concluded his reply by expressing the hope that the United States would offer another proposal 'more consistent with fairness and equity.' Faced with this rebuff, the President thereupon indicated that the time for temporizing and delay had passed once and for all. If England was not willing to compromise, the United States would advance and not retreat in pressing its claims. Polk could be assured that public opinion would now fully support the determined and unequivocal stand he forthwith adopted.

The conciliatory offer which had been made to England was promptly withdrawn, over the protests of the more pacific Secretary of State, James Buchanan, and, after refusal to accept England's oft-repeated suggestion that the issue should be submitted to arbitration, the President asked Congress for authorization to give the year's notice necessary for termination of the agreement for Oregon's joint control.[8]

In his annual message Polk then reiterated the principles first set forth by President Monroe and curtly warned England that the United States would permit no European interference on the North American continent, and that if such interference were attempted, we would be ready 'to resist it at any and all hazards.'

'It is due alike to our safety and our interests,' the President declared, 'that the efficient protection of our laws should be extended over our whole territorial limits, and that it should be distinctly announced to the world as our settled policy that no future European colony or dominion shall with our consent be planted or established on any part of the American continent.' [9]

This was a direct challenge to Great Britain. There was a threat of war in the air. Polk appeared determined to force the issue and the country as a whole was behind him. Public feeling ran high and jingoism had its day on either side of the Atlantic. Called upon to act after so many years of fruitless and apparently endless debate, Congress gave the President authorization for termination of the old Oregon treaty and provided for the extension of American jurisdiction over the Columbia Valley and for the military protection of American settlers in the Northwest. The agitation of the past two decades had at last borne fruit.

For all the excitement and bluster of this period which saw Oregon become a national issue of the first importance, there was nevertheless an undercurrent of anxiety in the country on the prospect of war with England. Congress reflected it by adding a conciliatory preamble to its resolution for termination of joint control, and from all sides pressure was brought upon Polk to abate his zeal. Nor was he himself blind to the dangers of the course he was following. He ran the risk he did, as he himself stated, because he was convinced that 'the only way to treat John Bull was to look him straight in the eye; that he considered a bold and firm course on our part the pacific one. Furthermore, he had every confidence in the success of his program. He noted in his diary that 'if we do have war it will not be our fault,' and on the evidence of Daniel Webster told a friend of the Whig statesman, shortly after his annual message but before the action taken by Congress, 'that he had not the slightest apprehension of War.' [10]

It was largely due to the fact that peaceful counsels prevailed in the ministry of Lord Robert Peel, and that the British Government had no mind to provoke hostilities with an aroused United States over so distant and relatively unimportant a colony, that Polk's course proved justified.¹¹ And even then it took conciliatory gestures on both sides. For while England made the first tentative move toward a renewal of the negotiations which Polk had broken off so abruptly, he himself let it become unofficially understood in London that the United States was not definitely committed to its maximum claim of the entire Oregon territory. If England was now prepared to consider our former demand for the forty-ninth parallel, it was hinted, a solution of the controversy might be possible.

This represented for Great Britain acceptance of our original position, but, convinced that at least some such concession was the only way of avoiding war, England was at last ready to surrender. The British minister in Washington was empowered to advance as a possible settlement of the boundary the forty-ninth parallel, the very line which he had so summarily rejected when Polk himself had proposed it. The President now took the novel course of seeking the advice of the Senate as to what policy he should adopt. It was not that any doubt existed in his own mind as to the necessity of accepting the British offer which he himself had invited, but that he wished to place upon the Senate the responsibility for retreating from our more advanced claims.

In the heated atmosphere which the slavery issue and the Mexican War created in the fifth decade of the past century, the President was bitterly criticized for being ready to give up so quickly rights which had been vociferously proclaimed from every housetop during the previous election. His willingness to compromise with England was contrasted with the truculence of his attitude toward Mexico. The Whigs sneered at a zeal for expansion which nothing could abate when potential slave territory was in question, but which subsided so easily when it was a question of northern lands. Even Senator Benton waxed sarcastic. 'Oh mountain that was delivered of a mouse,' he mused, 'thy name shall be fifty-four forty.'

But Polk was above all a realist. He knew exactly what he wanted and this was the natural extension of our boundaries to the Pacific. If it had been possible to secure all of Oregon, he would unquestionably have favored such a course, but it was obviously impossible to expect England peacefully to surrender all her rights in the Northwest and allow Canada to be shut off from any access to the Pacific. Nor would Polk have been warranted in running any further risk of hostilities over a part of Oregon to which we had never laid any serious claim, which was in no way vital to the United States, and where there were actually no American settlers. For the Columbia Valley the President would have fought. His annual message in 1845 was not a bluff in so far as it applied to this part of the Northwest, though perhaps he secretly hoped that it might force England into an even more conciliatory position than it actually did. Furthermore, he could have answered his Whig critics by pointing out that while he insisted upon the entire Columbia Valley, although it was obviously not territory which would promote the interests of the slavocracy, such statesmen as their own Daniel Webster had been prepared to sacrifice the northern bank of the Columbia and meet England's original terms.

In any event, the Senate approved his program and advised him to accept the boundary England had offered. For all his sarcasm Senator Benton was in essential agreement with the Administration policy and there were few but jingoistic hotheads who seriously thought the United States should further defy British power. The treaty, signed on June 15, 1846, provided that the line of the British–United States boundary should be extended along the forty-ninth parallel to where it met the Straits of Juan de Fuca and then follow these waters to the sea.[12] It thus gave the United States the entire Columbia Valley and the harbors of Puget Sound, but left England with Vancouver Island. It was a settlement which met the legitimate interests of both countries and was both logical and equitable.

Today the wisdom of Polk's course of action is generally recognized, but it is interesting to note the comment of an expansionist of a later day. 'No foot of soil to which we

had any title in the Northwest should have been given up,'
Theodore Roosevelt wrote many years later; 'we were the
people who could use it best, and we ought to have taken
it all.... We had even then grown to be so strong that we
were almost sure to win in any American contest for continental supremacy.' [13] Less belligerent students of history,
however, may be thankful that both in the United States
and in Great Britain more conciliatory views prevailed.

In bringing to a close the long-drawn-out controversy
over Oregon and carrying our northwestern frontier to the
Pacific, President Polk had not forgotten the other phase
of his program for expansion. Texas, with which we have
no immediate concern, had some time ago come into the
Union, but there still remained California. To a statesman
who saw the United States as the rightful claimant to all
the territory west of the Rockies and believed his country's destiny pointed to commercial and political supremacy in the Pacific, this Mexican province was as important
as Oregon.

As in the controversy with Great Britain, the President
hoped to achieve his goal by peaceful measures. At one
time he even appeared willing to give up California if
Mexico proved conciliatory on the boundary conflict in
relation to Texas, but it is probable that in his mind this
merely meant a postponement of action which he considered inevitable sooner or later. His policy clearly shows
a determination to acquire California at almost any cost on
the theory that it represented a logical extension of our
borders westward just as much as did the occupation of the
Columbia Valley. Certainly he was not swayed by any
consideration of Mexico's clear and unquestioned title to
California. Its acquisition by the United States was a final
expression of 'manifest destiny' and on these grounds he
was prepared to act, leaving to moralists the right or wrong
of the policy he was determined to follow.

At the time his evident willingness to carry through a
war with Mexico for the adjustment of the Texan boundary and the acquisition of California was charged to the

ambitions of the slave power and its determination to secure new territory for slavery. In Lowell's oft-quoted
stanza:

> They jest want this Californy
> So's to lug new slave-states in
> To abuse ye, an' to scorn ye,
> An' to plunder ye like sin.[14]

But nothing was farther from the truth, as it has been
recognized long since. Before the slavery issue had been
injected into the situation, it was the North, and especially
New England, rather than the South, which sought
California. Yankee traders had created and sustained our
interest in the Mexican province and it was the country's
commercial and not its planting interests which desired
San Francisco Bay for the development of Pacific trade.
Here again Polk might have pointed to the policy pursued
by Webster. The expansionists' desire to acquire California
proves more than anything else how important a rôle our
ambition to dominate the Pacific played in the whole movement which carried our national domain to that ocean's
shores.

President Polk was also even more concerned than had
been the previous Administration over the danger of
foreign intervention. He feared that, if we did not take
immediate steps to acquire California, either France or
Great Britain would forestall any action which we might
later contemplate. It was by now almost self-evident that
Mexico's hold upon the province could not last much
longer. It had become virtually independent. It does not
matter that as we now know neither England nor France
actually contemplated any intervention in this situation
and that the President's fears had little or no justification.[15] In 1845 the country thoroughly believed in the necessity for prompt and energetic action.

Polk's first move followed the line of his predecessors'
policy. He attempted to purchase California as part of the
general settlement of our boundary dispute with Mexico
growing out of the annexation of Texas. John Slidell
was sent to Mexico City empowered to offer as high as

$40,000,000 for New Mexico and California. To such a figure had our desire to obtain California mounted from the paltry $500,000 which President Jackson had offered for San Francisco Bay ten years earlier. Moreover, Slidell's instructions explicitly stated that 'money would be no object when compared with the value of this acquisition.' [16]

Coincident with this program for the peaceful purchase of the territory on the Pacific Coast, another plan was set in motion. We have seen that there was a growing restlessness upon the part of the Californians themselves to break away from Mexican rule and the steadily increasing influx of American settlers into the Sacramento Valley served to intensify this discontent.[17] It was Texas on a smaller scale. An annexationist movement was gaining weight which President Polk was not above encouraging. If California should of itself seek the protection of the United States, he was not the man to stand in its way. Consequently, the American naval commander on the western coast, Commodore Sloat, was ordered to be on the alert for any contingency demanding American action, Captain John C. Frémont was sent on a somewhat mysterious exploring expedition which carried him into Mexican territory, and Lieutenant Archibald H. Gillespie was rushed to Monterey with secret dispatches for Consul Thomas O. Larkin.

It is these dispatches which furnish the clue to what was going on in Polk's mind, for they lent themselves, to say the very least, to a rather broad interpretation. The United States could take no part in any possible struggle between California and Mexico, it could use no influence to induce the Californians to throw off the Mexican yoke, it had no territorial ambitions on the western coast. On these points the President was explicit. 'But if the people should desire to unite their destiny with ours,' Larkin was instructed, 'they would be received as brethren, whenever this can be done without affording Mexico any just cause of complaint.' 'Their true policy for the present,' the dispatches continued, 'is to let events take their course, unless an attempt should be made to transfer them without their consent to Great Britain or France.' [18]

Behind these two lines of action — purchase of the desired territory or the fomentation of revolt — was always the shadow of war. The immediate irritant was the bitter controversy revolving around our annexation of Texas, but our known designs in regard to California played their part in heightening the tension between the two countries. It would not perhaps be fair to say that Polk welcomed Mexican intransigency on the Texan boundary issue for the opportunity it offered him to strike out for California in the event his other plans failed, but his policy was determined and aggressive. Even though Slidell was originally instructed not to hold out for California should Mexico prove willing to reach an agreement on the other points at issue, the President indicated that he had little confidence in events taking this peaceful course. As early as his annual message of 1845 he expressed his belief that Mexico's attitude gave us just grounds for war, and in his instructions to his envoy in Mexico City he stated that, if the Mexican Government should refuse to receive him, 'the cup of forbearance will have been exhausted.' [19] In foreseeing trouble, the wish may or may not have been father to the thought, but no shadow of doubt exists as to Polk's intentions should hostilities break out.

As events gradually unrolled in the momentous year 1846, it became more and more clear that force was to be the final arbiter of our dispute with Mexico and that Polk was to have his opportunity. Slidell could make no headway in Mexico City in the face of the bitter anti-American feeling aroused by our annexation of Texas and aggressive attitude toward California. War became inevitable. 'Mexico wanted it; Mexico threatened it; Mexico issued orders to wage it,' the historian of that war has written.[20] Yet at the same time if it had not been for our aggressive determination to defend the furthermost boundary claimed by Texas, for the belligerent spirit of the West which was ready to fight England, Mexico, or any other country which seemed to stand in the way of our expansion, and for President Polk's own willingness to accept war for the furtherance of his annexation program, some

way might have been found in time to adjust the controversy.

In any event, the President now took military precau-
tions for the defense of the disputed Texan border and
ordered General Zachary Taylor to advance to the Rio
Grande. He was fully prepared to act upon Slidell's significant advice that 'nothing is to be done with these people
until they have been chastened.' [21] He moved slowly until
there were definite assurances that the controversy with
Great Britain over Oregon was to be settled peacefully.
War on two fronts — the northwest and the southwest —
would have been awkward. But when a new revolutionary
government in Mexico flatly refused to recognize Slidell as
our official envoy, the President with the support of his
cabinet decided that the time had come to open hostilities.
The date of this decision was May 9, 1846. By a fortunate
chance for Polk's policy, word was received later the same
day that Mexican troops had actually attacked a part of
the American forces on the Rio Grande. The President
was thereby able to announce to Congress on May 11 that
war existed by act of Mexico herself. The challenge was accepted and the country embarked upon its new imperialistic
venture.

It was a war welcomed by the Democrats and opposed
by the Whigs, enthusiastically supported by the West and
condemned by New England. Yet its real significance lay
in our designs upon California rather than in the settlement
of the Texan boundary. No one could have been more
frank than Polk in his acknowledgment of this objective.
Secretary Buchanan urged in a cabinet meeting the disavowal of territorial aggrandizement as a war aim. The
President flatly refused.

'I told him,' Polk wrote in his memorable diary, 'that
we had not gone to war for conquest, yet it was clear that
in making peace we would if practicable obtain California.'
If such an attitude annoyed either England or France, he
further quotes himself as telling the Secretary of State, he
was ready for them. Rather than make any pledge against
the acquisition of new territory, he declared that he was

prepared to 'meet the war either England or France or all
the Powers of Christendom might wage... and would stand
and fight until the last man among us fell in the conflict.' [22]

Upon the course of American operations in Mexico and
the final victory over that prostrate nation we cannot
dwell, but even before the military campaign opened, a
movement was under way in California which cast the
shadow of coming events. The careful program at which
Polk had hinted for encouraging the sentiment for annexation to the United States was bearing fruit. American
officials in the Mexican province, whether they were acting
upon instructions or upon their own responsibility, had
helped create a situation which almost surely would have
brought California into the Union even if the war had not
precipitated matters.

In the north the activities of Frémont and his refusal to
leave California, even when ordered to do so by the Mexican Government, had done nothing to allay the chaotic conditions which prevailed generally throughout the province.
In fact they brought this unrest to a head. Through his instigation, if not with his direct participation, a small band
of American settlers took matters into their own hands and
raised the banner of revolt.[23] On June 14, 1846, still ignorant of the war which had been declared a month earlier,
they captured the town of Sonora, declared the independence of California, and adopted a flag whose crude
figure of a bear gave to the uprising its name of the Bear
Flag Revolt.

For a time Frémont preserved an attitude of armed neutrality, though there was never any question as to where
his sympathies lay. But when the Mexican authorities
threatened a counter-attack upon the rebels, he openly
took the field. He was still without news from Washington, but, ready to gamble on the inevitability of war between Mexico and the United States, he adopted a bold
course looking toward California's conquest without waiting for any further developments.

Fortunately, events justified his actions. Word of the

outbreak of the war was received and the Bear Flag Revolt lost its significance in the face of the larger issues now involved. Commodore Sloat took Monterey and San Francisco and then, in coöperation with that naval officer's more aggressive successor, Commodore R. F. Stockton, the little army which Frémont had collected began to move southward. It met little resistance. Los Angeles was captured and that dream of so many pioneers on the western coast was at last realized — 'the Stars and Stripes were run up ... and the great province of California had a future.' [24]

'Frémont was not the liberator of California,' his biographer has written. 'It would in all probability have fallen safely and surely into American hands had he gone unambitiously north to the Oregon Trail in the spring of 1846. But he did play a gallant, daring, and useful rôle in expediting the American conquest, making it easy for the navy to act, preventing the possible occurrence of complications with Great Britain, and enabling California to be almost wholly pacified before the first overland forces under General Kearny arrived.' [25]

With the arrival of this latter officer, a certain measure of friction developed between the American army and naval forces. Frémont attempted to act independently and laid himself open to court-martial by his refusal to obey General Kearny's orders. Also there was an abortive attempt by the native Californians to overthrow their new masters which added to the confusion of the Californian scene. But peace and order were gradually restored, the Mexican province was organized as American territory, and when the Treaty of Guadalupe Hidalgo brought the Mexican War to a close and was ratified by the Senate on March 10, 1848, the seal of approval was set upon what was already an accomplished fact. California was ours.[26] We had secured by conquest that rich Mexican province which some forty years earlier one of its first American visitors had so significantly declared 'would fall without effort to the most inconsiderable force.'

Where diplomacy had succeeded in Oregon, war had succeeded in California. We had at last acquired that Pacific coastline which far-sighted statesmen had so long recognized as necessary for the full development of American power and influence. Expansion was everywhere victorious; 'manifest destiny' had carried the day. There may be criticism of the methods which President Polk adopted to achieve his program, but no American can today regret his achievement. It carried the United States to its final continental frontier and made possible the American empire in the Pacific toward which it was in fact the first step.

CHAPTER V

Perry Forecasts the Future

AFTER the acquisition of Oregon and California, it was to be some twenty years before the United States again made any successful advance toward territory in the Pacific. Yet in the decade from 1850 to 1860 there was a greater degree of interest in that ocean and more activity looking toward the extension of our Pacific trade and commerce than at any other time until 1898. The tightening of our political and commercial ties with the Chinese Empire, a tentative move toward the annexation of Hawaii, and other attempts to increase our influence in Asia came to a climax in Commodore Perry's formidable expedition to open up the mysterious island kingdom of Japan. So strong in fact was the urge to strengthen by any means possible our position in the Pacific that, had it not been for the turmoil and confusion at home resulting from the growing conflict over slavery, we might conceivably have anticipated by half a century our advance to the coast of Asia.

Two different factors were responsible for this mid-century activity in the Pacific. The first was the national urge for further expansion which had been reënforced rather than satiated by the pushing back of our frontier to the west coast; the second was the new significance of the Pacific based upon the rapid settlement of Oregon and California and the consequent development of closer communications with the Atlantic seaboard.

In commenting in 1846 upon 'the spirit of aggrandizement which has taken possession of this people,' John Quincy Adams had declared that it would 'hereafter characterize their history.' [1] So, too, had William H. Seward noted with full approval our entry upon a new stage of our national career in which our population was 'destined to roll its resistless waves to the icy barriers of the north, and to encounter oriental civilization on the shores of the Pacific.' [2]

And finally President Pierce stated in his inaugural address in 1852 that the policy of his Administration would not be 'controlled by any timid forebodings of evil from expansion.' [3] Everywhere there was the feeling that California and Oregon marked not the final but the initial stage of an extension of national power which hitherto had not been foreseen or even vaguely imagined.

To the representative of the slave interests — for expansion prior to the Civil War can never be disassociated from this rivalry between North and South — the next step seemed to be Cuba. But there were not wanting statesmen and politicians who firmly believed that it was toward the Pacific rather than the Atlantic that America's true destiny pointed. They recognized England as the United States' most dangerous rival, and felt that in the Western Ocean lay our best opportunity for effective competition against British trade and political power.

Their spokesman was Seward. He made himself the prophet of a new Pacific era in world history in which the United States was to play the predominant rôle. He urged surveys of the Pacific, supported every move for promoting our commerce with the Far East, and welcomed each new tie between Asia and the New World. He felt that the renovating influence of our institutions would soon be felt as far off as the shores of China and declared that our Pacific commerce had already 'brought the ancient continents near to us, and created necessities for new positions — perhaps connections or colonies there.' [4]

Nothing seemed more important to this statesman than the meeting of East and West on the Pacific shores. Our influence was fated to remould the 'constitutions, laws, and customs, in the land that is first greeted by the rising sun.' Carried away by an immense enthusiasm, he told the Senate that European commerce, politics, thought, and activity would sink in relative importance 'while the Pacific Ocean, its shores, its islands, and the vast regions beyond, will become the chief theater of events in the world's great hereafter.' [5]

His main warrant for a prophecy which even today may

seem extravagant, although the last word is still to be said on the relative importance of the Atlantic and the Pacific, was to be found in the phenomenal growth and development of California. For so close upon its conquest by the United States that it appeared to be a benediction upon the extension of our laws and institutions to the Californians, came the news of the discovery of gold. The steady stream of emigration to the coast was suddenly transformed into a wild rush for the new El Dorado. It was settled so rapidly that by 1850 it was ready for entry into the Union.

Although about half of the eighty thousand men who made their way to California in 1849 followed the overland trails now so deeply marked by the wheels of countless thousands of covered wagons, it was the development of other and far quicker routes to the coast which was the really significant aspect of California's settlement in so far as interest in the Pacific is concerned. Under the pressure of the impatient desire of gold-hungry prospectors to reach their goal, two methods of travel were developed which cut down to one and three months respectively the six months required on the overland trail.

The latter of these routes was the familiar passage about Cape Horn, but in place of those slow-sailing vessels in which Americans first sought California to trade in furs and hides, the Argonauts of the gold-rush days sailed in the new clipper ships. When in 1851 the *Flying Cloud*, that most perfect triumph of the great days of American shipbuilding, made the passage from New York to San Francisco in eighty-nine days, a run never surpassed and only twice equaled in all the history of sailing vessels, the Pacific seemed just around the corner.[6]

The second and even more rapid route was by way of Panama, with variations which led across either Mexico or Nicaragua. The California pioneers would take ship to the eastern port of the isthmus at Chagres, laboriously make their way by dugout and muleback through fever-infested swamps to the settlement of Panama, and there pick up whatever coastal vessel was available to take them on to some Californian port. It was a dangerous and comfortless trip at best, but it was the shortest line to the gold-fields. The San Francisco mails reached their destination in less than a month by way of Panama, though the average traveler could not make quite such good time. Moreover, it was a route which clearly pointed the way to a far more effective link between the Atlantic and the Pacific than any then in existence. Not only was the canal of half a century later envisaged, but it was taken so seriously that in the Clayton-Bulwer Treaty of 1850 the United States and Great Britain agreed that neither Power would seek exclusive control over its proposed route.

As the emigrants and gold-seekers swept across the plains, careened about Cape Horn in the clipper ships, fought off fever, thirst, and hunger on the trails across Panama, Nicaragua, and Mexico in their frenzied rush to the western coast, the movement further to project our influence in the Pacific gathered headway. And here still another element enters the picture — the advent of the steam vessel.

Even in this period of the glory of the clipper ship, steam foretold its eventual doom. In the very years in which the *Flying Cloud* was racing about Cape Horn beneath its great spread of billowing sails, it was recognized that the future belonged to its squat and puffing rivals. The settlement of California opened the prospects for a new direct trade between our western ports and those of the Asiatic coast. This pointed to the establishment of steamship lines across the Pacific. And these projected lines, because of the steamship's dependence upon frequent coaling stations, seemed to demand the immediate acquisition of ports of refuge along the lanes of Pacific travel and of naval bases for the protection of the commerce of the future. The movement for annexation of Hawaii was born, in far-off China an ambitious diplomat suggested the seizure of Formosa, and Commodore Perry would have had us establish naval bases in the Japan Sea.

It has been said of Seward's interest in the Pacific and of his subsequent activities as Secretary of State, that his contribution to our Far Eastern policy was greater than that of either Webster or Hay. And this same authority, Tyler Dennett, declares that Commodore Perry was the first official to view the commercial and political problems of the Pacific as a unity. 'No American before his time, and few after it,' Dennett writes, 'ever had such an extensive ambition.' [7] Seward was ready for empire in the Pacific; Perry was ready. There were some few others who saw the handwriting on the wall, but they were one and all far ahead of their day.

How directly the Japan Expedition was the result of these factors we have been discussing may be seen in the instructions given to Commodore Perry. Upon the expedition's dispatch in 1852 the acting Secretary of the Navy laid special stress upon the extent to which the Far East had been brought closer to the United States by 'the navigation of the ocean by steam, the acquisition and rapid settlement by this country of a vast territory on the Pacific, the discovery of gold in that region, the rapid communication established across the isthmus which separates the two oceans.' [8] But these were facts which it was not necessary to impress upon Perry. For while the objects of his expedition were to seek from Japan guarantees of protection for American seamen and property, permission to enter one or more ports for provisions and also for trade, and the privilege of establishing coal dépôts, Perry quickly demonstrated that his conception of his mission was far more ambitious.

He was no sooner at sea than he was reporting home on certain plans which he thought advisable should Japan prove at all backward about granting the privileges which the United States sought. In a dispatch from Madeira he gave his opinion that, if any delay was encountered in securing ports of refuge and supply for American vessels, it would be well to look over such islands adjacent to Japan as the Lew Chew group.

'Now it strikes me,' wrote the forthright commodore, 'that the occupation of the principal ports of those islands for the accommodation of our ships of war, and for the safe

resort of merchant vessels of whatever other nation, would
be a measure not only justified by the strictest rules of
moral law, but, what is also to be considered, by the laws of
stern necessity; and the argument may be further strengthened by the certain consequences of the ameliorization of
the conditions of the natives, although the vices attendant
upon civilization may be entailed upon them.' [9]

Here was a doctrine of benevolent imperialism which was
still somewhat new for an American citizen, but it was
certainly accepted by Seward. It was in that same year he
made his declaration of faith in the importance of America's
future upon the Pacific. Moreover, the two men were in
complete agreement upon another aspect of the situation
which strikes the familiar note of jealousy in regard to the
intentions of other powers. Just as we had been forced to
settle the Oregon dispute because of fear that England would
win control of the Columbia Valley, and had seized California to circumvent her designs in that direction, so both
Perry and Seward would have had us act in the Far East in
order to forestall British ambitions.

'When we look at the possessions in the east of our great
maritime rival, England,' Perry continued in his dispatch
from Madeira, 'and of the constant and rapid increase of
their fortified ports, we should be admonished of the necessity of prompt measures on our part.... Fortunately the
Japanese and many other islands in the Pacific are still left
untouched by this unconscionable government; and, as
some of them lay in a route of commerce which is destined
to become of great importance to the United States, no
time should be lost in adopting active measures to secure a
sufficient number of ports of refuge.' [10]

It is easy to see that this was no ordinary naval officer
whom the President had dispatched to open up Japan for
the advantage of Western commerce. Perry had ideas of
his own and the initiative to carry them out. Furthermore,
both by training and experience he was well equipped to
promote American interests in the Pacific whether by negotiations for the entry of American vessels into Japan or
by the acquisition of ports of refuge.

A younger brother of the Perry of Lake Erie fame, Matthew Calbraith had himself served in the War of 1812 and then started upon a career outstanding in that period even if it had not been crowned by the dramatic success of his mission to Japan. He had selected the original location for the American Negro settlement in Liberia, first demonstrated the efficiency of the naval ram, founded the naval apprenticeship system, been active in extirpating the slave trade, and served as a squadron commander during the Mexican War. Even more important, from the point of view of his activities in the Pacific, was his experimental work with steam vessels for which he has been called the 'father of the American steam navy.' [11]

As commander of the navy's first steam vessel, the *Fulton*, an awkward floating battery equipped with paddle-wheels and four great chimneys, he made a record run in Long Island Sound of 28 miles in 1 hour, 57 minutes. Also he was largely responsible for the building of the *Mississippi* and the *Missouri*, steam-propelled frigates. The former vessel, a sidewheel monstrosity of 1692 tons, was launched in 1841 and assigned to the squadron for the expedition to Japan.

These experiments with steam convinced Perry of the practicality of this new form of transportation, and before he left for the Far East he had given a careful study to the whole question of Pacific steamship routes. The naval bases and coal dépôts of the future unquestionably loomed larger in his mind as he sailed for Japan than any immediate trade developments which might result from his expedition, and if it had not been for what he considered their importance to American commerce and empire in the Pacific, his imperialistic ideas would probably have never been born.

After some six months of voyaging, the Perry squadron arrived off the Lew Chew Islands in May, 1853, and put into Napa. Following a careful program this port was then made the rendezvous for all the vessels in the expedition. But visits were also paid to the Bonin Islands, where at Port Lloyd, on Peel Island, an American-European settlement was discovered.

These two ports — Napa and Port Lloyd — were those which Perry had selected, together with the Hawaiian Islands, to provide 'connecting links, or suitable stopping places' for the line of mail steamers which he already saw drawing Asia and our own western coast together. Napa was the best harbor in that long string of islands which lies off the China coast stretching down from the southernmost tip of Japan almost to Formosa. Perry called them the Lew Chews, but as a formal possession of Japan they are now known as the Ryukyu Islands. Port Lloyd, the outstanding harbor of the Bonin Islands, now known as Ogasawara Jima, lay farther to the east, in line with Hawaii. The former archipelago was nominally a Japanese dependency in 1853; the sovereignty of the latter was somewhat uncertain.

Perry lost no time in coming to an agreement with the regent ruling over the Lew Chews to make Napa the base for his squadron, and began to evolve plans for the disposition of the Bonin Islands even more in line with his ambitions. 'The adventitious aid of their possession,' wrote one of the observers with his squadron, 'would prove of great advantage in a trade with Japan.'[12] Another reported, in connection with future coaling stations between California and China, that Port Lloyd was 'perhaps the only spot in the Pacific, west of the Sandwich Islands, which promises to be of real advantage for such a purpose.'[13]

The Commodore himself first suggested to Washington that an agreement might be reached with Great Britain whereby Port Lloyd could be made a free port. Under the flag of the United States or of England, or under a local flag, he reported, it could become a resort for the vessels of all nations 'and especially a stopping place for mail steamers.' But far closer to his own ambition of what should be done with the Bonin Islands was the definite hint that should the Navy Department deem it advisable to take immediate possession of them in the name of the United States, he was prepared to carry out such orders and would then adopt the best means for holding the desired port.[14]

Furthermore, he proceeded to pave the way for this

acquisition of an American colony off the coast of Asia
and his activities at Port Lloyd clearly demonstrate how
strongly he hoped Washington would authorize him to
raise the American flag. To understand this more fully,
however, it is essential to say something of the previous
history of the Bonin Islands and of the American-European
community Perry found at Port Lloyd.

The islands were known to the whalers of both the
United States and Great Britain earlier than 1827, but in
that year they were visited by Captain Beechey in the
H.M.S. *Blossom*, who named both Peel Island and Port
Lloyd and took possession of them in the name of George
the Fourth. He also gave the name of Bailey to a more
southerly island, although he did not in fact explore it and
it had already been visited by an American seaman, Captain Reuben Coffin, of the whaler *Transit*. Nothing came
of Captain Beechey's activities until three years later when
a group of foreign residents of Hawaii, accompanied by
twenty-five natives, decided to establish a European
colony at Port Lloyd. It was founded under British protection, but of the five whites who took part in the venture
two were Americans, one English, one Danish, and one a
Genoese. The latter, a man named Mazarro, was appointed governor of Peel Island by the British consul at
Honolulu, but upon his death soon after, it was one of the
Americans, Nathaniel Savory, who became the real leader
of the little settlement. When Perry reached the Bonin
Islands in 1853, the colony numbered thirty-one and Savory
was the only one of the original settlers still there.[15]

The American naval officer felt that England's claims to
sovereignty were somewhat nebulous in view of these circumstances and promptly took up with Savory the question
of Peel Island's future status. He drew up a code of government for the colony, saw to it that Savory was elected chief
magistrate, and raised the Stars and Stripes. A vessel was
dispatched to Bailey Island to take formal possession in the
name of the United States and a copper plate bearing witness to this act was affixed to a sycamore tree near the landing stage. Then Perry bought from Savory a parcel of land

fronting on the harbor at Port Lloyd for a future coaling
station and appointed the American an agent of the United
States Government with an assistant from among the seamen in the Japan squadron.

It was not Perry's intention to act over the head of his
Government or to assume a position from which he could
not retreat. He knew very well that his ports of refuge and
coaling stations could be established only with official support. But he was determined to do what he could toward
the realization of his plans pending further instructions.
'It is to be hoped that steps may ere long be taken to give
greater importance to Port Lloyd, and that the conditions
of the settlers may be improved,' he wrote Savory in the
last letter of their interesting correspondence, '[but] it must
be understood that the sovereignty of the Bonin Islands
has not yet been settled, and the interest taken by me in
the welfare and prosperity of the settlement has solely in
view the advantage of commerce generally.' [16]

Perry did not forward to Washington his full correspondence with Savory, but he did report that, after exploring Peel Island and giving the settlers certain supplies
in the way of livestock and seeds, he had gone so far 'as to
secure a suitable place for the erection of offices, wharves,
coal-sheds, &c.' Indeed the question of the Bonin Islands
was so much on his mind that in his dispatch describing his
first visit to Japan, where he sailed immediately after these
incidents at Port Lloyd, he returned to his favorite theme.
'Every day of observation strengthens the opinion so often
expressed in my communications to the department,' he
declared, 'that the large and increasing commerce of the
United States with this part of the world makes it not only
desirable, but indispensable, that ports of refuge should be
established at which vessels in distress may find shelter.' [17]

Washington proved somewhat cool to his suggestions.
His original plan for the establishment of a base at the Lew
Chew Islands for his own squadron had been approved by
the President, with strict stipulations for acting only with
the consent of the natives, and his dispatch in regard to
the Bonin Islands had been 'received and perused with

interest,' but the general tone of his instructions from the Navy Department were that 'too much prudence cannot be exercised.' [18] The Government, chiefly concerned in the success of the negotiations with Japan, rather feared that its emissary's excessive zeal in seeking to secure ports of refuge might defeat the major aims of his expedition by arousing the suspicions and distrust of the Japanese authorities.

Whatever effect it had in this quarter, Perry's activity served to arouse the interest of Great Britain. He could hardly have expected otherwise. When he was in Hongkong in the interval between his two visits to Japan, the British governor, Sir George Bonham, closely questioned him as to just what his intentions in regard to the Bonin Islands were. Sir George pointed out that Great Britain had substantial claims both to Peel Island and to Bailey Island based upon priority of discovery and settlement. Without official support for his own ideas, Perry was in an awkward position, but he had no intention of accepting the thesis of this 'unconscionable government.' In disputing the British claims he declared that Bailey Island had in reality been discovered by the American, Captain Coffin, and not by Captain Beechey of the *Blossom*, and that the colony at Port Lloyd had been settled by a group which included two Americans and only one British citizen. The question of the islands' sovereignty, he told the governor of Hongkong, would have to be discussed by the two Governments concerned. [19]

His correspondence with Sir George Bonham ended on a friendly note, but for his real feeling in the matter we must turn again to his dispatches to Washington.

'I shall in no way,' he reported to the Secretary of the Navy, 'allow of any infringement upon our national rights; on the contrary, I believe that this is the moment to assume a position in the east which will make the power and influence of the United States felt in such a way as to give greater importance to those rights which, among eastern nations, are generally estimated by the extent of military force exhibited.' [20]

By this time he had also visited Formosa, whose possibilities as a source of coal supplies for both naval and merchant vessels had caused him to play with the idea of setting up an American protectorate, and he definitely sought further instructions from the Government as to his general policy. With specific reference to the Lew Chews, he stated his opinion that it would be 'a merit to extend over it the vivifying influence and protection of a government like our own,' and declared, as have so many expansionists both before and since his day, that if we had any idea of extending our possessions we should act promptly and expeditiously lest 'some other power, less scrupulous, may slip in and seize upon the advantages which should justly belong to us.'

'It is self-evident,' Perry wrote, in a remarkable dispatch when we realize that it was penned in the middle of the past century, 'that the course of coming events will ere long make it necessary for the United States to extend its jurisdiction beyond the limits of the western continent, and I assume the responsibility of urging the expediency of establishing a foothold in this quarter of the globe, as a measure of positive necessity to the sustainment of our maritime rights in the east.' [21]

He had now done everything that he could to promote an American advance to the Asiatic shore. He had urged the advisability of securing ports of refuge and coaling stations along the China coast upon every possible occasion. He had made the Lew Chews a temporary American base, raised the flag at Port Lloyd, and suggested a protectorate over Formosa. The next move clearly enough was up to Washington.

It was never made. In the next dispatch which he received from his superiors, Perry read instructions which definitely brought to a close his ambitious projects. Coal dépôts he might establish and he was commended for the tone of his correspondence with Sir George Bonham, but there was no authorization for the annexation of Peel Island, for a Formosan protectorate, or for the acquisition of any other island or port in the Pacific. His proposal for

placing the Lew Chew Islands under the surveillance of
the American flag was directly vetoed, regardless of the
outcome of his negotiations with Japan over the opening
of her ports to American vessels.

It was altogether an embarrassing suggestion, the Secretary of State informed him, and the President was not inclined under any circumstances to occupy so distant an
island possession. If resistance to our course should subsequently develop, it was pointed out, it would be 'mortify-
ing to surrender the island,' and on the other hand it would
be both 'inconvenient and expensive to maintain a force
there to retain it.' Finally his instructions explicitly declared: 'It is considered sounder policy not to seize the
island as suggested in your dispatch.' [22]

Perry lost no time in vain regrets once he had received
these instructions. He accepted the decision of President
Pierce as irrevocable. His energies were concentrated upon
the immediate purpose of his mission, and the success of
his negotiations with Japan, shrewdly compounded of skillful diplomacy and a forcible demonstration of American
naval power, is too well known to need elaboration. The
Chinese wall of seclusion which the Japanese shoguns had
so carefully built up for their country's protection from
foreign aggression was finally pierced, and Japan thrown
open to intercourse with the Western world.

It was in a sense an ironic outcome to Perry's own ambitions in the Far East. He hoped to plant the seeds of
American power in the western Pacific and launch the
United States upon a career of colonial expansion. And he
did promote our commercial interests in Asia and raise
American prestige to new heights. Yet at the same time
the most significant result of his expedition was the impetus it gave to the rise of another Pacific Power which was
in time to become our most formidable rival for control of
the Western Ocean. If it had been possible in 1853 to foresee Japan's future rôle, Perry's program might have been
viewed at Washington in a far different light.

It was as an aftermath to the Japan Expedition that we

find another abortive attempt being made by an American envoy in the Far East to interest his Government in overseas expansion. Dr. Peter Parker, our commissioner in China, was an imperialist of the same school as Seward and Perry. And though his ideas were even more completely ignored at home than those of the more distinguished naval commander, they are nevertheless a part of the story of that decade from 1850 to 1860 which found the interest of the United States in the Pacific more pronounced than at any other period until the end of the century.

Commissioner Parker concentrated his attention upon Formosa. With an ambition which contrasted strangely with his own background — for he had first come out to China as a medical missionary — he was prepared to take every possible advantage of the disturbed conditions in the Chinese Empire during this period to wrest Formosa from its control. His first move in this direction was in connection with the attempts being made by England and France about 1856 to induce China to accept a revision of the treaties which she had been forced to sign with the Western Powers a decade earlier.

Although gravely menaced by the growing power of the Taiping rebels, who were ravaging the country in one of the most devastating civil wars the world has ever known, the Imperial Government was reluctant to make any further concessions to the 'foreign devils' who treated China so cavalierly. The Emperor refused to receive their importunate envoys in Peking. In these circumstances Parker saw his opportunity, and he urged the United states to coöperate with France and England in bringing China to terms by force. He was ready to seize Chinese territory as the most effective means to compel the mandarins to grant further treaty concessions, and specifically proposed that, if the Imperial Government continued in its obstinate refusal to welcome the Western emissaries, the French flag should be raised in Korea, the British flag in Chusan, and the American flag in Formosa. These territories, he declared, should be held until 'satisfaction for the past and a right understanding for the future are granted.' [23]

This policy, vaguely foreshadowing those later demands which were to be made upon China, but from which the United States was to disassociate itself, might seem to imply that Parker contemplated the occupation of Formosa as a temporary expedient. But subsequent dispatches to Washington proved otherwise. Before he had received word from Secretary Marcy that his program was out of the question and that the United States had no mind to become embroiled in a struggle with China, Parker was writing home of American interests in Formosa which in his opinion demanded permanent protection on their own account. He firmly expressed the hope that 'the Government of the United States may not *shrink* from the *action* which the interests of humanity, civilization, navigation, and commerce impose upon it.' [24]

Our contacts with Formosa to anyone but Commissioner Parker would hardly have justified this appeal in the name of those twin coadjutors of imperialism — civilization and commerce. The island had been explored by Americans in 1847 and visited by Commodore Perry whose own interest in its coal resources may have been Parker's inspiration. It had then become the field for the commercial activities of two American traders, Gideon Nye, Jr., and W. M. Robinet. They had constructed a port at the cost of some $45,000, entered into an agreement with the local authorities for a monopoly of the export trade, and loaded some seventy-eight vessels with cargoes of an estimated value of $500,000. This was the sum total of American interests in Formosa, but as a final crowning move the two ambitious traders had actually raised the American flag over their little settlement.[25]

Nye was an ardent advocate of American possession of Formosa. To two willing listeners, Commissioner Parker and Commodore James Armstrong, commander of the United States Squadron in the Pacific, he unfolded glowing plans for the island's development, and, taking his cue directly from Commodore Perry, stressed the value of Formosa's coal resources and its convenient location on the direct route of commerce between California, Japan, and

China. He promised to assist in the colonization of the island 'if I receive the assurance of the government of the United States that I shall therein be recognized and protected.' [26]

Parker now redoubled his efforts to impress upon Washington the arguments Nye had so judiciously 'drawn from considerations of humanity, commerce, and navigation' for the assertion of American title to Formosa. His next dispatch to Washington showed that his cup of enthusiasm was running over. He recounted the advantages which would accrue to the United States from such a step, advanced at length our moral right to seize the island in reprisal for the way China had treated us, and brought out the familiar argument that there was grave danger that if we did not act, and act promptly, England would. Finally he wound up his dispatch:

'Great Britain has her St. Helena in the Atlantic, her Gibraltar and Malta in the Mediterranean, her Aden in the Red Sea, Mauritius, Ceylon, Penang and Singapore in the Indian Ocean, and Hongkong in the China seas. If the United States is so disposed, and can *arrange* for the possession of Formosa, England certainly cannot object.' [27]

While waiting a reply from Washington upon his proposed policy, for he had not been daunted by Secretary Marcy's veto of his first suggestions, Parker conferred with Commodore Armstrong as to what they could do to forestall possible action by another Power. The new British governor at Hongkong, Sir John Bowring, was warned against taking any step to circumvent their program. He was told that the United States had a prior claim upon Formosa, should it by any chance become politically severed from China, because of the settlement 'over which the United States flag has been hoisted for more than a year.'

Apparently this did not worry Sir John Bowring. Either he was ready to have the United States do what it would with Formosa or he shrewdly realized that Commissioner Parker's reach far exceeded his grasp. In any event, he disavowed any British ambitions in that direction and said that he would gladly support any attempt to give to

American commerce in Formosa 'the strength and security of *legality*.' [28] It was a somewhat cryptic reply, but it satisfied the two eager imperialists.

They next considered further moves. They agreed that Formosa was a most desirable island and particularly valuable to the United States. They agreed that, in view of China's attitude on other questions, the raising of the American flag over the island could be fully justified and legally upheld. But, unfortunately for their schemes, they were also constrained to agree that there was nothing more they could do. Should the Chinese Government by any chance resist an attempt on their part to establish American authority in Formosa, they did not have at their disposal the forces necessary for their protection.[29] They had to wait for further instructions and tangible support from Washington.

They waited, these two ambitious colonizers, in vain. While Perry had at least received an official veto to his plans, Parker and Armstrong never received any word from Washington at all. In time they had to face the fact that their Government cared not one whit for Formosa and that their annexationist schemes were hopeless. The American flag was reluctantly hauled down from the island settlement and the matter forgotten.

That it was not through oversight, but because of a definite policy, that Washington had refused to sanction the seizure cf Formosa was, however, quite apparent. When through a change of administration Parker was superseded as commissioner to China by William B. Reed, the latter was given definite instructions which clearly demonstrated that neither the dispatches of Commodore Perry and Commissioner Parker, nor the eloquent speeches of Senator Seward, had convinced the Government that the time had yet come for acquiring new territory in the Pacific.

Reed's instructions from the Buchanan Administration explicitly stated that the United States was absolutely opposed to 'territorial aggrandizement or the acquisition of political power in that distant region.' The new commissioner was told to assure China that we had no intention of interfering in her affairs, that we would not become a party to any attack upon her sovereignty, and that under no circumstances would we attempt to gain a foothold in Chinese territory.[30]

Against the pressure of its representatives in the Far East, for Townsend Harris, who was carrying on in Japan the work started by Perry, followed the Perry-Parker lead in modified form by recommending the purchase of Formosa,[31] Washington held firm. It would not have the Bonin Islands, the Lew Chew Islands, Formosa, or even, as we shall subsequently see, Hawaii. The time had not yet come when those at home could agree with Perry that it was necessary for the United States to extend its territorial jurisdiction beyond the limits of the western continent, or with Seward that we should have connections or colonies off the shores of Asia. They were not prepared to assume the responsibilities of establishing a colony in the Western Pacific, however eloquently those on the ground might urge its desirability for the sake of protecting our maritime and commercial interests.

In the face of more immediate problems nearer home, the United States did not 'deem it needful to their national life,' as a later Secretary of State declared in regard to another but similar problem of territorial expansion, 'to maintain impregnable fortresses along the world's highways of commerce.'[32] In fact we did not deem it needful to have any naval bases or coaling stations. American foreign policy was still based upon the Jeffersonian principle that 'nothing should ever be accepted which would require a navy to defend it.'[33]

CHAPTER VI

Seward's Folly

THE end of the eighteen-fifties was marked by the triumph of the Republican Party and the outbreak of that irrepressible conflict which Seward had so clearly foreseen amid his other visions of an America stretching out its power to dominate the Pacific. The course of empire was rudely interrupted. But at the same time the Civil War did not mean an end to national expansion. Throughout the conflict settlers swarmed into the new lands west of the Mississippi, filling up the gaps left by the emigrants to Oregon and California, and with the end of hostilities the vast area lying between the old frontier and the coastal states began to take on form and substance.

With our national energies so absorbed in carving additional states out of the territory which the pioneers of the forties had scorned, it was only natural that the Pacific could not command the attention it had when Oregon and California were the new members of the American Federation. The final settlement of the slavery problem, the discovery of the West's mineral wealth, the growth of new communities along the line of communications between the East and the Pacific, served to turn our attention inward instead of outward.

If the questions arising from the creation of new states, the construction of trans-continental railroads, the Indian wars, and the rapid development of industry in the East and Middle West thus acted as a restraining influence upon overseas expansion, dreams of further empire were not entirely given up by the leaders of the Republican Party. They assumed the imperialistic mantle bequeathed to them by the Democrats, even though it lay somewhat lightly on their shoulders for almost half a century, and at least Seward, as Secretary of State in the immediate post-war period, labored mightily in the cause of expansion.

He tried to purchase the Danish West Indies, only to be rebuked by the Senate; to annex Santo Domingo, only to run foul of opposition in the House. Then, turning to the Pacific, he sought the Hawaiian Islands, and, so his opponents declared, would have added a part of China to the national domain.[1]

He himself recognized the changed aspect of national affairs and realized that he was fighting against the current. 'The public attention sensibly continues to be fastened upon the domestic questions, which have grown out of our late civil war,' he wrote somewhat despairingly. 'The public mind refuses to dismiss these questions, even so far as to entertain the higher, but more remote, questions of national extension.'[2] Yet he never forswore his ambitions because of the rebuffs to which he was forced to submit. He never wholly abandoned his dream of a United States which would absorb Russia's outposts in the Far North, the great provinces being developed in Canada, the republics of Central America, and even the islands of the Pacific.

Consequently, when circumstances gave Seward an opportunity to take one halting step toward the realization of his far-flung plans, he was ready. To him and virtually to him alone we owe Alaska. This was the one new possession which he succeeded in acquiring for his country while all his other projects floundered in a sea of public indifference. Alaska, however, was on the Pacific shore. It was a drawbridge to Asia. It represented an advance toward the mastery of that ocean which Seward had so eloquently declared would be 'the chief theatre of events in the world's great hereafter.'

Alaska had been discovered as a result of the exploring expeditions sent out by Russia early in the eighteenth century. To that stalwart Dane, Vitus Bering, who was dispatched first by Peter the Great and then by the Empress Catherine to discover whether Asia and America were divided, may be traced our first knowledge of this frozen land in the Far North which he sighted in 1741.

Trade soon followed exploration and the passion of the Russian court for the beautiful fur of the sea otter led to the same traffic with the Indians which the American Nor'-westmen were in later years to conduct in Oregon. Eventually the Russian American Company was organized with monopolistic privileges for trade throughout the entire territory, which was then and until 1867 known, not as Alaska, but as Russian America, and it was supposedly upon the instigation of this company that the Russian authorities in 1787 had blocked the proposed explorations of John Ledyard.

In time a permanent settlement was established by the Russians at Sitka and made the American headquarters of the Russian American Company. From this point Russia commanded the North Pacific, attempted at one time to bar all other nations from Bering Sea, and, as we have seen, gradually crept so far south as actually to maintain a colony just north of San Francisco Bay.

It was during the governorship, from 1790 to 1819, of Alexander Baranof, an amazing man whose warm-hearted cordiality to all visitors was matched by his cruelty to the Indians and whose successful administration of the affairs of the Russian American Company found a counterpoise in the roisterous revelry of life at Sitka, that the American fur traders of the Northwest Coast made their first contacts with Alaska. They were warmly welcomed at Sitka and made agreements with Baranof for coöperative trade with the Indians. It was their custom to borrow native hunters from the genial Russian factor, and these skillful Indians would put off from the American vessels in their small canoes and make a greater killing of sea otters than was possible by any other method. Such operations were carried on as far south as California.

For their part the Americans were useful to Baranof because they brought to Sitka supplies which the little colony could obtain in no other way. It was so distant from its Russian base and the visits of Russian vessels were so infrequent that on many occasions the Yankee ships saved the Alaskan colonists from actual want if not starvation.

Common interests during this period drew the Russians and Americans together in the friendliest spirit, and one of John Jacob Astor's objectives in the foundation of Astoria had been a definite trade agreement with Baranof.

The Russian authorities did not continue to look upon this coöperation with friendly eyes for very long. They soon began to realize that the American fur traders represented commercial competitors whom the Russian American Company could not afford to welcome at Sitka. Consequently, some ten years after the question of Alaska's territorial boundaries had been settled between Russia and the United States by the treaty of 1824, definite restrictions were put into effect. American privileges of trade, navigation, and fishing in Alaskan waters were withdrawn.[3]

Owing to the decline in the fur trade consequent upon the extinction of the sea otters, these new regulations did not greatly concern the United States and it was many years before any real interest was again shown in Alaska. The whalers, which in the middle of the nineteenth century swarmed through the icy waters of the Arctic Sea, occasionally put into Alaskan ports, and with the establishment of American settlements on the Pacific Coast a slight trade in ice was inaugurated, but on the whole our contacts with Russian America were so tenuous that to the country at large Alaska did not really exist. Comparatively few persons in the United States, except in Oregon and California, could have known anything whatsoever about this cold northern territory. The movement for its purchase from Russia sprang from no background of national interest. There were certain definite reasons for Russia's desire to rid herself of Alaska; except in the mind of Secretary Seward the United States seemed to have none for wishing to acquire it.

Nevertheless, suggestions of the possible transfer of Alaska to the United States may be traced back to the time of the settlement of the Oregon controversy with Great Britain. Robert J. Walker, who was President Polk's Secretary of the Treasury, is reputed to have said at one

time that in 1846 Russia was willing to cede the territory
to the United States if we acquired from England the entire Oregon country.[4] Then at the time of the outbreak of
the Crimean War in 1854 it was more authoritatively rumored that Russia wanted to sell it. There was actually
no basis for these latter reports except in so far as they
represented an attempt upon the part of Russia to forestall
any possible British attack upon her unprotected colony.
And this objective was more directly secured by a mutual
neutrality agreement between the Russian American Company and the Hudson's Bay Company.[5]

The exposed situation of Alaska as brought home to
Russia at the time of the Crimean War did, however, start
a definite movement for its sale, and in 1857 the Grand
Duke Constantine strenuously urged the transfer to the
United States of a territory which Russia could not possibly
defend should it ever be attacked. He was vigorously supported in this policy by the Russian minister to the United
States. Baron de Stoeckl agreed with the Grand Duke that
Alaska was completely defenseless and he also pointed out
that it might well become a source of needless friction with
the United States through controversies over fishing and
other rights in Alaskan waters. There were at this time
rumors that the Mormons contemplated establishing a
settlement in Alaska, and the Russian minister foresaw
endless complications between his Government and the
United States should they prove to be true.

Upon the basis of these arguments the Russian Government decided in 1860 to initiate informal negotiations
in Washington, and Baron de Stoeckl first discussed the
question with Senator Gwin of California. He proved
moderately responsive to the Russian minister's proposals
and after taking the matter up with President Buchanan
reported that the Administration was open to consideration of Alaska's transfer. Yet no real importance seems to
have been attached to the matter and Secretary of State
Cass was never even informed of what went on. A possible
price of $5,000,000 was mentioned by Gwin, the Russian
envoy had some talks with an assistant Secretary of State,

but before negotiations conducted along such vague lines could come to anything, the Civil War intervened.

In succeeding years the United States had no time to consider anything so remote from national needs, but Russia did not let the matter drop entirely. It began to grow more and more apparent in St. Petersburg that Alaska was a liability and not an asset. Affairs in the distant colony had been badly handled, its trade was no longer profitable, and the Russian American Company was slowly but surely drifting into bankruptcy. Retention of Alaska under these circumstances appeared unwise unless it was demanded by strategic considerations. And they proved unmistakably, as the Grand Duke Constantine and other Russian officials had pointed out, the advisability of selling the territory if the United States could be prevailed upon to buy it. It was strongly felt that another war such as the Crimean would mean its loss in any event, while in the meantime so isolated a possession might easily involve Russia in a conflict which would not vitally affect her interests, but in which national prestige would demand that she take a firm stand.

It was at a council of ministers in 1866 that this whole question was thrashed over and a definite decision reached to press the sale of Alaska upon the United States by every means possible. Baron de Stoeckl was instructed to return to Washington and carry out this policy to the best of his ability.[6]

The moment could not have been more propitious. Seward was still Secretary of State. He was the one American on whom Russia could have counted at this time as being receptive to a proposal for purchasing territory in the North Pacific. It was the year in which above all others he was giving free rein to his expansionist ambitions. Looking toward the Atlantic, he was ready to annex Santo Domingo and purchase the Danish West Indies; looking toward the Pacific, he hoped to negotiate a treaty either of annexation or of reciprocity with the Hawaiian Islands, had proposed to the French minister a Franco-American expedition in Korea, and was quietly appropriating Midway Island. An opportunity to secure a foothold in the North Pacific, which he had always considered essential to the full development of our national power, fitted into his schemes more neatly than the Russians could have imagined. Alaska, in fact, rounded out his ambitious plans perfectly.[7]

To discover many other Americans who felt as Seward did is a difficult task. In 1864 the Western Union Company conducted some surveys in Alaska with a view toward laying a telegraph line to Europe by way of this territory and Siberia, but this project was abandoned when the Atlantic cable was laid. Two years later, a San Francisco Company considered a proposal for taking over the charter of the Russian American Company.[8] Yet there was no real interest in Alaska unless it was that of the communities on the west coast in possible fishing rights in the northern waters.

It was from this latter source that Seward got the inspiration to take up the possible purchase of Alaska even before the Russian minister officially suggested it. A memorial was received by President Johnson from the legislature of Washington Territory which urged a new Russian treaty giving to American vessels the right to visit Alaskan ports and take fish off the Alaskan coast. Not even this memorial represented any public demand. It was solely the work of one Joseph Lane MacDonald who had organized the Puget Sound Steam Navigation Company and was acting in his own interests.[9] The Secretary of State seized upon it, nevertheless, to make a move which played directly into the Russian minister's hands.   In his own words the inconsequential suggestion of Joseph Lane MacDonald was made the 'occasion in general terms for communicating to Mr. de Stoeckl the importance of some early and comprehensive arrangement in the Russian possessions.'[10]

Here were two willing partners for the possible transfer of Alaska and no further time was lost in opening direct negotiations. Seward obtained the unenthusiastic approval of President Johnson and the cabinet for his plans and then proceeded in March, 1867, to reach an agreement with de

Stoeckl, swiftly and secretly. Neither Congress nor the country had the slightest inkling of what a large addition to American territory the ambitious Secretary of State contemplated.

Seward at first offered $5,000,000 for Alaska. The Russian minister asked $7,000,000. A compromise between these two figures appeared logical and Baron de Stoeckl was actually prepared to accept, as he reported to his Government, from $6,000,000 to $6,500,000. But he reckoned without Seward's enthusiasm and impetuosity. There was no need to reduce the price for such an eager buyer. Not only did the Secretary of State almost immediately indicate that he was prepared to meet Russia's maximum demands, but when the question of concessions and franchises leased by the Russian American Company arose, he offered de Stoeckl an extra $200,000 if Alaska came to the United States free of all such encumbrances. The bargain quickly sealed under these circumstances, the Russian minister cabled St. Petersburg for the necessary authorization to conclude a definite treaty. Even more impatiently than de Stoeckl, Seward waited for the official reply.

'On Friday evening, March 29,' as the next step in our acquisition of Alaska has been described by the Secretary of State's son, 'Seward was playing whist in his parlor with some of his family, when the Russian minister was announced.

'"I have a dispatch, Mr. Seward, from my Government by cable. The Emperor gives his consent to the cession. Tomorrow if you like, I will come to the department, and we can enter upon the treaty."

'Seward with a smile of satisfaction at the news, pushed away the whist table, saying:

'"Why wait till tomorrow, Mr. Stoeckl? Let us make the treaty tonight."' [11]

And so the arrangement whereby Alaska was transferred to the United States was officially drawn up in this hasty and informal fashion. Startled secretaries were routed out and summoned to the State Department and with Charles

Sumner, chairman of the Senate Foreign Relations Committee, as almost the sole witness, the final instrument em-
bodying Seward and de Stoeckl's agreement was signed at
four o'clock in the morning. Passers-by, wondering why
the State Department should be so brilliantly lighted at
such an unusual hour, could little have suspected that it
signified their country's acquisition of new territory total-
ing some 590,884 square miles, an area more than twice the
size of Texas and equal to nearly one fifth of continental
United States.

Nor could any legislative body have been more surprised
than was the Senate on the following day when a special
message from President Johnson, which the members of
that august body wearily expected to be but still another
veto of some phase of their reconstruction program, briefly
submitted for their approval 'a treaty for the cession of
Russian America.' [12]

The public announcement of Seward's dramatic *coup*
was generally greeted throughout the country with howls
of derision and scorn. No step in our national expansion
had ever appeared to be so unnecessary and ill-advised.
We had a natural sympathy for Russia, largely born of the
friendly appearance of Russian fleets in New York and
San Francisco at a critical moment during the Civil War
when British recognition of the Confederacy seemed imminent, and we did not wish to do anything to disturb our
cordial relations with that Power. But to take Alaska off
Russia's hands seemed a rather large order in the interests
of international comity, and otherwise there appeared in
the public mind no logical reason for paying what was then
the huge sum of $7,200,000 for a territory in which the
United States had no real interest and which in no way
seemed necessary to our national development.

So little was known about Alaska that the press could
not discuss the physical features of the country with any
intelligence, but this did not stop it for a moment from
treating with ridicule every phase of Seward's project.
Russian America was universally characterized as barren

and worthless. It was confidently stated that the ground
in that distant territory was everywhere frozen six feet
deep, that its streams were all glaciers, and that its only
products were icebergs and polar bears. Our prospective
possession was joyously termed 'Seward's Folly' and
'Johnson's Polar Bear Garden,' while caustic editorials in
anti-Administration papers glittered with such phrases as
'bad bargain,' 'egregious folly,' 'shrewd Russians,' and
'silly administration.' [13]

Seward alone knew what he wanted and marshaled his
forces to justify his treaty and repulse the attacks which he
knew would be made upon it. He undertook to educate the
public as to the real value of Alaska, and, furnishing that
section of the press friendly to his policy with extracts from
the campaign of abuse and vilification which had marked
Jefferson's purchase of Louisiana, he endeavored to prove
by analogy that opponents of the purchase of Alaska were
following the same short-sighted and provincial tactics as
had the critics of the earlier acquisition. He must have
realized, as James G. Blaine declared, that 'in the general
judgment of the people the last thing we needed was additional territory.' [14] He had himself written that 'the desire
for the acquisition of territory has sensibly abated... we
have come to value dollars more, and dominion less.' [15] But
his inner conviction that Alaska was in reality an outpost
which would assure our control of the North Pacific gave
him the courage to wage a vigorous offensive in favor of
his treaty.

Fortunately for his plans, he secured the support of
Senator Charles Sumner. The Massachusetts Solon had a
broad vision of America's future, but it is doubtful if it had
ever embraced Alaska.[16] It was his friendship for Seward,
and more particularly his friendship for Russia, which
were the chief factors in the support he gave the Administration at this juncture. 'The Russian treaty tried me severely,' he later wrote; 'abstractly I am against further
accessions of territory, unless by the free choice of the inhabitants. But this question was perplexed by considerations of politics and comity and the engagements already

entered into by the Government. I hesitated to take the responsibility of defeating it.'[17]

Nevertheless, having once made up his mind to uphold Seward, Sumner did not do it half-heartedly. He made himself an authority on everything to do with Alaska, its physical resources and potentialities no less than its past history. When he came to defend the treaty in the Senate, his speech proved to be a masterpiece of eloquent reasoning and was so packed with information that it is still a valuable source of Alaskan history.

His espousal of Seward's program was predicated upon the stern dictum that 'this treaty must not be a precedent of a system of indiscriminate and costly annexation,' but with this notice served upon the Secretary of State that he could not count upon senatorial support for his other plans in regard to American expansion, Sumner vigorously urged prompt ratification of Alaska's cession. He believed in the extension of republican institutions and the dismissal of one more monarch from the American continent; he thought that in acquiring Alaska we might actually be anticipating similar action by Great Britain; he felt that our friendship for Russia and an obligation growing out of her cordial attitude during the Civil War made it imperative for the United States to fall in line with Russia's desire to dispose of Alaska even though we might not otherwise want it. 'It is difficult to see,' he declared in emphasizing this latter point, which unquestionably bulked largest in his mind, 'how we can refuse to complete the purchase without putting to the hazard the friendly relations which happily subsist between the United States and Russia.'[18]

More in line with Seward's own policy he also raised the question of our future position in the Pacific and spoke of our rivalry with Great Britain over that ocean's trade routes. He pointed out the strategic importance of Alaska in the northern Pacific and the possibility of its ports drawing to this country the trade of China and Japan. 'The western coast,' he told his fellow senators, 'must exercise an attraction which will be felt in China and Japan just in proportion as it is occupied by a commercial people communicating readily with the Atlantic and with Europe.' [19] Consequently, he characterized our acquisition of the Aleutian Islands, that adjunct to Alaska which stretches far out into the Pacific, as 'extending a friendly hand to Asia.' Sumner was not fired with Seward's vision, he would never have purchased Alaska upon his own initiative, but he made himself the Secretary's staunchest ally.

So decisive was the attitude of the Foreign Relations Committee chairman, in fact, that no opposition to the treaty could develop in the Senate even though support for it was actually so lukewarm. It was accepted as a *fait accompli*, and when the vote upon ratification was held, there were only two dissenting voices. Seward moved on to the next hurdle. There was still the House of Representatives. Even though it had no authority to question the Russian treaty as such, its consent was necessary for the appropriation to pay for Alaska and it was in the House that the real fight over the cession developed. Eventually it, too, swung into line, but it was not until nine months after the actual transfer of Alaska to the United States — for Seward had lost little time in carrying out this operation after his treaty's ratification — that the $7,200,000 due Russia was finally appropriated on July 14, 1868.

For a time the House showed itself so reluctant to make the appropriation necessary to reimburse Russia that Baron de Stoeckl despaired of ever seeing his country paid for Alaska's cession. He even suggested to his Government that it offer to forego payment in the hope that such a gesture would shame Congress into taking action, but the Russian Foreign Minister did not dare take any such chance.[20] He was none too confident of American generosity.

He had in this instance good reason for a wary policy, as it developed that the claims of certain American citizens against the Russian Government were being brought up as an offset to the money due on the Alaskan transaction. Even though these claims were not recognized, it soon became apparent that their injection into the situation might block the House bill. Just what happened we do not know, but no doubt exists as to the fact that bribery was used to smooth the path of congressional action. The whole transaction was tainted with that aroma of corruption which was to become so familiar to post-war Washington.

Seward later testified, with rather skillful evasions, that he had no knowledge of any corrupt deals and that in his efforts to secure the appropriation 'no engagement was ever made with anybody for any part of the purchase-money, or any other fund.' [21] But on the other side is a dispatch from de Stoeckl to his Government reporting that he had used up the greater part of the $200,000 provided him for 'secret expenses,' and an even more significant memorandum which was found among the papers of President Johnson.[22] In this latter document the President quotes Seward as having told him that Russia had paid in connection with the Alaskan treaty $30,000 to John W. Forney, $20,000 to R. J. Walker and F. P. Stanton, $10,000 to Thaddeus Stevens, and $8,000 to N. P. Banks.[23] If there was some justification for certain of these pay-ments, such as that to R. J. Walker, who was admittedly acting as de Stoeckl's chief lobbyist, this could not be said of the others. It is not a pleasant aspect of our purchase of Alaska to have to recognize the unsavory atmosphere in which it was completed or to note Baron de Stoeckl's final plea to his Government to transfer him to some place where for a while he could 'breathe an atmosphere purer than that of Washington.'

Apart from all this, however, the propaganda inspired by Seward in favor of his treaty and the debates in the House when the appropriation bill was discussed in the open rather than in the lobbies and committee rooms, are revelatory of the state of public interest in the further extension of our Pacific empire. The Secretary of State found only a handful of supporters for his own ambitious schemes, but they at least had the advantage over Alaska's critics of being able to take the offensive and urge action for which precedents could be produced from every previous accession of territory.

From the American minister at St. Petersburg, C. M. Clay, came word that Alaska was really worth $50,000,000 and that it was impossible to overestimate the importance of 'our ownership of the western coast of the Pacific in connection with the vast trade which was springing up with China and Japan and the western islands.' [24] Robert J. Walker, even though his statements may not have been disinterested because of his connection with de Stoeckl, proved to be an imperialist after Seward's own heart. 'The ultimate struggle for command of the commerce and exchanges of the world,' he wrote at this time, 'is to be decided mainly upon the Pacific, and, the acquisition of Alaska, including the Aleutian isles, has immeasurably strengthened our position in that ocean.' [25]

Even more reminiscent of Seward's own apotheosis of the Pacific was the speech made in the House in the course of the Alaskan debate by another of de Stoeckl's supposed protégés. 'That ocean will be the theatre of the triumphs of civilization in the future,' N. P. Banks, chairman of the Foreign Relations Committee, declared. 'It is on that line that are to be fought the great battles of the hereafter. It is there that the institutions of the world will be fashioned and its destinies decided. If this transfer is successful, it will no longer be an European civilization or an European destiny that controls us. It will be a higher civilization and a nobler destiny. It may be an American civilization, an American destiny of six hundred million souls.' [26]

Unfortunately, Representative Banks did not fully explain how the purchase of Russian America was to bring Asia's millions within the orbit of American civilization and American destiny. That apparently was for the future. But in the meantime Alaska was the key to the Pacific and the Aleutian Islands were 'this intermediate communication between the two continents, this drawbridge between America and Asia, these stepping stones across the Pacific Ocean.'

So, too, did Representative Maynard of Tennessee look eagerly forward to the day when 'the civilization of this world will be transferred from the Atlantic to the Pacific.'

He caught Seward's beatific vision of empire which would give the United States 'commercial and naval supremacy on the Pacific as complete as Great Britain has for two centuries enjoyed on the Atlantic Ocean.' For him Alaska was 'but a part of our great Pacific system.'

In the face of the enthusiasm and exuberance of spirit shown by this small band of Seward's allies, the opponents of the Russian treaty struck a flat and discordant note. They were bitter and sarcastic. They caught no glimpse of Pacific empire. They foresaw no future for the United States in which Alaska could play its part. All they could see in this distant Russian territory was a completely valueless but very burdensome expanse of snow and ice. If our obligations to Russia demanded a payment to her of $7,200,000, they were prepared to make it, but they were against taking Alaska even as a free gift.

Russia was welcome to keep her colony, Hiram Price of Iowa declared, 'in all its hideous proportions and native churlishness... until the last echoes of the trump of time shall have died away among the hills of eternity.' C. C. Washburn of Wisconsin blandly suggested 'that we could have bought a much superior elephant in Siam or Bombay for one hundredth part of the money, with not a ten thousandth part of the expense incurred in keeping the animal in proper condition.'

'Alaska, with the Aleutian Islands,' Representative Ferris of New York caustically remarked, 'is an inhospitable, wretched, and God-forsaken region, worth nothing, but a positive injury and incumbrance as a colony of the United States.'

'Have the people desired it?' demanded Representative Williams of Pennsylvania. 'Not a sensible man among them had ever suggested it. The whole country exclaimed at once, when it was made known to it, against the ineffable folly, if not the wanton profligacy, of the whole transaction.'

A more telling and significant argument than anything brought out in these rabid denunciations of Seward's policy was advanced by Representative Shellabarger of Ohio. He pointed out that Alaska was non-contiguous territory and that its acquisition would mark an entirely new departure in our program of national expansion. The real issue at stake, he told the House, was whether the United States was prepared 'to step now for the first time upon the policy of acquiring possessions across the world, far remote, and of creating a system of foreign colonies.' Thirty years later, debates on this point were to arouse the nation. The halls of Congress were to echo and reëcho with bitter comment upon foreign colonies and republican principles. But in 1868 the issue did not seem important. The purchase of Alaska appeared so quixotic that it was not believed it could establish any dangerous precedent.

The favorable vote upon the appropriation of the moneys due Russia which was finally wrung from the reluctant House was consequently far from being an expression of any real national interest. Political influence and the subtle pressure of the Russian minister played a more important part in the result than the eloquence of Seward's allies and their dreams of empire.

Nevertheless, many of the enthusiastic statements made by the Secretary of State and his friends as to Alaska's potential value were quickly realized and the country soon became reconciled to possession of 'Johnson's polar bear garden.' Within a few decades the $7,200,000 which the United States had paid for its new territory, a sum which amounts to 1 19/20 cents an acre and constitutes a striking comparison with the $25,000,000 which we were to give half a century later for the Virgin Islands, had been repaid many times over in the form of taxes upon Alaskan industries. The expansion of the northern fisheries, the development of the fur seal industry, and especially the discovery of gold soon gave an entirely different aspect to this 'inhospitable, wretched, and God-forsaken region, worth nothing.'

In the period from 1880 to 1893 the gold production of Alaska equaled the price set upon the territory by the Russian Government and by the end of the century one mine alone had paid its stockholders an approximate $7,200,000 in dividends. The total value of the annual catch of the fisheries for the thirty years following the Russian treaty was almost ten times this figure, while upon the expiration of its monopoly in 1890, the Alaska Commercial Company had paid into the United States Treasury some $6,000,000 from its profits in the fur seal industry.[27]

Views of Alaska's potential wealth became for a time as exaggerated as had been the earlier conception of its worthlessness. When these profits from the gold-fields and from the fishing and sealing industries first began rolling in, it was difficult not to consider the country an inexhaustible treasure-house of easily available wealth. Yet even if this was not quite justified, there is no question that Seward's bold stroke obtained for the United States a territory worth many times the sum paid for it and a possession which the country would not now willingly relinquish.

Whether its strategic importance has justified the claims Seward made for it is another question. It has not yet proved to be a 'drawbridge between America and Asia' nor have the Aleutian Islands developed into 'stepping stones across the Pacific Ocean.' But has the last word been said? The air routes of the future have not been plotted, and it is far from inconceivable, in fact such an opinion is held in many quarters, that in time the Aleutian Islands will mark the stages of an air transport system linking America and Asia and furnish the aviation bases for future air fleets.

Seward may prove to have been justified when as a part of his Pacific policy he acquired Alaska to assure our domination of the northern seas. Even though circumstances have changed since his day and the international agreements providing for the divided control of the Pacific by the naval Powers should obviate the necessity of developing great seaplane bases in the Aleutian Islands, we cannot be too sure of this. 'If the United States were again to set out by isolated action to protect its interests in Eastern Asia,' Tyler Dennett has written in discussing our retention of the Philippines, 'it is probable that the line of advance would be over the bridge to which "Seward's Folly" points.'[28]

Had the United States not purchased Alaska in 1867 it is highly probable that sooner or later it would have fallen into British hands. Yet it is interesting to conjecture what would today be our attitude if this northern territory had remained a Russian possession and represented an outpost of the Soviet Government on the American mainland. The potential threat to our interests of a Communist base which stretched down the western coast to within seven hundred miles of the Northwest States would cast the politics of the Pacific in a far different mould.

Freedom from these possible complications we owe to Secretary Seward. Our westward expansion to the coast and the occupation of Oregon and California may be viewed as the inevitable expression of 'manifest destiny.' President Polk was the willing instrument of forces greater than himself. But our first acquisition of non-contiguous territory was almost wholly due to the initiative and determination of one man.

CHAPTER VII

The Navy Discovers Samoa

THE purchase of Alaska marked the last actual acquisition of territory on the Pacific until the end of the century. Yet this does not mean that there was a complete cessation of expansionist activity. There was still, as we shall see, Hawaii, while within five years of the signature of the treaty with Russia, the visit of an American naval officer to an obscure island in the Samoan Archipelago set in motion a train of events which some thirty years later was to add another outpost to our growing empire. This new accession was an island possession which in the minds of its advocates was to do for American power and influence in the South Pacific what Seward had hoped the possession of Alaska would do for our position in the North Pacific.

Even though Samoa is one of our least important acquisitions, moreover, the history of the successive stages through which it came into our possession is unusually significant. It reflects over a period of thirty years the slow growth of a feeling in the United States that we were not yet done with national expansion. Our involvement in the affairs of so remote and relatively unimportant an island marked a new departure in our foreign policy which was still further emphasized by entanglements with Germany and Great Britain which seemed to cast the United States in the unexpected rôle of a rival to their colonial activity. It is easy to realize, as we trace the course of our policy toward Samoa, how those national ambitions were developed and strengthened which made possible the imperialistic spirit of the closing days of the century and the birth of a new conception of America's destiny.

American interest in the South Pacific was born almost as early as that in the North Pacific. Just as the first voyages along the coast of Oregon and California were an offshoot of the old China trade, so were the first voyages among the isles of the South Seas. They were a projection of the indefatigable search of New England's merchant seamen for products which could be exchanged at Canton for China's teas and silks. At the Marquesas, the Fijis, the Carolines, the Admiralty Islands, the Friendly Islands, and Tahiti the Yankee traders bartered with eager natives for such strange commodities as sandalwood, tortoise-shell, edible birds' nests, and *bêche de mer*. Sometimes these romantic South Sea voyages brought great profits in terms of full cargoes of China goods; sometimes they ended in disaster with wrecks on hidden coral reefs or sudden, treacherous attacks by the savage islanders.[1]

Occasionally, too, these pioneers of trade played with the idea of establishing American colonies in the South Seas. None of their fanciful schemes ever came to anything. The usual motive behind them was nothing more than an urge to find a way of living, as one of the early voyagers wrote, free from 'the toils, and cares, and constant miseries of a moneyed slave.' Among such schemes, however, was an attempt by an American naval officer to annex a group of the Marquesas. It received no support from his Government, but foreshadowed the somewhat similar action taken sixty years later in Samoa by another naval officer, action which was to have more permanent results.

This early attempt to annex a Pacific island was made by Captain David Porter, in command of the frigate *Essex*, during the course of the War of 1812. American ships had been effectively driven from the Pacific by British war vessels during this conflict, but Captain Porter, after a series of memorable attacks on enemy shipping in the Atlantic, rounded Cape Horn without orders and proceeded to wage a retaliatory war upon British whalers. Forced at length to seek supplies and repair his vessel, he took refuge among the Washington Islands, a group of the Marquesas which had been discovered by an American trader, Captain Joseph Ingraham, in 1791. Here he beached the *Essex* at Nukahiva Island and sent his crew ashore for rest and recuperation.[2]

It proved to be a wonderfully pleasant resort. Captain

Porter found such plentiful supplies of hogs, breadfruit, and coconuts that his men 'rioted in the luxuries which the island afforded,' while the natives were so cordial that the naval officer wrote in his account of his experiences that he was fully inclined to believe 'that a more honest, or friendly and better disposed people does not exist under the sun.' The most happy relations were quickly established between the Americans and their Marquesan hosts from which the native women were by no means excluded. 'With the common sailors and their girls,' Captain Porter reported succinctly, 'all was helter skelter.' ³

But this able officer was not drugged into inactivity by the lazy delights of South Sea life. He apparently dreamed of establishing a naval base in the Marquesas. After setting the natives to work upon a village to house his men and upon a fort for their protection, he determined to annex Nukahiva in the name of his Government. It was renamed Madison Island and its broad harbor called Massachusetts Bay, the American flag was raised over the fort, and on November 19, 1813, an official proclamation was made to the mystified but acquiescent natives.

'Our right to this island being founded on priority of discovery, conquest, and possession,' Captain Porter announced, 'cannot be disputed. But the natives, to secure to themselves that friendly protection which their defenceless situation so much required, have requested to be admitted into the great American family whose pure republican policy approaches so near their own.... I do declare that I have in the most solemn manner, under the American flag displayed in Fort Madison, and in the presence of numerous witnesses, taken possession of said island, called Madison Island.... And that our claim to this island may not be hereafter disputed, I have buried in a bottle, at the foot of the flagstaff in Fort Madison, a copy of this instrument, together with several pieces of money, the coin of the United States.' ⁴

The act of annexation could not have been carried out more efficiently. Every requirement for the seizure of new territory was duly fulfilled and the reference to the na-

tives' desire for the protection of the United States, because the great American family's 'pure republican policy
approaches so near their own,' showed a subtle understanding of the processes of expansion which should have stood
Captain Porter in better stead. For this is the end of the
story. When the *Essex* left Madison Island to renew the
chase of British whalers and was defeated in a spectacular
encounter with enemy frigates in the harbor of Valparaiso,
the Marquesan natives seem to have forgotten their mem-
bership in the great American family.

A few years later, another vessel, the U.S.S. *Dolphin*,
called at Nukahiva and found that all traces of American
occupation had disappeared. What had once been the
village of Madison was a tangle of underbrush and the
jungle had pulled down in ruins the walls of the American
fort.[5] Captain Porter himself never returned and there is
no record of discussion or official action at Washington
upon his ambitious project. Thirty years later, France
undertook to annex the Marquesas and the United States
entered no protest.

No other definite move for acquiring a naval base in the
South Seas marks the early history of our maritime activity in that part of the Pacific until the agitation over
Samoa. But there is plenty of evidence of our growing interest in these distant waters. Trade among the islands
increased, the whalers explored the length and breadth of
the South Sea, the navy established a Pacific station in
1821, and American war vessels called at almost every port
in the Western Ocean including our subsequent possessions
in the Philippines, Hawaii, and Samoa. There was even at
one time vague rumors that we contemplated extending
our influence over the Fiji Islands because of debts owed
American merchants which the native chiefs refused to
honor. In 1858 the Fijis offered their islands to Queen Vic-
toria in order to forestall such action, and again in 1869
Lord Granville had occasion to refer to the 'risk of the
United States assuming the protectorate.' Such action
was never seriously contemplated in Washington, however,
and England in any event settled the question by annexing
the Fijis herself in 1874.[6]

Samoa first swung within the orbit of official American interest in 1839 when the islands were visited by Commodore Charles Wilkes in the course of an expedition of exploration through the South Seas. Lying in the Southwest Pacific on a line between San Francisco and Australia, the Samoan Archipelago consists of some fourteen islands. Savaii, Upolo, and Tutuila are the largest, but the total area is only about twelve hundred square miles. They were first sighted by the Dutch navigator Jacob Roggeveen in 1722 and explored by Louis de Bougainville in 1768, who called them the Isles of the Navigators. For long they were carefully avoided by traders of the South Seas because of a reputation for cruelty which the natives won as a result of an attack on French explorers, but this obscure incident had created a false impression of Samoan character. When English missionaries sought out the islands in 1830, they found the people peaceful and friendly. Nowhere was Christianity embraced more eagerly than in Samoa and nowhere were the traders who followed in the missionaries' wake welcomed more cordially.[7]

Commodore Wilkes found virtually the entire population converts of the new faith in 1839 and was immensely impressed by their piety. Their strict observance of Sunday reflected in this exotic tropical atmosphere all the austere decorum of New England. It was a day devoted to church-going and hymn-singing. All other activity was tabu, including the chief Samoan pleasure of bathing and the imported delight of cricket. But at the same time the American visitors discovered that church-going in Samoa, as is sometimes the case in other parts of the world, meant in addition to piety a recognized occasion for social display. The wife of one of the chiefs to whom Commodore Wilkes had distributed certain gifts seized the opportunity of a Sunday service to appear in all her new finery. The temperature was 87°, the Commodore tells us in his official report, but this important lady was dressed in a red calico gown, four or five colored petticoats, woolen socks, green slippers, a cap and a bonnet, a plaid blanket shawl and polar gloves, topped off with a red silk umbrella.[8]

The trade of these childlike people was a matter of simple barter. Commodore Wilkes discovered a lively commerce under way in copra and coconut oil for which the foreign traders visiting the islands exchanged various gaudy articles of European and American manufacture. He considered this commerce worth promoting and drew up with the native chiefs formal articles of agreement for the reception of foreign vessels and the admission of foreign consuls. On the island of Tutuila, where he noted particularly the great possibilities of the fine bay of Pago Pago, he found resident an American trader whom he named as agent of the United States.

For some thirty years after this visit no further step was taken linking the United States and Samoa except the appointment of a consul. The foreign community in the islands and its trade expanded gradually during this period, but the archipelago seemed destined to be dominated by Germany. The Hamburg firm of Goddefroy made Apia, the Samoan capital, the headquarters for all its extensive operations in the South Seas, and the German consul asserted a rising influence over certain of the native chiefs. Then in 1871 the project of a steamship line between San Francisco and Australia, for which Samoa appeared to be a natural way-station, created a new and active American interest in the islands.

Upon the instigation of W. H. Webb, a New York shipbuilder, Captain E. Wakeman paid a visit of investigation to Samoa and examined with particular care the possibilities of making the harbor of Pago Pago into a naval and coaling station. His report was enthusiastic. Pago Pago was described as 'the most perfectly land-locked harbor that exists in the Pacific Ocean.' [9]

A copy of this document was sent to Secretary of the Navy Robeson, who replied that the navy was fully aware of Pago Pago's great value, and another to Rear Admiral John A. Winslow, in command of the Pacific station, whose answer was more specific. He dispatched Commander Richard W. Meade to Samoa with orders to locate a coal dépôt at Pago Pago and secure a treaty with the chiefs of Tutuila 'to frustrate foreign influence which is at present very active in this matter, seeking to secure the harbor.' Here were already evident the portents of future friction between the United States and Germany. For it was true that German residents in Samoa were growing ambitious. Their consul had suggested either annexation of the islands or establishment of a naval base, although Bismarck had rejected his schemes and ordered him 'to avoid any friction with the United States.' [10]

Commander Meade carried out his mission with thoroughness and dispatch. In February, 1872, the great chief of Pago Pago, persuaded of the unique advantage of securing the friendship and protection of the United States, signed an agreement which granted this country possession of the desired harbor. Three months later, the Senate was confronted with this new treaty which would have involved the United States in the affairs of a more distant part of the world than even Seward or Perry had ever contemplated as a field for American activity.

The treaty was submitted by President Grant. He was an expansionist, as his attempt to annex Santo Domingo proves, but the Senate's recent rejection of his Dominican treaty made him somewhat cautious about supporting the Samoan agreement. He informed the Senate that it had been made without authority and declared he was hesitant about sponsoring it in view of the obligations it appeared to impose upon the United States. Nevertheless, he stressed the value to this country of the harbor at Pago Pago, and finally stated that 'with some modification of the obligation of protection which the agreement imports, it is recommended to the favorable consideration of the Senate.' [11]

That august body, however, was still in no mood for anything even as remotely resembling annexation as a coaling station. It was governed by the same feelings which had induced the House, after its reluctant approval of the purchase of Alaska in 1868, to pass by a two-thirds majority a bill against any further purchases of foreign territory. Consequently, Commander Meade's treaty was never ratified.

The advocates of American control over Samoa were not entirely disheartened by this rejection of their plans. They continued to advance their arguments stressing the value of Pago Pago to the United States, secured by fair means or foul a petition from a group of Samoan chiefs which asked President Grant 'to annex these our islands,' and at length prevailed upon the Government to send a special commissioner to look into Samoan affairs. A. B. Steinberger was appointed to this post, and his instructions from Secretary of State Hamilton Fish stated, despite the recent action of the Senate, that 'it is not unlikely that perhaps in the not distant future the interests of the United States may require not only a naval station in the Samoan group, but a harbor where their steam and other vessels may freely and securely frequent.' The 'not unlikely' and the 'perhaps' of Secretary Fish would seem to indicate a certain doubt of the reasonableness of an extension of American influence to the South Seas, but nevertheless he asked Steinberger to render a full account of conditions in Samoa 'to enable the government here to determine as to the measures which may be advisable toward obtaining that object.' [12]

Steinberger's career in Samoa was a dramatic, and, in its close, somewhat unsavory, episode in what was fast becoming the complicated and pathetic history of the islands' relations with the outside world. The rivalry of the German, British, and American traders at Apia was combining with the internal strife among the Samoan chiefs to create a situation fraught with endless friction. The United States was fast becoming involved in problems which the State Department could hardly hope to understand and of which the country at large knew nothing whatever.

With Steinberger's first visit to Samoa there was nothing out of order. He may have given the chiefs a somewhat false impression of the possibility of the United States extending a protectorate over them, but at least he took no definite action. He returned to Washington after a few months' stay with a full and interesting report of the islands and a letter from the leading chieftain repeating the former plea for annexation. That influence was exerted by interested parties in securing this letter is rather ironically demonstrated in the innocent chief's expressed desire for American jurisdiction because he knew of our 'paternal care of the Indians.'

The American commissioner's second visit to Samoa was another matter. He was sent back at his own request after declaring that he could 'with facility control these people; and to me it would be a labor of love.' His instructions counseled caution in raising false hopes among the chiefs, and Secretary Fish now stated that, despite the importance to the United States of the Samoan group, it was doubtful 'whether these considerations would be sufficient to satisfy our people that the annexation of these islands to the United States is essential to our safety and prosperity.' In view of these circumstances, he further declared, it was deemed inexpedient 'to originate a measure adverse to the usual traditions of the Government, and which, therefore, probably would not receive such a sanction as would be likely to secure its success.' [13]

Feeling this way about Samoa, it is curious that the Administration sent Steinberger back at all, but it is only too evident that the islands had a magnetic influence upon Washington. A treaty having once been signed with a native chief, it was apparently impossible to forego the hope that eventually something might come of it. For not only was Steinberger sent back. He took with him a collection of presents made up of guns and ammunition, one hundred sailors' suits, and three American flags — a choice of gifts hardly calculated to have a calming effect upon the Samoan chiefs.

The American envoy's actions upon his arrival at Apia were even more disturbing. Within a month the American consul was reporting that Steinberger was everywhere giving the impression that the United States was about to establish a protectorate and he quite logically asked for an explanation of the commissioner's 'assumption and exercise of arbitrary and unauthorized power quite inconsistent with your instructions.' These charges Steinberger quickly denied, but in July, 1875, news of another sort reached Washington. Its erratic envoy calmly announced that he had accepted the position of premier of the Kingdom of Samoa, while from other sources it was learned that he had entered into an agreement with the German firm at Apia and that his influence in the local government was being exerted in favor of the American traders' chief rivals.

There is no question that Steinberger was an out-and-out adventurer in his Samoan career. His orders against encouraging the protectorate idea were explicit and certainly Washington had nothing to do with his assumption of the Samoan premiership. When he had the grace to submit his resignation as special commissioner, it was accepted without question. When his subsequent activities aroused the opposition of the foreign element in Samoa and the American consul asked about his status in behalf of those wishing to have him deported, no finger was raised for his protection. The State Department informed its representative at Apia that Steinberger had completed his mission, made his report, and tendered his resignation. The incident was closed.[14]

The protectorate idea could not be disposed of as easily as could Steinberger. The handful of Americans in Samoa, including the consul, were more than anxious that the United States should actively intervene in Samoan affairs, and feared that, if this country did not act quickly, either Germany or England would. The islands seethed with rumors of foreign aggression, and either of their own volition or through the influence of the foreigners, the chiefs alternately offered their country to England and to the United States. On two occasions, in 1877 and 1878, when the prize seemed about to fall into British hands, the American consul actually raised the American flag. His action was immediately disavowed by his Government, but nevertheless it indicated how high feeling was running in Samoa. Also in the midst of this local excitement the Samoan chiefs, with the assistance of their American friends, made a new attempt to win the protection of the United States by dispatching one of their number to

Washington with a definite offer for either annexation or a protectorate.

This native envoy was received by Under-Secretary of State Frederick W. Seward, son of William H. Seward, who has left an interesting account of his unusual visitor. Seward was thoroughly in sympathy with the idea of annexation of Samoa, but naturally felt dubious about the possibility of getting such a treaty through the Senate. He explained to the Samoan that, whereas the United States had formerly sought new territory, there had been a change in its policy and 'extension of the national boundaries was now looked upon with disfavor,' while even the purchase of Alaska 'was still a subject of reproach and ridicule, and pronounced a gigantic folly.' [15] Nevertheless, he introduced the island chief to President Hayes and Secretary of State Evarts and annexation was debated in a cabinet meeting.

Both the President and the Secretary of State, Seward wrote, believed 'that my father's policy in this regard had been wise and judicious. But they also saw that it would now encounter the same opposition that it had during the administration of President Johnson and subsequently under that of President Grant.' When opinion was sounded out, the Administration's views were confirmed, and like a true son of his father Seward lamented that 'it seemed to be a mark of patriotism to oppose any addition to our own country.' [16]

The South Sea envoy was not, however, sent home empty-handed. The Samoan magnet had not lost its attractive powers. On January 16, 1878, a treaty was drawn up providing for the naval station at Pago Pago for which Commander Meade had first contracted and granting the United States certain commercial and extra-territorial privileges. The only clause even indirectly suggesting anything in the nature of a protectorate was one in which the United States proffered its good offices in the event of any differences arising between the Samoan Government and that of any Power with which we were on friendly terms. [17]

This treaty the Senate ratified. It seemed innocuous enough and aroused neither enthusiasm nor opposition. Seward reports that the public was completely indifferent and Congress made no appropriation for developing a coaling station. In naval circles, however, a different feeling prevailed, and two years later Commodore Robert W. Shufeldt, an expansionist of the Perry school, was coupling the treaty with our other moves for controlling the Pacific. 'The acquisition of Alaska and the Aleutian Islands, the treaties with Japan, Sandwich Islands and Samoa,' he wrote in 1880, 'are only corollaries to the proposition that the Pacific Ocean is to become at no distant day the commercial domain of America.' [18]

In Samoa the action of the United States was soon followed by the negotiation of similar treaties by both England and Germany. The two countries secured naval stations and other privileges comparable to those of the United States, while still further to equalize their position in the islands a joint agreement was reached in 1880 by the three foreign consuls and the Samoan Government setting up in Apia a foreign-controlled municipality. Thus, instead of finding themselves securely under the protection of one Power, the Samoans had allowed themselves to be maneuvered into a position in which three rival countries all had equal but somewhat vaguely defined rights in their islands definitely infringing upon Samoan independence.

They themselves were too completely innocent of the significance of international relations and too ignorant of the outside world to have the slightest idea of the trouble they were storing up for themselves. But the combination of foreign rivalries and native wars was to make Samoa at intervals during the next two decades a cockpit for the suspicion, jealousy, and open hostility of the three Powers. On that Lilliputian stage was to be played a drama which almost brought about international war.

We must now turn to the chronic strife among the Samoan chieftains for the dubious honor of the kingship,

a continuing quarrel in which the foreigners were hereafter always embroiled. This rivalry had its origin in
a complicated question of honorary 'names,' somewhat
corresponding to titles, which carried with them certain
attributes of power, but rendered it almost impossible for
any one Samoan to have a clear right to the kingship. In
1880 the recognized King was Malietoa, but his death a
year later brought about a renewal of native warfare with
Malietoa Laupepa and Tamasese, rival claimants to the
throne. The foreign consuls intervened in an attempt to
bring about peace, and a treaty was finally signed between
the two opposing factions on board the American ship
Lackawanna whereby Malietoa Laupepa was declared
King and Tamasese made Vice-King.[19]

It was a clever compromise, but four years later the
storm again burst and the protectorate ambitions of the
foreign consuls made common intervention impossible.
New Zealand was frantically urging the British Government to annex the islands. The German consul, reflecting
Bismarck's new colonial policy and interest in the South
Seas, was intriguing for a German protectorate. And if
the United States was not officially interested in extending
its influence, it was not for lack of agitation on the part
of its representatives in Samoa.

The rivalry culminated when the German consul forced
upon King Malietoa, without even allowing him to read
the document he had to sign, a new agreement which
would have provided a German adviser for his Government and a Samoan-German council of state. The native
chieftain appealed to England and the United States for
protection and disregarded the pact. Whereupon the
German consul took over control of Apia, raised his
country's flag, and virtually deprived Malietoa of all
power. Further than that, he did not hesitate to foment
a native revolt against the King under the leadership of
Tamasese.[20]

'The fact is notorious,' wrote the British consul in
regard to these developments, 'that the rebellion was
taken under German protection to forward the plans which

they had failed to bring about in a peaceful manner through Malietoa; so they were determined to try other means, even if it cost another war.'[21]

It is not difficult to imagine the light in which the British and Americans in Samoa viewed these high-handed proceedings and the apparent evidence of Germany's determination to seize control of the islands. Yet when Malietoa had turned to the two friendly consuls for protection, they could only counsel peace. They had no recourse but to rely upon their Governments to settle the international questions involved and to protect both their own and Samoa's interests. And during this period of excitement and native war in the islands, the diplomatic wires between Washington, London, and Berlin began to hum. Samoa had suddenly become a problem which could not be ignored.

When word reached Washington that the German consul had hauled down the Samoan flag, the United States protested promptly and vigorously to Berlin. President Cleveland was now in office. While his Republican predecessors had never entirely given up the idea of annexing new territory, this first Democratic President since the Civil War was firmly opposed to any such move. The respective positions of the two parties, considering the Republicans as the successors of the Whigs, had been completely reversed. But at the same time Cleveland was fully alive to the existence of American interests in Samoa and to the potential value of the naval base at Pago Pago. It is certainly open to question whether he would otherwise have believed that the United States was obligated to preserve Samoan independence. His attitude in view of the European colonial policy of that day might have been fairly described by Germany as that of a dog in the manger. He felt it constitutionally and ethically wrong for the United States to annex the islands, but he was determined to prevent any other Power from doing so.

'The moral interests of the United States with respect to the islands of the Pacific, necessarily dependent in greater or less degree on our own American system of commonwealths,' Secretary of State Bayard wrote the American consul at Apia, 'would counsel us to look with concern on any movement by which the independence of those Pacific nationalities might be extinguished by their passage under the domination of a foreign sovereign.'[22]

The attitude of the German Government at this period, or more precisely that of Bismarck, was one of official opposition to colonial development and its secret encouragement.[23] Consequently, the Chancellor's reply to the American protest on the activities of the German consul in Samoa was an immediate disavowal of any annexationist program. Behind this the United States could not go, for it, too, was soon constrained to issue a similar denial of aggressive designs when the American consul attempted without authorization to proclaim an American protectorate over the islands. It may well be that this local move was more effective in blocking Germany's designs than our official protests. It was believed to be at the time, as we find reflected in the biography of Sir George Grey, a former governor of New Zealand and friend of Samoa, whose authors do not hesitate to state that had it not been for the action of the American consul in placing Samoa under the protection of the American flag, the islands 'would have been seized by Germany and incorporated in the German Empire.'[24]

In any event, it became all too clear in both Washington and Berlin that affairs in Samoa were getting out of hand and that the situation there demanded some change in the treaty relations of the Powers concerned. Secretary Bayard consequently suggested a conference in Washington to consider a program which involved recognition of a new king, a fresh deal of consuls all around, and a joint declaration against either annexation or the establishment of a protectorate by any one of the three Powers. To this both England and Germany agreed, and after special commissioners had been sent to Samoa to examine the situation, a conference was held in Washington in the summer of 1887.

The specific proposal now advanced by the United States was a tripartite agreement for temporary control of Samoan affairs through the appointment of three foreign representatives to the Samoan executive council. Secretary Bayard may have been actuated solely by an altruistic desire to preserve Samoan independence; he may have been influenced by the recommendation of the American commissioner. The latter had strongly stated his opinion that, since the United States had acquired a foothold in the South Pacific, 'it would be shortsighted indeed if we were to permit the advantages of this action to slip away from us by leaving the way open to European domination in this group.' [25]

Whatever the motive for tripartite control of Samoa, the American program found no favor with either England or Germany. The British viewpoint, which hitherto had coincided with that of the United States, had changed because of an agreement which England and Germany had reached in 1886 limiting their respective zones of influence in the South Pacific. Samoa was excepted from this arrangement, yet England seemed prepared to give Germany a free hand in the islands. The latter nation's proposal to the conference was that the Power having a predominant interest in Samoa should appoint an adviser to the King, whose position would be upheld by all three Powers. Obviously this meant Germany, whose traders controlled the bulk of Apia's commerce with a far greater volume of exports and imports than those of the United States and England combined. This solution of the problem might not mean annexation by Germany, but it was construed as a thinly disguised step toward that goal. The United States would not accept it and the conference was adjourned without results. [26]

In the meantime events had begun to move fast in Samoa. Although it had been understood that the *status quo* would be maintained while the negotiations at Washington were under way, friction among the foreigners could not be eliminated and the situation in Apia grew steadily more dangerous. The fact was that the consuls and the officers of the foreign naval vessels in the harbor were too far out of touch with their Governments — Samoa had no cable communications with the outside world — for them to feel subject to as much restraint as would have been good for them. They were one and all governed more by the demands of the moment, colored by all the suspicion and hostility which Samoa seemed to breed, than by considerations of international comity.

Germany had dispatched a squadron of four vessels to the islands for the safeguarding of its interests, and with their arrival the German consul declared a 'personal war' against Malietoa Laupepa on the pretence of alleged insults to Germany and certain outstanding debts to German traders. After landing six guns and seven hundred men, the helpless King was deposed and in his stead Tamasese installed as new head of the Government with a German named Brandeis acting as his premier. Driven to the bush, Laupepa soon surrendered to 'the invincible strangers' and was thereupon deported. Behind him he left two pathetic documents, a farewell to his country sadly declaring that he had surrendered to avoid bloodshed, but that he did not know 'what is my offence which has caused their anger to me and to my country,' and a farewell to the American and British consuls, recalling their promises of protection and expressing the hope 'that you will so far redeem them as to cause the lives and liberties of my chiefs and people to be respected.'

These two consuls refused to recognize the puppet administration which Germany had set up; so did the Samoans. A native revolt broke out, headed by a new claimant to the throne, Mataafa, and the chiefs declared that they were 'worn out with the constant wickedness of Tamasese and Brandeis.' The insurgents received the passive if not the active support of the Americans and British, while the Germans made no pretense of denying the fact that they were backing Tamasese. The two hostile forces clashed in September, 1888, and the Mataafa adherents routed the Tamasese forces, which were unable to

rally until they reached a point on the shore under the protection of the guns of the German vessels.[27]

The American and British consuls now recognized
Mataafa as King, but the Germans continued to support
Tamasese and supplied his followers with guns and ammunition. It looked more than ever as if Germany were
determined to keep its candidate in power as a means of
gaining domination over the islands. The American
consul grew frantic. 'Could not the United States get in
ahead till things are settled?' he hysterically asked
Washington. 'Must act at once. Please telegraph instructions via Sidney.'[28] Permission to make any drastic move
was not accorded him, but President Cleveland ordered
two war vessels to proceed to Apia at once to protect
American interests.

Germany next attempted a risky step to bolster up the
crumbling position of its puppet king. A naval force was
sent ashore to disarm the followers of Mataafa. Someone
blundered, the landing party was ambushed, and 'the
invincible strangers' were routed with heavy losses —
fifty-six killed and wounded out of one hundred and
forty. Here was a new crisis. 'Germans swear vengeance,'
reported the American consul. 'Shelling and burning
indiscriminately, regardless of American property. Protests unheeded. Natives exasperated. Foreigners' lives
and property in greatest danger. Germans respect no
neutral territory.'[29]

There was now, in January, 1889, open war between
Germany and Samoa, ridiculous as a contest between two
such ill-matched rivals must seem. Martial law had been
proclaimed in Apia and the German flag flew everywhere.
But neither the British nor American consuls would
recognize the validity of the steps taken by their German
confrère. They warned their nationals that only at the
consulates themselves could they be assured of protection.[30] It was a period which Robert Louis Stevenson,
interested observer of this absorbing drama from his
retreat at Vailima, described as that of 'furor consularis.'
But the real danger in the situation lay in the fact that

behind the consuls stood a strong array of warships —
three German, three American, and one British vessel.
No one knew what might happen next, where the spark
might light which would start a conflagration whose
destructive ravages could not be confined to Samoa.

CHAPTER VIII

An Entangling Venture

WHILE the foreign consuls and naval vessels stood warily on guard over the smouldering volcano in Samoa, a sharp exchange of diplomatic notes between Washington and Berlin gave evidence of the concern with which the United States and Germany regarded these obscure quarrels between their representatives in the South Seas. Even though the tension between the Governments did not reach a point comparable to that existing in Samoa, a measure of friction developed which caused definite alarm. Bismarck might regret that 'the two nations should differ as to affairs on those remote and unimportant islands, while their relations elsewhere were so friendly,' [1] but regretting could not wave away the problem. Samoa was an international issue.

Germany protested first. Her resentment at the supposedly anti-German activities of the American consul in Apia was expressed in vigorous language and a point was scored against American policy by drawing attention to Germany's moderation in not making the preponderance of German subjects in Samoa an excuse for demanding special commercial privileges 'as the United States have recently done in Hawaii.' The deportation of Malietoa was explained by stating that the continuation of his government 'was incompatible with our dignity,' and an attempt was made to place upon the United States all responsibility for 'the redress of a misunderstanding which has no foundation in the actual reciprocal friendly relations between the two countries.' [2]

Secretary of State Bayard answered this note in a sharp and unequivocal fashion. He declared that President Cleveland, like Bismarck, regretted what had occurred in Samoa, but that the United States had consistently tried to maintain friendly relations with the other Powers involved in Samoan affairs, and in its endeavor to prevent native dissension had been solely actuated 'by a benevolent desire to promote the development and secure the independence of one of the few remaining independent territories and autonomous native governments in the Pacific.' He questioned whether as much could be said of Germany's policy. Then, after characterizing the Tamasese Government 'as nothing else than the government of the islands by the local German commercial and landed interests,' the American dispatch bluntly stated that Germany's course could not be regarded 'as having been marked by that just consideration which the ancient friendship between the United States and Germany entitles this Government to expect.' [3]

Here the matter rested for a time, but American public opinion, hitherto so apathetic as to everything concerning Samoa, gradually became aroused. Reports of German interference in the islands' affairs, of destruction of American property by Germany's naval forces, of supposed insults to the United States symbolized by the mutilation of an American flag, awoke a storm of indignation throughout the country. It did not matter that the public scarcely knew that the Samoan Islands existed and had no idea of what we were doing there or why we so unexpectedly found ourselves quarreling with Germany. The fact remained that another Power was interfering in a situation in which somehow or other our interests seemed to be involved. Congress was awakened to its duty and passed two measures providing $500,000 for the protection of American lives and property in Samoa and $100,000 for the development of the long-neglected harbor at Pago Pago.

The debates consequent upon this action brought up the whole question of our Samoan policy and soon indicated that for all its previous indifference to the question, Congress had no idea of abandoning the islands. Its attitude was a striking example of how once American interest in such a matter as Samoa's status had been asserted, no matter how tenuous our actual contacts with the islands, there could be no withdrawal and no surrender of our position. In a long report which counseled moderation in our dealings with other Powers and decried the jingoistic clamor on the part of the press for an active rejoinder to German 'insults,' Senator John Sherman declared that American policy nevertheless demanded a friendly agreement for Samoan autonomy combined with recognition of our exclusive right to Pago Pago.

His stand was supported by a senatorial group which took up, along the lines with which we are already so familiar, America's need for naval bases and overseas possessions in order to strengthen and maintain our position in the Pacific. The appearance of Germany as a new rival to our ambitions for supremacy in that ocean awoke the gravest fears, and again and again in the Samoan debate we seem to hear the voice of Floyd, of Benton, of Seward himself warning the United States to safeguard its rights in the Pacific from the encroachments of foreign Powers.

Senator Frye declared that the Hawaiian and Samoan Islands were the only two resting-places left to us in the Pacific and that the harbor at Pago Pago was absolutely invaluable. Senator Dolph drew an alarming picture of European countries gradually absorbing the bases so essential to our trade, while 'we, feebly protesting, allow our treaty rights to be disregarded; the lives of our citizens to be jeopardized, their property destroyed, the Monroe Doctrine to sink into innocuous desuetude.' Senator Reagan solemnly advised the President 'to assert our rights in such a way that there could be no mistake about what his meaning and his powers are.' [4]

There was opposition to any further involvement in Samoa. The value of our interests in the islands was disputed and our need for a naval base in so remote a part of the world was seriously questioned. The wisdom of appropriating $500,000 for the protection of American property in the islands did not appeal to liberal sentiment. Voicing the opposition to Congress's action, the *Nation* ironically spoke of 'running this wild goose chase respecting a group of islands in the South Pacific Ocean more dis-

tant from our shores than Berlin itself,' and flatly proposed
that we abandon Samoa altogether and let Germany do
with the islands whatever it chose. 'The more the matter
is looked into,' the editors of the *Nation* wrote, 'the more
plainly does it seem, on our part, an outbreak of sheer
Jingoism and meddlesomeness in other people's affairs.' 5

In a sense this was undoubtedly true. It was hard to
substantiate a claim to any vital American interest in
Samoa. But public feeling as reflected in the Congressional appropriation was something more than an outbreak of jingoism and meddlesomeness. It was a sign of
a reawakening of old ambitions which had remained
dormant during the reconstruction period. As the country
became less absorbed in domestic issues and more alive to
opportunities for asserting its place in world affairs, there
was a growing popular demand for an aggressive foreign
policy. Interest in Samoa was a straw which showed
which way the wind was blowing, and it is not without
significance that the unfolding of these events coincided
with the successful movement for building up a new navy.

Under such circumstances it is evident that even with a
Democratic Administration in power the next move for
settlement of the Samoan controversy would have to come
from Germany. It was made soon after Congress had
passed its bill for defending our Samoan interests, significantly soon. Secretary Bayard was informed by the German minister that Prince Bismarck felt that something
should be done to relieve the existing tension, and with a
frank disclaimer of any intention to place in jeopardy the
independence of the Samoan Islands or to challenge the
equal rights of the three treaty Powers, his Government
suggested a resumption in Berlin of the abortive negotiations of 1887.6

This proposal met with President Cleveland's immediate
approval. His term of office was about to expire and he
was anxious to leave the Samoan question with some sign
of settlement in sight. He did not subscribe to the views
of those who hoped to make the islands an outpost of
American influence in the Pacific, but, as we have noted, he

was interested in preserving their independence and decidedly suspect of German policy. This was not publicly revealed, but how strongly he actually felt on the subject is graphically shown in the manuscript of a draft of his final message to Congress which was subsequently modified.

Germany may be expected to set up her own government in Samoa, he declared in this undelivered message, and thus accomplish 'the purpose which Germany, in my opinion, has long held in view, being nothing less or different than the inauguration of a condition of government in the Islands of Samoa entirely in accord with German interests and standing for German supremacy. This purpose has colored any proposition of adjustment made by Germany and furnishes the key to all her acts.' [7] With the pacific Cleveland feeling so strongly on this subject, it is not surprising that the country at large was determined to forestall German designs upon little Samoa.

This, then, was the situation in March, 1889. The Powers themselves were moving toward a conciliatory solution of Samoan problems and a change in Germany's policy seemed to be foreshadowed by Bismarck's request for another conference. But in the islands the representatives of the Powers were still at swords' points. Any move made by any one of them was viewed by the others with suspicion and hostility. It is no exaggeration to say that the Americans and the Germans in Apia, backed by their respective consuls and the officers of the three naval vessels by which each country was represented, were virtually semi-belligerents. The most casual incident might at any time have undone all the work of the diplomats in Washington and Berlin by precipitating a clash which would have involved those dangerous intangibles of international politics — prestige and national honor. A German assault imperiling the safety of the American consulate, a quarrel between the seamen of the two countries, might have had repercussions which would have made the proposed Berlin conference impossible. But upon this troubled situation there now fell literally a bolt from the blue, a sudden storm of hurricane force which either sank or drove upon the Samoan beach with tragic loss of life six of the seven warships which lay in Apia harbor.

'In what seemed the very article of war,' wrote Robert Louis Stevenson, who has left us a vivid description of this dramatic climax to the situation in Samoa itself, 'the sword-arm of each of the two angry powers was broken; their formidable ships reduced to junk; their disciplined hundreds to a horde of castaways, fed with difficulty and the fear of whose misconduct marred the sleep of their commanders. Both paused aghast; both had time to recognize that not the whole Samoan Archipelago was worth the loss in men and costly ships already suffered.' ᵃ

The American ships in the harbor were the *Nipsic*, the *Vandalia*, and the *Trenton*; Germany was represented by the *Adler*, the *Eber*, and the *Olga*; England had only the one vessel, the *Calliope*. The storm had come up on the night of March 15, and morning found the seven vessels at the mercy of mountainous seas which swept ceaselessly into the little harbor, alternately burying the ships from the view of those on shore and tossing them high on the crest of the billows. Dragging their anchor chains and unable to maintain any headway, the helpless craft continually threatened to ram each other as their frantic seamen endeavored to keep up steam with engine-rooms awash and water pouring into the holds. The *Nipsic* even lost her smokestack and smoke and sparks were pouring along the level of her deck.

The *Eber* was the first to go. Striking a treacherous reef, she sank stern foremost, carrying all but four of her crew of eighty with her. The *Nipsic* then met a more kindly fate. Swept hopelessly toward the shore, she miraculously escaped the reef and was beached upon the sand, most of her crew making their way to safety. Not so the *Adler*. Seeking to follow the *Nipsic's* example, the German vessel was hurled high upon the fatal reef, her back broken, and twenty of her seamen tossed into the sea. Throughout the rest of the day and the following night the survivors clung to the wreck, while the Samoans, forgetting in this emergency that they were at war with Germany, valiantly endeavored to bring them off.

With the four vessels left, the greatest danger was from self-destruction. The *Vandalia* was almost cut down by the *Calliope*, while the *Olga* and the *Trenton* collided dangerously. Attempting to beach beside the *Nipsic*, the captain of the *Vandalia* had his vessel sink under him and was swept with forty-two of his men off the deck as the rest of the crew took refuge in the tops. The *Olga*, which had appeared to be the only vessel with a chance of riding out the storm until she had crashed into the American man-of-war, now ran ashore and was beached without loss of life; the *Trenton* was driven stern foremost upon the partially submerged *Vandalia*, but only one of her crew of four hundred and fifty was lost.

This left only the *Calliope* still afloat. Somehow this English vessel managed to keep up steam, and while the other ships were tossed helplessly about the bay she slowly but steadily crept toward the harbor's mouth in the face of the storm. By the narrowest margin she escaped the *Trenton* on the one side and the reef on the other, while to the agonized onlookers she appeared at every moment about to be cast on the shore. But almost by inches she crept forward. When at last she passed the already doomed *Trenton*, the American seamen hailed her success with a ringing cheer which the British answered in kind as they made their perilous way to the open sea and safety.

On the morning of the seventeenth, the little harbor of Apia, which had been crowded with shipping the day before, presented a desolate scene. The *Eber* had sunk completely, the *Vandalia* was partially submerged, the *Trenton* lay piled upon the latter vessel herself sunk to the gun-deck, the *Adler* was broken on the reef, the *Olga* and the *Nipsic* were beached, and the *Calliope* had escaped to sea. On the shore were also the broken remains of many smaller vessels, both foreign and native. Not a single sail was afloat. The hurricane had done its work with a deadly precision.[9]

Both in Samoa and in the foreign countries whose ves-

sels had been lost, the effects of the hurricane had a sobering influence. In Berlin and Washington there was a new
will for a friendly settlement of the questions at issue between the two Governments, while in Apia the natives
made no attempt to take advantage of their enemy's
plight and the foreigners were generous in their aid and
sympathy to each other. A new and unexpected peace
descended upon Samoa while its residents awaited whatever solution of their problems might be agreed upon at
the Berlin Conference.

The American delegation to this Berlin meeting in 1889
had as its objectives the preservation of our rights in
Samoa and defense of the islands' autonomy, a somewhat
difficult if not antithetical combination of aims. Its instructions from Secretary of State James G. Blaine, for the
Harrison Administration had now succeeded that of
President Cleveland, laid somewhat more stress upon the
latter objective, but at the same time it was clearly apparent that fear of an extension of German influence in
the South Seas rather than an interest in the Samoans for
themselves motivated our policy. Germany's war against
Malietoa was termed 'an abrupt breach of the joint relations of the treaty powers to each other and to the Government of Samoa,' and it was definitely stated that it was
not the American policy 'to subordinate the right of this
amiable and dependent people to the exigencies of a grasp-
ing commerce, or to the political ambition of a territorial
extension on the part of any one of the treaty powers.'
Somewhat reluctantly, Secretary Blaine accepted, as
the only way out of the *impasse* which seemed to exist in
the relations of the treaty Powers, the scheme for tripartite
control of the islands which had been suggested at the
Washington Conference in 1887. He felt that such an en-
tanglement with two foreign Powers was not 'in harmony
with the established policy of this Government,' yet
should such an agreement prove necessary he instructed
the conference delegates to accept it on the distinct understanding that it should be only a temporary arrangement,

preparatory to the complete restoration of Samoan autonomy. In no event, Secretary Blaine declared, was Germany to be permitted to win control of the islands.[10]

Our participation in the Berlin Conference and our willingness to enter into an 'entangling alliance' with Germany and Great Britain marked a radical departure in our foreign policy, as Blaine himself suggested, and we were still far from eager for a commitment so far afield. Otherwise we might have given some encouragement to the suggestions made by England for that division of Samoa which was actually made a decade later. For the idea of tripartite control was accepted with equal reluctance by all concerned. It was a temporary makeshift in which no one had very much confidence. The United States, still only dimly conscious of its destiny in the Pacific, felt it had to block German aggressiveness, but it did so with a good many doubts and qualms.

The actual negotiations revealed an unexpected harmony in the general views of the Powers and the meetings proceeded in an atmosphere of friendliness and coöperation. Germany no longer insisted upon a single German adviser to the Samoan Government as she had two years earlier, was ready to abandon her support of the Tamasese régime, and even agreed to Malietoa's return to the islands as the lawful king. This meant a complete repudiation of the aggressive policy of the German agents in Samoa. It meant that Germany peacefully gave up any idea of seeking redress for the losses which her naval forces had suffered during the days of active intervention. The conference demonstrated, therefore, a complete change in Prince Bismarck's attitude. Upon review of the years of blundering, bullying, and failure in Samoa, as Stevenson wrote in 1892, the Iron Chancellor seemed 'magnanimously to have owned his policy was in the wrong.' It would perhaps be more accurate to say that expediency rather than magnanimity dictated Bismarck's course, but the effect was the same.

What difficulties there were over the detailed arrangements of the new system to be inaugurated in Samoa came as much from dissensions which cropped up within the American delegation itself as from any other cause. Its three members had very divergent views. John A. Kasson was decidedly pro-German and not very interested in Samoa, William Walter Phelps followed a more middle-of-the-road policy, and George H. Bates, who had been the special commissioner to Samoa three years earlier, was a vigorous and outspoken critic of German policy. Furthermore, Bates believed that with the construction of an isthmian canal, Hawaii would have to yield to Samoa 'the key of the maritime dominion of the Pacific,' and he was determined that our position there should be maintained. Secretary Blaine on the whole stood behind Bates and approved his firm insistence that the tripartite agreement should not allow too much control to slip into the hands of either Great Britain or Germany.

On one occasion, when Kasson reported that England and Germany were objecting to certain details insisted upon by the United States and declared that 'the President does not know the irritability of those who believe they have yielded already in all essentials to claims of the United States,' the Secretary of State administered a sharp rebuke. 'Irritability on the part of your English and German associates,' he cabled, 'is not a determining factor with the Government of the United States.' The popular belief that Blaine defied Bismarck on the Samoan settlement is not warranted by the facts, for Germany retreated from her former high-handed policy on her own initiative, but he did demand and obtain full protection of American interests.[11]

The Berlin General Act, as finally accepted by the United States, Great Britain, and Germany, conformed on the whole to American desires, although the supposedly temporary character of the accord was not proclaimed. It provided for the neutrality and independence of Samoa with recognition of Malietoa as the islands' lawful king. It established a supreme court with inclusive jurisdiction over Samoan laws, elections, and foreign disputes, and set up a municipal administration for Apia, both of these

institutions to be headed by appointees of the three
treaty Powers, or, failing agreement, by appointees of the
King of Sweden and Norway. Any further alienation of
Samoan land was prohibited except under very special
circumstances, a land commission was appointed to adjust
existing claims, the importation of arms and alcohol was
forbidden, and a new schedule of import duties was
agreed upon.[12]

The assent of the Samoan Government was declared
necessary to the validity of this pact, but it was obviously
nothing more or less than the establishment over the
islands of a joint protectorate in which the United States,
Great Britain, and Germany participated upon equal
terms. So far at least had the United States departed from
its traditional policy of no entangling alliances and no
overseas possessions.

For a time all went well in Samoa under this new dis-
pensation, but it soon began to be apparent that peace
and coöperation among the residents of the South Seas
were impossible whatever the Powers might solemnly decree in Berlin. Intrigue and jealousy among the foreigners,
the ambitious rivalry of the native chieftains, could not be
abolished by international fiat. Inevitably a situation
developed which came to bear so close a resemblance to
that existing prior to the Berlin Act that only new negotiations and another international agreement could liquidate
it.

Actual native strife broke out when the chieftain
Mataafa, for whom no provision had been made by the
Powers, raised the banner of a new revolt and attempted
to set up an authority counter to that of the king upon
whom the foreigners were agreed. But for once such unity
prevailed among the foreigners that they could take concerted action. Their prompt intervention in the interests
of peace squashed Mataafa's hopes and the unlucky chieftain himself was deported.

This instance of foreign unity, however, was the exception which proved the rule, for in their relations with each

other the consuls of the Powers and the newly appointed
officials at the head of the supreme court and the municipal administration were soon completely at loggerheads.
The natives were treated to the engaging spectacle of
Chief Justice Conrad Cedercrantz and Council President
Baron Senfft von Pilsach — names and titles which only
heightened the comic-opera flavor of their absurd and
petty quarrel — squabbling over their respective powers
and privileges to the endangerment of all law and order.
They tilted vaingloriously for greater influence in the
islands, interfered with the duties of the consuls, and
brought such confusion into Samoan affairs that the
shrewd natives took quick advantage of the situation to
refuse to pay any taxes and completely ignore the writs of
the supreme court.[13]

The climax of these new troubles which forced the recall
of Chief Justice Conrad Cedercrantz and Council President
Baron Senfft von Pilsach coincided with Cleveland's return to office in 1893, and, viewing the disorder in Samoa,
the President found little satisfaction in the previous
Administration's solution of the problem he had left on its
hands. Even though the tripartite agreement was in substance the suggestion of his own Secretary of State in 1887,
he now recognized its impracticality. And even more
emphatic in disapproval was the new Secretary of State,
W. Q. Gresham. He considered Samoa of little value to
the United States, saw no justification for the Berlin convention, and felt that some change in the islands' status
had already become absolutely necessary.

In a report on the whole situation, Gresham characterized our adherence to the Berlin Act as 'the first departure
from our traditional and well established policy of avoiding
entangling alliances with foreign powers in relation to
objects remote from this hemisphere,' and said that
Samoa's 'autonomous government' was in reality not even
a protectorate, but 'a tripartite foreign government, imposed upon the natives and supported and administered
jointly by the treaty powers.' He condemned the whole
business. 'Soberly surveying the history of our relations

with Samoa,' his report concluded, 'we may well inquire what we have gained by our departure from our well established policy beyond the expenses, the responsibilities, and the entanglements that have so far been its only fruits.' [14]

It was at this same time, as we shall subsequently see, that President Cleveland and Secretary Gresham were also objecting to Republican maneuvers for the annexation of Hawaii. The Democratic Party had deserted its pre-war rôle as the party of expansion and was resolutely setting its face against the rebirth of that imperialistic spirit upon which it had ridden to power in 1844. As the Republicans became more and more convinced that the time had come for a vigorous foreign policy and a possible expansion of our power and influence, the Democrats constituted themselves an unbending opposition to tendencies which they considered dangerous to the fundamental principles on which the United States was founded. They saw in our attitude toward both Hawaii and Samoa signs of a colonial venture with which they would have nothing to do.

Acting on this principle, President Cleveland sought some way out of the Samoan imbroglio and lost no occasion to characterize the way the Berlin treaty was working out 'as signally illustrating the impolicy of entangling alliances with foreign powers.' On this point the Republicans would have agreed with him, but no such solution of the problem as that which they eventually adopted occurred to so staunch a Democrat as Cleveland. He wanted to see the United States out of Samoa altogether, and in 1894 bluntly asked Congress to consider a complete withdrawal from the tripartite control.[15]

Congress ignored this suggestion. It never showed any real interest in Samoa except when the country was aroused by Germany's aggressive tactics in the islands, but abandonment of the position we had assumed there was another matter altogether. Moreover, the feeling was growing that, despite their size, their distance from our coasts, and their slight commercial importance, the islands might be more valuable than these considerations seemed to indicate. If no other Power had wanted Samoa, the President might have prevailed upon Congress to authorize American withdrawal, but it was because England and particularly Germany were so interested in the islands that what public opinion there was on the question tended to oppose the surrender of our treaty rights.

Writing in the *North American Review*, for example, Henry C. Ide, who had served as an official in Samoa, argued ably that our interest in the islands was a sustained and deliberate policy, and that the fundamental purpose of the Berlin Act, aside from all protestations in regard to Samoan autonomy, was the preservation of our rights in Pago Pago. He stressed, as had so many visitors to Samoa before him, the value of this potential naval base, dwelt upon the growing importance of trade in the Pacific, and declared that Samoa should be our sentinel in the south as Hawaii was in the north. 'When we once relax our grasp,' he wrote, 'we do so forever.' [16]

Nothing further occurred in the Cleveland Administration but in the year 1898, whose far more momentous events left little time for President McKinley's consideration of Samoan affairs, the friction and dissensions which had continued to characterize the situation in the islands came to a head in an open clash between the representatives of the treaty Powers. Malietoa had died in that year and the old question of the kingship was again in dispute. His nominal successor was one Malietoa Tanu, but the rebellious Mataafa had by now been brought back from exile and he promptly took the field in an effort to seize the power of which he felt himself unjustly deprived. The British and American consuls supported Malietoa Tanu, whose right to the throne was recognized by the Samoan chief justice, but the German consul took up the cause of Mataafa. Even though it was this chieftain who had overthrown the puppet king Germany had upheld ten years earlier, and his followers who had ambushed Germany's landing party, the antagonism between the German consul and his British and American colleagues drove the former into this obstructive position.

The ill-feeling of the previous decade was now repeated as this silly quarrel over the precedence of two insignificant native chiefs developed, and proclamations and counter-proclamations flew back and forth between the consulates. The Malietoa and the Mataafa factions were in arms and their foreign adherents could not keep out of harm's way. When Admiral Albert Kautz of the U.S.S. *Philadelphia* arrived upon the scene, he decided upon active intervention in behalf of the Anglo-American candidate to the throne.

Still the German consul proclaimed the rights of the rival candidate and protested vigorously against intervention in favor of Malietoa. When the Americans shelled the Mataafa forces and in firing across the town of Apia destroyed some German property and supposedly endangered German lives, he became frantic.[17] It was the situation in 1889 all over again with the rôles reversed. The United States was now playing the more active part in intervening in island affairs, even though Admiral Kautz believed he was on the side of law and order, and it was Germany who felt herself the aggrieved nation. And as ten years earlier a climax was reached when a foreign landing party was ambushed by the Samoans, but this time it was American and British dead who were left on the field.

News of these events created a mild sensation in the United States, but the immediate reaction was a determination not to let so petty a quarrel get out of hand and to take prompt steps to pacify both the Samoan natives and the islands' foreign residents. Washington now knew only too well how dangerous it was to leave the conduct of affairs in this part of the world to consuls and naval officers, and the proposal was therefore made to Germany and Great Britain that a joint commission should be sent to Samoa at once. Its chief function, as the three Powers quickly agreed, would be to investigate the causes of Samoa's new troubles and propose some means for dealing with the situation in the future, but the commission was also empowered to establish peace and order in the islands by assuming upon its arrival paramount authority over the local government.[18]

The three foreign commissioners reached Apia together in the spring of 1899, to find the natives and foreigners still at swords' points. Three British, two American, and one German warship lay in the harbor, marines patrolled Apia with the aid of native guards, and two thousand of Malietoa's followers were stationed in outposts facing three thousand of Mataafa's henchmen entrenched in an improvised fort. The islands were a battle-field.

The commission promptly took hold of the situation and despite the ominous outlook succeeded in persuading all concerned of the necessity for peace. The native chiefs accepted a truce, professed allegiance to 'the great voices,' and agreed to acknowledge whatever king the commission appointed. Whereupon events took an unexpected turn. Malietoa was recognized and resigned immediately, perhaps realizing only when it was actually within his grasp how empty and precarious was the honor for which he had been striving. But the commission did not then turn to his rival. It seized the opportunity to abolish the kingship, which had proved to be only a source of rivalry and civil strife ever since its establishment, and the three foreign consuls were empowered to assume the king's prerogatives until a more generally satisfactory system of government could be evolved. Within a month of the commission's arrival, the American representative, Bartlett Tripp, was able to report to his Government that 'everything is now peaceable and quiet in the islands.'

'The chiefs and warriors have returned to their homes,' read his lyrical dispatch to the State Department. 'The smoke is now ascending from the native cabins and plantations in every portion of the islands. The war song is discontinued, the war camp abandoned, and the happy joyous nature of this unrevengeful people manifests itself in the ready forgiveness of their enemies and their glad welcome of returning peace.'[19]

What to be done next was the difficult problem. The commissioners worked out a new governmental program which included permanent abolition of the kingship, abolition of extraterritoriality, and the establishment of a governing body of three commissioners and a chief executive. This plan they believed in theory would do away with the chief causes of past difficulties, but no one of them had any real confidence in its practicality. Past experience seemed to indicate that on no terms could the three Powers carry out their joint protectorate without friction, and even though the Samoan chiefs were prepared to accept the new government, there seemed to be little warrant to believe that intrigue and jealousy on the part of the foreign residents would not again lead them to indulge their natural proclivity for fratricidal warfare.

Commissioner Tripp was outspoken in his belief that no conceivable system of tripartite control could possibly work. 'I cannot forbear to impress upon my Government,' he wrote in his final report, 'not only the propriety but the necessity of dissolving the partnership of nations which has no precedent for its creation nor reason for its continuance.... Considerations of national welfare should terminate this unusual alliance at the earliest possible moment that it can be done with proper regard for the rights and interests of the powers concerned.' [20]

So far he had adopted the attitude of President Cleveland and Secretary Gresham, which might not be expected to satisfy a Republican Administration which had by now annexed Hawaii and was fighting the insurgents of the Philippine Islands. But Tripp did not stop here. He was convinced of the value of Samoa, not on commercial but on geographical grounds, and he believed that the importance of its position on the great future pathway of commerce could not be overestimated. He felt that the harbor of Pago Pago, throughout the whole history of our relations with Samoa the only part of the islands in which we really had a vital interest, should be in our undivided possession and that we should lose no time in letting the world know that we intended to keep it under our control and fortify it. [21]

Events now moved rapidly toward that division of the islands which the failure of the tripartite protectorate seemed to indicate. We were at last prepared to abandon the theory that Samoan independence was our primary objective. Times had changed. Imperialism needed no cloak to disguise its intentions, but moved openly toward achieving its goal. 'Manifest destiny' had swung out across the Pacific to embrace Hawaii and the Philippines and there was no reason why Samoa should not be included as a southern outpost for the empire which had now come into being. Whether it was due more to chance or to design that the United States had this stake in the South Seas, the emergence of the Samoan problem in such acute form in 1899 left little doubt of what disposition of the islands would now be made.

It was from Germany and not from the United States, however, that the proposal for a division of the islands first came. That Power must have realized that the only way in which she could now protect her interests in Upolo, the island wherein lay Apia and the plantations of the German firms, was to grant the United States and England the other parts of the archipelago. In the prevailing temper of 1899 there was not the remotest chance of Germany being allowed to retain all of Samoa. Consequently, Berlin suggested that the United States take over the island of Tutuila in order to have full title to Pago Pago, and allow Germany and England to divide the rest. The United States would perform 'a very real service' for Germany, declared the dispatch in which this proposition was first made, if it 'would prevail with its whole powerful influence on England' to induce the British Government to grant Germany the island of Upolo while retaining Savaii for itself.[22]

To this proposal, falling in line so closely with the recommendations of Commissioner Tripp and representing such a convenient escape from the embarrassments of the tripartite protectorate, the United States consented without hesitation. It gave us Pago Pago. More we did not want; less we could not have accepted with imperialism so strongly in the saddle. As President McKinley declared in his annual message: 'To relinquish our rights in the harbor of Pago Pago, the best anchorage in the Pacific, the occupancy of which had been leased to the United States in 1878 by the first foreign treaty ever concluded by Samoa, was not to be thought of as regards the needs of our navy or the interests of our growing commerce with the East.' [23]

It was more difficult for England and Germany to come to an understanding. A multitude of questions relating to the colonial policies of the two countries throughout the world were involved. For a time it even appeared that Germany might actually surrender Samoa in return for compensation elsewhere, but in the event it was England which withdrew from the islands. A sentimental interest in Samoa as the field of Germany's first colonial activity, the importance of Germany's commercial interests in the South Seas, and von Tirpitz's insistence upon the strategical value of Samoa, compelled Germany to continue to hold out for the objective which she had pursued so obliquely and so unsuccessfully for the past thirty years.[24]

The Anglo-German agreement as finally reached relinquished Tutuila in favor of the United States and provided for England's surrender of her rights in the other islands in favor of Germany. As compensation, Germany ceded to England the Tonga Islands and a part of the Solomon Islands, agreed to a rectification of boundaries in West Africa, and gave up extraterritoriality rights in Zanzibar. A convention giving effect to this pact was signed on December 2, 1899, by the United States, Great Britain, and Germany, and at long last the Samoan question was settled.[25] In place of tripartite control, the United States had won Tutuila and a few smaller islands; Germany had acquired Upolo and Savaii.*

There was little opposition to ratification of the treaty and it was approved by the Senate in the midst of more exciting debates over what was to be done in the Philip-

* As a result of the World War the islands held by Germany have now become a mandate of New Zealand.

pines. An attempt on the part of Senator Pettigrew, a violent anti-imperialist Democrat, to have a commission of
inquiry sent to Samoa was sidetracked, but his protest
against our policy had a significance which at any other
time would have been more widely appreciated. 'We blot
out, then,' he declared bluntly, 'a sovereign nation, a people with whom we have treaty relations, and divide the
spoils.' [26] The Republicans did not deign to answer.

The McKinley Administration was thoroughly satisfied
with the settlement. Secretary of State Hay coupled our
acquisition of Samoa with that of Hawaii and the Philippines as giving the United States interests in the Pacific
as great as those of any other Power and 'destined to
infinite development.' Writing to Joseph H. Choate, the
American ambassador in London, he gave his opinion that
we had profited from the new deal far more than either
Germany or England, and that Pago Pago was 'absolutely
indispensable to us.' [27]

As evidence that it was not only in the United States
that this extension of American influence in the South
Seas was considered significant, the views of a French
commentator might also be cited. Writing in the *Annales
des Sciences Politiques*, Paul Lefébure said that Samoa was
fully as important as either Hawaii or the Philippines
and that America had now become the great Power and
arbiter of the Pacific. Echoing Seward's famous speech
of half a century earlier, he further declared that it was
in the Pacific 'que va se décider désormais la grandeur ou
la décadence des nations.' [28]

Curiously enough, it was to be many years before the
exact status of what we must now call American Samoa
was established. In July, 1900, the native chiefs formally
ceded to the United States the island of Tutuila and four
years later that of Manu, but Congress took no action to
give practical effect to these cessions. An executive order
placed the islands under the control of the Navy Department with authority to establish a naval station and afford
Tutuila the necessary protection, and an opinion of the
Attorney General declared our exclusive sovereignty over

the territory, but nevertheless the instructions to the naval commandant in 1902 stated that 'the occupancy of Tutuila is quite distinct from the sovereignty exercised at Porto Rico, Hawaii, and Guam.'[29] Even as late as 1926, Congress was still refusing to define Tutuila's status,[30] and it was not until 1929, fifty-seven years after Commander Meade signed the first treaty with the great chief of Pago Pago, that Congress took the requisite action to accept the cession of the islands allotted to us, and American Samoa at last found its destined place among our Pacific possessions.

CHAPTER IX

Early Contacts with Hawaii

IN POINT of time final settlement of the Samoan problem had been preceded by two far more important acquisitions of territory in the Pacific. After a full century of progressively closer contacts, the Hawaiian Islands had been gathered into the American fold, while the Spanish War had left a surprised country with the Philippines on its hands. We were fully launched upon that colonial expansion for which our activities in Samoa had to some extent pointed the way even before the South Sea island had itself become a part of the American system.

The accession of Hawaii shared the characteristics of both of the great periods of American expansion in the Pacific. It was in a sense a projection of the westward movement of the middle of the century, for the islands came to be regarded as geographically a part of the American continent; it was also a move to secure one of those naval bases and strategic outposts which the Pacific-minded in the nation were so urgently demanding. The old conception of our 'manifest destiny' as it was recognized in 1848, and our new 'imperial destiny' as it was proclaimed in 1898, joined forces at the end of the century to plant the American flag over Hawaii and stamp the final seal of ownership on a group of islands which for long had been almost wholly American in everything but name.

To account for our possession of Hawaii, it is consequently necessary to turn back to the close of the eighteenth century and trace a development which ran parallel with that which brought us Oregon, California, Alaska, and Samoa. Upon the occasion of each of these advances toward control of the Pacific, we also reached out for Hawaii. It eluded our grasp because of our own timidity when in the middle of the nineteenth century Commodore Perry sought naval stations in the Pacific, when the ambitious Seward bought Alaska, and when a hesitant Republican Administration was actually testing its imperialistic wings in Samoa. But each tentative approach toward control of Hawaii brought the islands' ultimate absorption by the United States that much nearer.

They were discovered in 1778 by Captain James Cook, the English explorer, and soon became well known to all ships sailing between the west coast of America and the ports of Asia under the name of the Sandwich Islands. Their early American visitors were those same little vessels which made our first contacts with Oregon and California in the early days of the China trade. Both the *Columbia* and the *Lady Washington* called at 'Owhyhee' on their first voyage to the Northwest Coast and they set up a precedent which was thereafter regularly followed by all vessels sailing between Oregon and Canton. It was not only that Hawaii proved to be an idyllic spot for the rest and recuperation of sea-weary crews and a convenient source for fresh supplies. It had in sandalwood a valuable product which could be exchanged almost as profitably as sea-otter furs for China's teas and silks. A thriving trade developed which soon gave the Americans what they considered a proprietary right in the island kingdom.

At this time, the close of the eighteenth century, the Hawaiians were an unspoiled, gay, and carefree people who welcomed their white visitors cordially. It is true that there were occasional instances of native treachery, for which the foreigners were not entirely unresponsible, but on the whole no people could have shown the traders greater hospitality. The logs of the American vessels bear continual witness to the relief and pleasure which the Yankee seamen felt in putting into the Hawaiian ports after their harsh experiences with the dour Indians of the Northwest Coast.[1]

John Boit, Jr., the fifth mate of the *Columbia* in 1792, spoke of 'these beautiful Isles, the inhabitants of which appear'd to me the happiest people in the world';[2] a few years later Ebenezer Townsend, Jr., wrote that the islanders were 'neat in their persons, respect their legislators and their laws, are cheerful and obliging to each other'; [3] and still again we find Richard Cleveland referring to their 'activity, gayety, volatility, and irritability' in contrast to the 'heaviness, melancholy, austerity, ferocity, and treachery' of the Northwest Indians. [4]

In the person of the Hawaiian King, the forward-looking and, for all his childish interests, highly intelligent Kamehameha, the Americans found an enthusiastic host. He welcomed them for their trade and for the assistance they were able to give him in his efforts to bring all the islands of the archipelago under his rule. He learned with remarkable rapidity the ways of the West. At first we read of this island potentate as a natural savage eager only for the gewgaws and knickknacks which the traders offered him in exchange for fresh supplies and sandalwood. He would board their ships, accompanied by one or more of his favorite wives, and gayly take part in festivities which usually ended in all concerned getting very drunk, not excluding those ladies of striking beauty but 'unmeasured size' who made up his *entourage*. But soon he was adopting other customs of the strangers. Even though firearms and rum were always those tokens of civilization which most appealed to him, other more substantial products of the West eventually found their way out to Hawaii in the holds of the China traders, and the beginning of a new culture grew up in the islands under Kamehameha's leadership. [5]

This was to prove a mixed blessing for the Hawaiians, however much it pleased the American traders. As early as 1791, Joseph Ingraham of the brig *Hope* confided to his log that 'these islands, as well as many others in this ocean, have abundant reason to lament they were ever discovered.' [6]

Still a third element in Hawaiian life attracted the Americans in addition to the general cordiality of the natives and the gay hospitality of Kamehameha. This was a custom not unusual in the Pacific islands, as noted by Commodore Porter in the Marquesas, whereby the natives freely offered to visitors the favors of their wives and daughters. The Hawaiian girls were considered 'quite handsome' by the seamen of the American ships, and they were usually more than ready to take advantage of the chiefs' customary suggestion that they might choose whom they would from among the women. When Kamehameha received Townsend on shore, he took him to a circle of sixty girls and 'by very expressive signs told me if I had come for a wife I could take which I pleased.'[7]

As a result of these conditions it is not surprising that the captains of the merchant ships found it increasingly difficult to hold their crews whenever they touched at Hawaii. Desertions became more and more frequent, and it was these sailors who found themselves unable to resist the languorous delights of Hawaiian life who formed the nucleus of the American colony which slowly grew up in the islands. They did not form as stable or respectable a community as might have been desired and one early visitor did not hesitate to characterize the white population of Hawaii as being, generally speaking, 'of the very worst order';[8] but after a time the settlement in the islands of a number of traders, and of the agents of those Boston firms which found Hawaiian trade worth cultivating, began to work some improvement in the status of the foreign community. Then in 1820 two events occurred which entirely changed the character of Hawaii and clearly foreshadowed an American interest in the islands which was to be satisfied only by annexation.

These two events were the arrival of the first American missionaries and the first American whalers. The former were destined not only to convert the Hawaiians to a new faith, but to dominate their government and make of the islands an outpost of American civilization in the Pacific. The latter were to give the islands a commercial importance which soon aroused the attention of Washington and made politically possible those successive steps by which Hawaii approached its eventual fate. Missionaries and whalers were always in bitter conflict and no love was ever lost between the stern New England men of faith and the roisterous seamen of the whaling ships, but in unconscious coöperation they gave to Hawaii its predominantly American character.

The missionaries' arrival could not have been made under more dramatic circumstances. King Kamehameha had just died, but a development for which he had prepared the way by his whole-hearted reception of Western customs promised the newcomers a more cordial welcome than even he could have offered them. The Hawaiians had abolished their superstitious tabus; they had broken their idols and hurled them by the thousand into the sea. They had become almost overnight a people without a religion, 'lying ready, like a fallow ground, to receive the seed of a new husbandry.'[9] Under the impact of new ideas their chiefs had carried through one of the most remarkable movements in the history of primitive religion.

The missionaries did not know how propitiously they had timed their arrival, but they were quick to seize upon the miraculous opportunity presented them. They carried the message of the new faith throughout the islands and were rewarded by wholesale conversions; they set up schools and within ten years 44,895 Hawaiians had become their pupils. With unparalleled enthusiasm the natives embraced Western customs and showed the extraordinary influence of the missionaries on their lives by aping everything that their preceptors did. 'They imitated the manner, tones, and the very appearance of the missionaries themselves,' wrote one English resident... 'their soft feline style of approach, their very seat in the saddle, the sun-burnt black suit, all were exactly counterfeited — nothing escaped them.'[10]

Furthermore, this influence was extended to the councils of the chiefs and the rule of Kamehameha's successor. The missionaries made themselves self-appointed advisers to the Government and brought all the pressure to bear of which they were capable in favor of stricter laws and regulations. They combated the prostitution which was so widely prevalent, forced upon the natives a strict observance of the Sabbath, forbade many of the games and sports which the natives were accustomed to, and in every way endeavored to give lax and easy-going Hawaii an atmosphere more in keeping with their own Puritanical traditions.

This brought them into sharp and bitter conflict with the other elements in Hawaii's foreign community and the natural antagonism between the missionaries and the merchants and sailors became more and more intensified. The missionaries believed that the seamen were debauching the Hawaiian people, as they undoubtedly were; the seamen believed with equal reason that the missionaries were interfering with native liberty. So bitter grew the feud that all foreign residents took part in it.

'These bloodsuckers of the community,' wrote the American consular agent in an attack upon the missionaries which shows all too plainly his violent partisanship, 'had much better be in their native country gaining their living by the sweat of their brow, than living like lords in this luxurious land, disturbing the minds of these children of Nature with the idea that they are to be eternally damned unless they think and act as they do.'[11]

So, too, did the British consular agent find the missionary influence a disturbing and upsetting factor in Hawaiian life. He held their harsh laws, prohibition of games and sports, and other reforms responsible for the depopulation of the islands which was already setting in. He saw no hope for Hawaii when these newcomers were able to set up a régime which was an iniquitous combination of the blue laws of Connecticut and the tyranny of a Turkish pasha.[12]

It is difficult to judge the rights and wrongs of this feud upon which not a single visitor to the islands during this period fails to comment. The missionaries brought Christianity to Hawaii and attempted to guide the natives on the path toward a higher civilization. They had the welfare of the people at heart, which is more than can be said for the merchants who were looking to their profits and the seamen who were looking to their pleasure. Yet at the same time the missionary policy was often ill-advised, hasty and unjust. They were personally inclined in some instances to be arrogant and overbearing, ruling their converts with a rod of iron. They did not hesitate to ride roughshod over the customs of an older day in their fixed determination to set up in Hawaii a theocratic régime which would allow no law 'at variance with the word of the Lord Jehovah.'

Disregarding the violent attacks on the part of the rowdy element in Hawaii and such an infamous example of anti-missionary feeling as that shown by Lieutenant John Percival of the U.S.S. *Dolphin*, who upheld his seamen when they rioted in protest against the missionary-inspired regulations against prostitution,[13] many visitors with less prejudiced views are found who criticized missionary control as too theocratic, too intolerant, and too oppressive.

Commodore John Downes, of the United States frigate *Potomac*, did not hesitate to advise the missionaries to help the natives and let trade and government take care of themselves.[14] Sir George Simpson, of the Hudson's Bay Company, gave his opinion that the missionaries exercised their best judgment for the welfare of Hawaii, 'but in their over zeal, they counselled the enactment of some very strange and unusual laws which foreigners find irksome and vexatious; and as might be expected, they not infrequently divert the streams of justice from the proper course to favor their own friends and countrymen.'[15]

Many tributes to their work could also be cited, such as that of Captain Thomas ap Catesby Jones, who, in arbitrating the dispute growing out of the 'frolic' of the *Dolphin's* crew, declared that 'not one jot or tittle, not one iota derogatory to their character as men, as ministers of the gospel of the strictest order, or as missionaries, could be made to appear by the united efforts of all who conspired against them.'[16] But perhaps the least prejudiced estimate of their rôle in Hawaiian life was made by an English observer, Manley Hopkins.

In his discussion he notes with high praise the success of the missionaries' work in converting and educating the natives, and defends their going into the government

as the only way in which they could exert the influence
necessary for carrying out their program.   But like
Sir George Simpson he found that their zeal had often
led them to adopt an intolerant and oppressive attitude,
and from the point of view of the natives he criticized
them for presenting Christianity as a severe, legalistic,
Jewish religion which in its prohibitions and restrictions
had much the effect of restoring some of the Hawaiians'
own superstitious tabus.[17]

With this reasoned comment on missionary influence
we may well leave the feud to burn itself out, for in the
meantime the islands were undergoing a remarkable
metamorphosis for which trade and whaling were fully
as responsible as the missionaries.   Each group might decry
the other's influence on Hawaii, but its Americanization
was almost equally due to both.

The arrival of the first whaling ship in 1820, the *Maro* of
Nantucket, was followed by that of many others.   Sixty
whalers put into Honolulu in 1822 and twenty-two years
later the number of arrivals was four hundred.[18]   It was the
great era of Pacific whaling in which it could again be said
in regard to the seamen of New England, as had Burke
half a century earlier, that there was 'no ocean but what is
vexed with their fisheries, no climate that is not witness to
their toils.'   Hawaii was the ideal source of supplies for the
whaling fleet as it had been for the Northwest traders, and
it was these new visitors who between 1820 and 1850
boomed Hawaiian trade and gave to the islands a new importance.

'The business of this place is increasing from year to
year,' wrote Sir George Simpson, 'principally dependent
on the whalers and other vessels that rendezvous here....
It is chiefly with reference to the supply of these civilized
wants, that foreign merchants and foreign mechanics have
established themselves in the group.'[19]

In 1843 it was variously estimated by different authorities that the American residents in Hawaii numbered
from two hundred to four hundred, but they were all
agreed that this group far exceeded the citizens of any

other country. The value of American property in the
islands was placed at one million dollars, while that of
the American ships touching at Hawaii was put at anywhere from four to seven millions. Everything centered
about the visits of the whaling fleet and when as many as
fourteen hundred seamen might be in port at the same
time, the vast majority of them from American vessels,
Honolulu took on all the aspects of an American coast
town.[20]

In 1816 a little village of thatched huts shaded by coconut trees, with some forty-two American residents,[21] Honolulu had become some thirty years later a thriving town
whose American-style homes, church steeples and school-
houses bore witness to its prosperity. It had its fort,
government house, foreign consulates, shops and stores.
Two weekly newspapers were published. Through the
influence of the seamen of the whaling ships, commercial
houses, taverns, and grogshops had sprung up like mush-
rooms.[22]

Everything about the town bore so plainly upon it the
stamp of America that visitors from the United States
were immediately at home in its pleasant atmosphere.
Commodore Wilkes upon his visit in 1840 noted the influence of the missionaries. He declared that Sunday was
ushered in 'with a decorum and quietness that would
satisfy the most scrupulous Puritan' and for himself he
felt at once 'identified and connected with the place and its
inhabitants.'[23] 'Could I have forgotten the circumstances
of my visit,' wrote another seaman, 'I should have fancied
myself in New England.'[24]

Within a decade of the coming of the missionaries and
the whalers, Samuel Eliot Morison has written, Hawaii
had become the commercial Gibraltar of the Pacific and
Honolulu, 'with whalemen and merchant sailors rolling
through its streets, shops filled with Lowell shirtings, New
England rum and Yankee notions, orthodox missionaries
living in frame houses brought around the Horn, and a
neo-classic meeting house built of coral blocks, was becoming as Yankee as New Bedford.'[25]

There was another side to this picture, however. Just as the Hawaiian natives found themselves swamped in the engulfing wave of this alien civilization, so did their chiefs find the independence of the government constantly assailed by foreign countries which looked with covetous eyes upon so strategic an outpost in the Pacific. The United States was not the first offender. As in every instance of American expansion, it took a threat of seizure of the islands by some other Power to arouse the United States to the necessity of protecting its own rights. And even when we began to fear that England or France might seize the archipelago, the principle upon which we long acted was that on which we first stood in the case of Samoa. We declared that we had no designs upon Hawaiian independence ourselves, but that we could not allow any other nation to infringe upon the sovereignty of the island kingdom.

The first attempted assault on Hawaii's independence occurred in the period immediately following its discovery. The islands came within the orbit of the voyages of the English explorer, Captain George Vancouver, and in 1794 he won a strong ascendancy over King Kamehameha through the advice he gave him and particularly for bringing about a reconciliation between the native chieftain and his favorite wife. As a result the King, with the consent of his chiefs, resolved to place the island of Hawaii under British protection. It is not likely that the Hawaiians knew just what they were doing, but Vancouver at any rate formally accepted the cession of the island and raised the British flag.[26] Somewhat as in the case of Commodore Porter in the Marquesas, however, no official confirmation of this act was ever forthcoming. England was not yet awake to the value of Hawaii and lost an opportunity to acquire an important naval base which in 1794 she could have held without any other nation being able to dispute her rights. It was an oversight only too rare in the history of British colonial expansion.

The next move upon Hawaii had no more permanent results, but it came from an unexpected quarter and if successful might have greatly changed the history of the Pacific. It was made by Russia.

About 1811, it may be remembered, the Russian colonists in Alaska had dreams of extending their influence southward and actually established a station in northern California. Hawaii also entered into their plans. It is probable that Governor Baranof thought of nothing more than a close trade relationship which would enable him to obtain in the islands supplies for the colony at Sitka, but his agent, one Dr. Georg Scheffer, had more expansive ideas. He induced one of the native chieftains to cede to Russia an island, to which he had no real title; raised the Russian flag, and defied Kamehameha to dispute his possession of the territory. His own Government, however, refused to take the slightest cognizance of his action and in 1816 the Russians were forced to withdraw.[27] Twice Hawaiian independence had been preserved because the Governments concerned failed to support the acts of their agents and felt no real urge for the islands' occupation.

The third early attack on Hawaiian liberties came from France, thus completing the circle of European colonizing Powers of that day, and though it fell far short of occupation it had more permanent results than either of the two previous episodes. In 1831 a law was passed by the native Government, for which the French held the American missionaries largely responsible, banning Catholic priests from Hawaii. France chose to take this act as a national affront and Captain Laplace was dispatched in the sixty-gun frigate *Artemise* in 1839 to impress upon the native chieftains the necessity of affording equal treatment to all foreigners. With a show of force he compelled the Hawaiian Government to accept an ultimatum which recognized Catholicism, provided that there could be no prohibition of wine imports, and set up a system whereby French offenders against local laws could be tried only by a jury of foreign residents. In threatening to open fire upon Honolulu unless this ultimatum was immediately accepted, Captain Laplace informed the American consul that the American clergy in the islands would be treated as part of the native population should hostilities prove necessary. He was fully alive to the growing American influence in the islands and with remarkable prescience reported to his Government that 'of necessity, the Sandwich Islands will belong some day to the masters of California.'[28]

By now it was growing clearly apparent that foreign rivalry for control of Hawaii was becoming an important issue and both in the islands themselves and in the United States a movement arose for the protection of American interests. 'If caution is not used,' we find one American resident of the islands writing in 1843, 'if the fair bud which has thus far been fostered by American citizens, is not nurtured and strengthened by the government, a rival nation will pluck the fruit.'[29] It was a metaphor which was to occur again and again in the discussion of Hawaii. Some forty years later, Secretary of State Bayard, advocating toward the islands a policy of *laissez-faire*, declared our acquisition of Hawaii 'was simply a matter of waiting until the apple should fall'; and in 1893 our minister in Honolulu, changing the fruit but not the metaphor, reported to Washington that 'the Hawaiian pear is now fully ripe, and this is the golden hour for the United States to pluck it.'[30]

Even before 1839 there had been memorials from Nantucket shipowners for the protection of American rights in Hawaii, and our consular agent had sent to his Government repeated requests for the visits of American ships-of-war in view of the islands' importance to our commerce and value to the whale fisheries. The U.S.S. *Dolphin* had been sent on such a mission, and so had the U.S.S. *Peacock* and the U.S.S. *Vincennes*. The commander of the *Peacock*, in fact, succeeded in negotiating with the Hawaiian King his first foreign treaty. However, this pact of trade and friendship was never ratified by the Senate, although the United States maintained cordial relations with Hawaii and Captain William B. Finch of the *Vincennes* took out to the King a Presidential letter of friendship and one of those curious collections of presents Washington was accustomed to sending native chieftains. We were to let both England and France enter into treaty relations with the Hawaiian kingdom before we took any definite action.[31]

The island Government, however, was anxious to conclude foreign agreements which would guarantee its independence and was aroused by the Laplace incident to dispatch a mission to both Europe and America. It succeeded in persuading France and England to conclude a convention mutually guaranteeing Hawaiian independence as between themselves, which was followed by new treaties with the island kingdom, but in the United States a different conception of our relations with the islands already prevailed. We were determined fully to protect our growing interests, to enter into no compact with other Powers which might restrict our freedom of action, and to move slowly in whatever we did. There was no tendency at this time, 1842, when the country was on the eve of its effective expansion to the Pacific Coast, to enter into any such entangling alliances in respect to Hawaii as we were later to conclude in the case of Samoa.

The Hawaiian commissioners were cordially enough received in Washington. Their contention that the islands were of special importance to the United States as the center of the whale fisheries in the Pacific and as an indispensable port of call in the China trade was fully admitted. But no formal guarantee of their independence was forthcoming. Secretary of State Webster did not hesitate to tell the commissioners that it was the sense of the United States that Hawaii should not be brought under the exclusive control of any foreign Power, but he would go no further.[32]

This statement in regard to any encroachment upon Hawaii by a European Government was, nevertheless, the first official indication that we considered American relations with the islands in a somewhat different category from the relations between Hawaii and the rest of the world. It was a bold stand. We had not yet formally acquired any territory on the Pacific Coast and on the grounds of propinquity could make out no better case for interest in the Hawaiian Government than could England. Ships from American ports could reach Honolulu only by the long and hazardous voyage about Cape Horn. It was our commercial activities in the Pacific, and the growing feeling that at no cost should we allow ourselves to be shut off from potential control of that ocean, which made us even at this early date move cautiously in our Hawaiian commitments. As President Tyler declared, in a statement further amplifying Secretary Webster's reply to the Hawaiian commissioners, the United States would view with dissatisfaction 'any attempt by another power, should such attempt be threatened or feared, to take possession of the islands, colonize them, and subvert the native Government.' [33]

Pressure from the New England merchants engaged in the China trade, from the whaling industry, and from those elements in our national life interested in the missionary enterprise in Hawaii, had brought home to the Government a strong realization of the islands' importance. Its action, furthermore, was supported by Congress. The report of the House Committee on Foreign Affairs, written by John Quincy Adams, gave an idealistic picture of our influence in Hawaii, and the consequent moral necessity of extending it, which indicated the growth of our proprietary attitude in Hawaiian affairs.

'It is a subject of cheering contemplation to the friends of human improvement and virtue,' Adams wrote, 'that by the mild and gentle influence of Christian charity, dispensed by the humble missionaries of the gospel, unarmed with secular power, within the last quarter of a century, the people of this group of islands have been converted from the lowest debasement of idolatry to the blessings of the Christian gospel; united under one balanced government; rallied to the fold of civilization by a written language and constitution, providing security for the rights of persons, property and mind, and invested with all the elements of right and power which can entitle them to be acknowledged by their brethren of the human race as a separate and independent community. To the consummation of their acknowledgement, the people of the North American Union are urged by an interest of their own, deeper than that of any other portion of the inhabitants of the earth — by a virtual right of conquest, not over the freedom of their brother man by the brutal arm of physical power, but over the mind and heart by the celestial panoply of the gospel of peace and love.' [34] Naturally no reference was made to the fact that the blessings of civilization were also leading to a depopulation of the islands which seemed to foreshadow the probable extinction of the native race.

It was not long before the new American policy toward Hawaii was put to the test. While the island commissioners were actually engaged in seeking guarantees of their country's independence in England, France, and the United States, alleged insults and injuries to British subjects in Honolulu caused Captain Lord George Paulet of H.M.S. *Carysfort* to make certain demands upon the Hawaiian Government which no sovereign power could accept. Confronted with an ultimatum radically infringing upon native liberties, but which he was powerless to combat, the Hawaiian King adopted a shrewd course of action. He declared he was unable to meet the British demands as an independent ruler and therefore made formal cession of his kingdom to Great Britain.

This act, taken under the direction of his American advisers, was accompanied by an eloquent plea for justice in which he called upon his people and the native chiefs to have faith in their country. 'I make known to you that I am in perplexity by reason of difficulties into which I have been brought without cause,' his declaration read; 'therefore, I have given away the life of the land, hear ye! But my rule over you, my people, and your privileges will continue, for I have hope that the life of the land will be restored when my conduct is justified.' [35]

Nevertheless, Captain Paulet accepted the cession of the islands and raised the British flag without regard for the possible international complications into which he might be plunging his country. He acted as if his annexation of the islands would be automatically confirmed, and, after organizing a governmental commission headed by himself, he even went so far as to form a native regiment, the 'Queen's Own.' It was officered by British subjects, paid out of the Hawaiian treasury, and required to take an oath of allegiance to Captain Paulet's own sovereign. Nor did the English naval officer pay any attention to the protests of Commodore Lawrence Kearny, commander of the American naval forces in the East Indies. The latter officer arrived upon the scene fresh from his success in winning for the United States those commercial privileges which Great Britain had just wrung from China as a result of the so-called Opium War, and he was determined that England should not obtain any exclusive control over Hawaii.

The Hawaiian King in the meantime appealed to the United States for aid and the State Department lost no time in forwarding a protest against Captain Paulet's action to London. Secretary Webster, deeply involved in negotiations with England on other questions, was rather mild in his attitude, but before anything could be done he was succeeded in office by H. S. Legaré and a firmer stand was taken by the United States. Writing to the American minister in London, Edward Everett, on June 13, 1843, the new Secretary of State declared that 'there is something so entirely peculiar in the relations between this little commonwealth and ourselves that we might even feel justified, consistently with our own principles, in interfering by force to prevent its falling into the hands of one of the great powers of Europe.' [36]

Still further evidence of the strong feeling in the United States that we had to be on guard in the Pacific is afforded by an additional statement significantly linking Oregon, California, and Hawaii. It shows to what extent possession of these territories was associated in the middle of the past century with the idea of American power in the Pacific. For in referring to possible foreign seizure of

Hawaii, Legaré told Everett that it was doubtful 'whether even the undisturbed possession of the Oregon Territory and the use of the Columbia River, or indeed anything short of the acquisition of California (if that were possible), would be sufficient indemnity for the loss of these harbors.' [37]

Whether or not England would have followed a different course had we not protested is open to question, but the fact remains that Paulet's acceptance of the cession of the Hawaiian Islands was completely disavowed. Upon the visit to Honolulu of Rear Admiral Thomas there was a formal restoration of native sovereignty and the incident was closed with the lowering of the British flag and the running up of that of Hawaii.

A diplomatic agent, Commissioner George Brown, was now sent to Hawaii by the United States, our vital interest in the islands' complete independence was reaffirmed, and in 1845 negotiations were started for a formal treaty of friendship and commerce between the Hawaiian Kingdom and the American Republic. It granted the United States most favored nation treatment and settled a number of minor issues between the two countries, such as the arrest of deserters from American ships, privileges for whaling vessels, property rights, etc., but it was not signed until 1849. The personal attitude of the American commissioner and also that of his successor made them *persona non grata* to the Hawaiian Government and they had to be recalled, but when at last concluded, the treaty constituted a complete recognition of Hawaiian independence.' [38]

Its signature, curiously enough, almost coincided with another assault on native sovereignty by a foreign power which brought out even more clearly than had the Paulet episode the growing predominance of American interests in the islands. For France was again having difficulties with the local authorities and when they refused to accede to her demands for compensation for a supposed infraction of the French treaty, a force of marines was landed by Admiral de Tromelin and possession taken of the fort, customs house, and administration quarters. Pro-

tests were made by both the British and American consuls
and again Hawaii sought American aid.

As it had in the case of threatened British aggression,
the United States immediately carried its protest to the
Government concerned. Our minister in France was instructed to offer his friendly offices for an adjustment of
the Franco-Hawaiian quarrel, but a diplomatic warning was
also conveyed to the French Government that, while the
United States did not covet the islands for itself, it would
never allow them to pass under the dominion or exclusive
control of any other power.[39]

The *impasse* continued in Honolulu, however, and in
March, 1851, the Hawaiian Government thereupon took a
step somewhat reminiscent of its action in the Paulet episode, but at the same time indicative of how greatly conditions had really changed. For the King placed his kingdom under the protection of the United States and declared
that if a satisfactory agreement could not be reached with
France, 'then is our wish and pleasure that the protection
aforesaid under the United States be perpetual.'[40] As a further sign of the fine hand of the King's American advisers,
a sealed cession of the islands' sovereignty was delivered
to the American commissioner which was to be opened and
acted upon should the United States flag be raised above
that of Hawaii as a sign and symbol of French aggression
against which Hawaii was unable to protect herself.

By this time the control over the native government
of the American residents in the islands had grown so
complete that, faced by the possible loss of independence,
it was entirely natural that Hawaii should turn to the
United States in place of France. There was a strong
feeling in the islands that American annexation was in any
event the only way of securing for the islands an un-
troubled future free from the constant menace of foreign
aggression. With Americans dominating the Government
and one of them serving as Secretary of State, with Americans constituting a large majority in the popular legislature which the King had by now been prevailed upon to
grant, with Americans controlling at least three fourths of

the islands' business, the eventual merging of Hawaii into the American system appeared so highly logical that even though there had been no occupation by French forces, a strong case could have been made out for the wisdom of the King's tentative cession of his sovereignty.

The American commissioner in Honolulu was outspokenly anxious for American annexation. He hoped against hope that French aggression would enable him to open the sealed cession of the islands which had been handed over to him and he rather naïvely reported to Washington that in such an eventuality he feared his inclinations might lead him to transcend his authority. 'We must not take the islands in virtue of the "manifest destiny" principle,' he wrote with forced moderation, 'but can we not accept their voluntary offer? Who has a right to forbid the banns?' [41]

The situation proved rather embarrassing to Washington. We had so recently secured Oregon and California that the spirit of expansion was still strong, and, as we have previously noted, there was a greater degree of interest in the Western Ocean than there was to be again for half a century. After having pushed our frontier to the Pacific, it appeared an easy and logical step to gather in these islands which lay such a comparatively short distance off the new coastline, particularly when Hawaii seemed so agreeable to accepting the American flag. But it was not President Polk or even a Democratic Administration which was now in office. The Whigs were back in power under President Fillmore and the banner of expansion had been lowered. Furthermore, Daniel Webster, once again back in the State Department, had not been converted to the cause toward which he was so lukewarm as Tyler's Secretary of State, and he still believed that the United States could not hope to hold Oregon, let alone establish effective control over Hawaii, without running the risk of disunion.

Consequently, we find Washington pressing for a solution of Hawaii's controversy with France and gently soft-pedaling the enthusiasm of its envoy in Honolulu, who continued nervously to finger his precious deed of cession without quite knowing what to do about it. Officially Webster put up a brave show. He instructed our Hawaiian commissioner, first, that the United States would continue to honor Hawaiian independence; second, that it could never consent to see the islands taken over by either of the two great commercial Powers of Europe; and, third, that it would not permit demands, 'manifestly unjust and derogatory and inconsistent with a *bona fide* independence,' to be enforced against the Hawaiian Government.

Privately a more conservative tone was employed. Webster informed the commissioner that the war-making power rested with Congress and that he should carefully bear this in mind. He ordered him to express no opinion on annexation to the Hawaiian Government, to return at once the deed of cession, and by no means to encourage or in any way promote annexationist sentiment.[42]

This was the end of the unsuccessful cession of 1851 and fortunately it also marked the end of the French controversy. A solution to that problem was reached without any further intervention by the United States. Hawaii had successfully survived a series of attacks upon its independence, and by the middle of the century it was apparent that if it were to lose its autonomy, it would be only by a gradual development of what was already virtually an American protectorate into an American colony. That this was to be Hawaii's eventual fate at least one European statesman had no doubt. Lord Palmerston is reported to have advised the Hawaiian commissioners who visited him in 1850 to look forward to seeing their country become an integral part of the United States.

'Such was the destiny of the Hawaiian Islands,' he is reputed to have said, 'arising from their proximity to the State of California and Oregon and natural dependence on those markets for exports and imports, together with the probable extinction of the Hawaiian aboriginal population, and its substitution by immigration from the United States.' [43]

CHAPTER X

Toward Annexation

IF THE Fillmore Administration made no effort to extend American influence in Hawaii and was content with a reaffirmation of our interest in the islands' independence, the return of the Democrats under President Pierce in 1853 marked that change in policy which we should expect from the party of annexation. Even without the excuse of a voluntary offer of the islands such as that with which President Fillmore and Secretary Webster had been confronted, the new Administration lost no time in exploring the possibilities of outright annexation. After all, it was that period of mid-century interest in the Pacific which we have already examined in connection with the Perry Expedition to Japan, and there was a widespread feeling that Hawaii should be brought within the American Union as quickly as possible. In fact, the Perry program for naval bases and coal dépôts in the Bonin Islands and Formosa had been virtually predicated on the theory that we were soon to take over Hawaii.

Secretary of State Marcy made the first step in this direction before he had been in office ten months by instructing our minister in Paris to sound out the attitude of the French Government toward American annexation. Even though only a year or two before we had been expressly denying any suggestion of seeking exclusive influence over the islands, Marcy now spoke of the inevitability of their coming under our control and gave his opinion that 'it would be but reasonable and fair that the powers should acquiesce in such a disposition of them, provided the transference was effected by fair means.'¹

On the Pacific Coast particularly there was strong support for the program which the new Secretary of State contemplated. The legislature of Washington Territory, organized that very year, passed a resolution in 1853,

stating that 'great advantage would result to this Territory and to the United States of America, by the annexation of the Sandwich Islands'; [2] while in California
favorable opinion toward such a step was even more emphatic. It appeared for a time that the residents of the
latter State might take the matter in their own hands. Rumors were rife of the organization of filibustering expeditions to overthrow the Hawaiian Government and
bring the islands into the Union much as Texas had been,
or as California itself might have been as a result of the
Bear Flag revolt.

Farther east the question did not excite so much interest, but scattered support for Hawaii's annexation
could be found. Describing the islands as a halfway point
between California and China and the chief resort of our
whaling fleet, the *New York Herald* declared: 'Let us have
the Sandwich Islands, small pox, missionaries, volcanoes,
and King Kamehameha, admitted into the Union without
delay.' [3]

The strongest friend of annexation in Congress was a
member from so distant a State as Maine. Bespeaking
his mistrust of 'manifest destiny in the raw and rampant
forms in which they have been advocated so frequently of
late,' Representative Washburn nevertheless wanted the
Hawaiian Islands, not as a colony, but as a Territory and
potential State. He urged upon the House their value to
commerce and to the fisheries, their naval importance, and
the imminent danger of their seizure by some other
Power. 'The question of the annexation of the Sandwich
Islands,' he concluded in a speech on January 4, 1854, 'is
one of necessity, of time, and of justice.' [4] There were to
be scores of speeches on this question before the action
which Representative Washburn advocated was finally
taken forty-four years later, but few new ideas were introduced. If his address had been remembered, Senate and
House could have been spared a great deal of oratory.

It was against this background, and undoubtedly influenced by the reports Commodore Perry was sending
home on the necessity of securing naval bases in the

Pacific, as well as by an earlier report of Admiral du Pont which declared the acquisition of Hawaii would be intimately connected with our commercial and naval supremacy in that ocean, that Secretary Marcy proceeded with his annexation program. Early in 1854 he instructed the American commissioner in Honolulu 'to treat with the present authorities of the Hawaiian Government for the transfer of the Sandwich Islands to the United States,' and he urged him to obtain a treaty as quickly as possible in order that it might be submitted to the Senate before adjournment of the current session.[5]

Conditions in the islands were not quite as favorable for such a move as they had been a few years earlier. On the one side was the feeling of insecurity in the islands created by the recent threats of foreign aggression, the fear of filibustering expeditions from California, and the growing discontent with native rule on the part of foreign residents. But on the other were the existence of an English party in the islands decidedly unfavorable to American influence, and the vigorous opposition to any surrender of Hawaiian sovereignty expressed by the native heir apparent to the throne.

A treaty was signed despite the objections of the anti-Americans, but the negotiations were several times delayed and before he was through the American commissioner had been compelled to grant various concessions which were not contemplated in his instructions. The instrument at last agreed upon provided annuities of $300,000 for the ruling family, whereas Secretary Marcy had set a limit of $100,000 for such payments, and, far more important, it stipulated that Hawaii should be at once admitted to the Union as a State.[6]

Obviously this latter clause created difficulties with which the Administration was not anxious to cope at a time when slavery and States' rights had raised a problem so completely overshadowing Hawaiian annexation as to render the fate of the treaty a negligible consideration. Marcy felt obliged to postpone his plans for the time being, and had so informed our commissioner in Hawaii when events in the islands also served to kill whatever chance for success the treaty might have had. The Hawaiian King suddenly died, and his successor, whose opposition to the treaty as heir apparent has already been noted, raised in Hawaii obstacles to ratification of the treaty as insurmountable as those raised in the United States by the question of statehood.

The independence of the islands, which had seemed to be so much more seriously endangered by the friendly overtures of the United States than it ever had been by the threats of England or France, was thus accorded a new lease on life. But although our advance into the Pacific had received such a severe set-back, it was now impossible to doubt that it would some day be carried through with greater determination.

During the Civil War we should naturally expect Hawaii to be forgotten, but it was not altogether neglected and an unsuccessful attempt was actually made to conclude a reciprocity treaty with the native Government. 'In every light in which the state of the Hawaiian Islands can be contemplated,' we find President Lincoln stating in one of his messages to Congress, 'it is an object of profound interest for the United States. Virtually it was once a colony. It is now a near and immediate neighbor.' [7]

Following the war, with Seward as Secretary of State, annexation again came to the fore. The seer of Pacific expansion could no more ignore an opportunity to acquire these islands than he could resist the temptation to purchase Alaska. They fitted into his scheme of things even more neatly than the distant northern territory. Consequently, when our minister in Honolulu, Edward McCook, privately asked Seward for permission to take up with the Hawaiian Government the possible purchase of the islands, the Secretary of State gladly gave him free rein.

Political considerations prescribed caution and so we find these communications confidential and couched in somewhat mysterious terms. 'You are at liberty to sound the proper authority on the large subject mentioned in your note,' Seward wrote McCook on July 13, 1867, 'and ascertain probable conditions. You may confidentially receive overtures and communicate the same to me.' Later he supplemented these instructions by stating, again confidentially, 'that a lawful and peaceful annexation of the islands to the United States, with the consent of the people of the Sandwich Islands, is deemed desirable by this Government.'[8]

The ill-success of his other imperialistic ventures and his difficulties in securing congressional approval for the purchase of Alaska, however, caused him reluctantly to give up this plan for extending our influence in the Pacific. He could discover no popular support for his ambitious program of expansion and was forced to accept the implications of his own mournful observation that public attention continued to be fastened upon domestic questions to the exclusion of 'the higher but more remote questions of national extension and aggrandizement.'[9]

This did not mean that Hawaii was entirely overlooked in Washington. President Johnson favored annexation and President Grant transmitted to Congress, though without comment, a dispatch from our minister in Honolulu recommending such a move. But the official attitude veered from the annexation program of the immediate pre-war period to a policy of commercial reciprocity, which in the words of President Johnson would serve as a guaranty of good-will 'until the people of the islands shall of themselves, at no distant day, voluntarily apply for admission into the Union.'[10] For ten years such a free-trade treaty was debated arousing both the support and the opposition to which every commercial agreement is subject.

In the United States it was generally favored, but the treaty actually negotiated in 1867 was defeated in the Senate through opposition from two different quarters. It was attacked by the country's sugar interests which saw their industry undermined by Hawaiian competition, and it found little favor among the friends of annexation on the ground that reciprocity would forestall or at least indefinitely postpone the achievement of their real objective. The attitude of the former group could not be changed, but that of the latter was modified when a second reciprocity treaty submitted in 1875 provided that no Hawaiian territory should ever be leased or disposed of to any other Power, and that none of the privileges of the American treaty should be conferred elsewhere. In the belief that this treaty thereby paved the way for eventual annexation, it was finally ratified.' [11]

In Hawaii a vigorous opposition to the treaty also had to be overcome. Paradoxically enough, it was opposed for a time by both the friends and enemies of annexation, the former fearing, as had the annexationists in the United States, that it would block their program, and the latter interpreting it as the first step toward the absorption of the Hawaiian Kingdom by the United States. The leader of the anti-Americans was a Frenchman whom the King had appointed as his foreign minister, and though he was at length prevailed upon to accept reciprocity because of the pressure brought to bear by Hawaiian planters seeking an American market, he remained the spokesman of an anti-American *bloc* which was not without influence in island affairs. [12]

When in 1884 this reciprocity treaty came to be renewed, it included a new clause which marked a further progress toward our expansion into the Pacific. It provided for the cession to the United States of Pearl Harbor, on the island of Oahu, a potential naval base which General J. M. Schofield had urgently recommended we should acquire, in a report submitted in 1873. [13] If we had not yet formally annexed Hawaii, we had brought it by this treaty within the American commercial system and arranged for an American outpost in the islands which would serve to protect them against intervention from any other quarter.

Our policy toward Hawaii during the period which saw the tightening of these commercial bonds, but no further political connections between the two countries, was well summed up by James G. Blaine during his first term of office as Secretary of State in 1881. Faced with a choice between material annexation and commercial assimilation, he declared, we had chosen the less responsible alternative, but nevertheless Hawaii had become an integral part of the American system, we could never consent to share what responsibility we had, and our position in the islands had to be maintained both because of our duty to the Hawaiians and because the islands represented the key to the dominion of the Pacific. Benevolent neutrality rather than either annexation or a protectorate was our policy, he concluded, but should this be found impracticable 'this Government would then unhesitatingly meet the altered situation by seeking an avowedly American solution for the grave issues presented.' [14]

Still further was this proprietary attitude exemplified when in 1887 both England and France formally protested Hawaii's cession of Pearl Harbor and suggested a joint declaration by the United States, England, and France guaranteeing Hawaiian independence and neutrality. It was the very year in which the Samoan controversy had come to a head and the United States had itself suggested a form of tripartite control over the South Sea islands shared by England and Germany. Yet when this somewhat similar undertaking was suggested for Hawaii, we would have nothing whatsoever to do with it. Secretary of State Bayard made it clear that we could admit of no foreign restraint upon our Hawaiian policy whatever course we chose to adopt. He denied that either the reciprocity treaty or the cession of Pearl Harbor infringed in any way upon Hawaii's independence, but he refused any undertaking to guarantee in conjunction with England and France the islands' sovereignty. [15]

In this policy he had the complete support of President Cleveland. While favoring Hawaiian autonomy as he favored that of Samoa, the President nevertheless expressed 'his unhesitating conviction that the intimacy of our relations with Hawaii should be emphasized.' [16] It was somewhat ironical that in the case of Hawaii, as in the case of Samoa, Cleveland's first administration was responsible for action which definitely paved the way for a subsequent program of annexation. For this was a policy to which the forthright Democratic leader was absolutely opposed, in conformity with the reversal of his party's attitude toward expansion since the war, and one which he vainly tried to block during his second term of office. His ineffectual efforts to bring about our withdrawal from Samoa, and his fruitless opposition to the Hawaiian annexation treaty of President Harrison, bear telling witness to the inevitability of the processes of expansion once they were set in motion.

There was a danger in the passive attitude toward Hawaii in effect in the eighties to which the statesmen in Washington were far from oblivious. This lay in the instability of the island kingdom. Secretary Blaine among others had clearly seen the risks inherent in the decline of the native rulers and the gradual dying out of the native people, and in the years following the conclusion of our reciprocity treaty, it was this situation which aroused the concern of the proponents of annexation in this country and of the American residents in Hawaii. It became more and more apparent that an independent Hawaii was really an anachronism.

That the native Hawaiians were a dying race had been noted as early as the eighteen-forties, and by 1857 their survival was almost despaired of according to the report on a questionnaire which had been sent to all foreign residents in the islands by the British-born Hawaiian foreign minister. 'It is doubtful,' he wrote in summing up the answers he received, 'whether the native race will be able to withstand the shock which the overwhelming wave of Anglo-Saxon energy, enterprise, and cupidity has given it.' [17]

All the writers of that period drew attention to the native depopulation and ascribed various causes for the phenomenon which often reflected their stand on the old missionary-traders feud. In other words, each group held the other responsible for changes in Hawaiian life which had a bad effect upon the natives' health, and failed to realize that both traders and missionaries had a part in developments which always accompanied the impact of Western civilization upon the natives of the Pacific islands.

The commercial elements in Hawaii's foreign community declared that the restraints imposed upon the natives by the missionaries, the labor to which they were forced in order to meet the tax levies of a missionary-inspired government, the ill effect upon native health of the introduction of foreign clothing, and the prevalence of abortion due to the harsh punishment meted out for breaches of chastity, were responsible for depopulation. The missionaries, on the other hand, held the traders chiefly guilty for the weakening of the native strain and cited three chief causes — the distribution of firearms which had caused a great increase in the casualties resulting from native wars, the wide sale of alcoholic drinks to which the Hawaiians became universally addicted, and the introduction of venereal disease.

Without question all these causes contributed to the decrease in the native population during the nineteenth century and neither missionaries nor traders can be held exclusively responsible for it. It was a phenomenon all too common wherever Europeans came in contact with peoples of a less advanced civilization, and while the higher death rate among the Hawaiians may have been directly due to the vice and disease introduced by the foreigners, their lower birth rate is usually explained by impaired reproductive powers resulting from a lack of adjustment in the course of a too rapid transition from a natural to an artificial mode of life. For this the foreigners were indirectly as responsible as they were for the more immediate causes of the decline, but the most shocking example of their influence remained in the widespread prevalence of venereal disease, first introduced at the time of Captain Cook's visit in 1778.[18]

Whatever the explanation, however, a native popula-

tion, which in 1832 had already fallen to 130,313 from
original estimates of anywhere from 200,000 to 400,000,
continued to decline at an alarming rate. By 1860 it had
been cut almost half to 69,800, and in the next thirty
years it was again halved to show a total in 1890 of
34,436.[19]

Foreigners were taking the place of natives so that at the
end of the century Hawaii's total population was about
the same as it had been at the beginning. Europeans and
Americans were the dominant element in this influx of
newcomers, and they won control over island affairs to
an extent far greater than their numerical proportion
entitled them to exercise. The land was largely theirs;
control of commerce and industry almost entirely in their
hands. But the bulk of Hawaiian immigrants were
laborers imported by the planters for the field work of
which the native Hawaiians were incapable — first Portu-
guese from the Azores, then Chinese, and finally Japanese.
Hawaii was fast losing its native character and becoming
a country of white traders and planters supported by
Oriental labor.*

This development served to make the idea of a native,
independent Hawaiian kingdom a contradiction in terms,
and the declining power of the long line of kings descended
from the great Kamehameha served still further to emphasize the islands' ambiguous status. For the native
rulers had become more and more acquiescent to foreign
advice and in the legislature it was the foreigners, Europeans and Americans, who commanded an overwhelming
majority on every occasion.

For a time after the advent of the foreigners the ability
of the Hawaiian kings and the influence of the chiefs
gave a native character to the administration. The first
Kamehameha had been a remarkable man. Supported by
an able group of chieftains and by his influential wife,
Kaahumanu, who acted as his premier, he had consoli-
dated his kingdom and prepared the way for Christianity

---

* This process has continued, but the final fate of the native race seems destined to be not total extinction, but merger with the Chinese and Japanese.

and Western civilization. His successor, Liholiho, or
Kamehameha II, was himself a drunken debauchee, but
the influence of the old chiefs and of Kaahumanu, who for
long acted as regent, made possible further advances
along the road of progress and material development
demanded by the foreigners.

Kamehameha III then ushered in a brief period of
reaction, in which the childishness and licentiousness of
the natives were given full sway, but he subsequently
recognized his responsibilities and with the aid of missionary advisers ruled ably and well until his death in
1854. Even though a suggestion that he visit America had
to be vetoed because his advisers feared that his intem-
perance would provide a shocking spectacle for the
American public, it was he who gave Hawaii its first
constitution in 1839 and then in 1852 modified it so as to
extend still further the principles of representative government. He was consistently friendly to the United States
and personally favored the annexation treaty engineered
by Secretary Marcy.

The brief reign of Kamehameha IV, from 1854 to 1863,
was unimportant, but it was his early death, a direct
result of the dissipated life he led at court, and the even
more premature death of his heir, which brought home to
foreigners a realization that the Hawaiian royal line was
dying out. An elder brother of the last king was now
placed on the throne as Kamehameha V, but when he died
within nine years leaving no successor, it became necessary to elect a king. First Lunaliho and then Kalakaua
were chosen in this manner, but there were now disputes
over the lawful succession and trouble was being stored
up for the future.

United States marines had to be landed for the sup-
pression of riots at the time of Kalakaua's accession in
1874 and during his reign there was resort to peaceful
revolution to win a new constitution providing the reforms demanded by the foreign element. Furthermore,
international rivalry was introduced into the situation.
Kalakaua was a strong adherent of the United States,

which he twice visited and where he died in 1891, but his rival for the throne, Queen Emma, had pronounced British sympathies and looked for support from that quarter. A confused, dangerous situation was developing which began to seem ominous to the Americans in Hawaii, especially when to existing uncertainties was added a movement of 'Hawaii for the Hawaiians' which gained great strength in 1891 when Queen Liliuokalani, sister of Kalakaua and last of the native rulers, ascended the throne.[20]

Her attempt to revive the power of native rule and to break away from foreign influence came at a critical time. The dying-out of the old chiefs and the disintegration of the royal line had brought into power a group of native reactionaries who were allied with a number of unscrupulous foreign adventurers ready to use the natives as tools for satisfying their own selfish ambitions. The court had become thoroughly corrupt; bribery and favoritism were the order of the day, and misgovernment was weighing heavily upon both natives and foreigners. 'During these years,' writes a native historian with shrewd irony, 'the politics and government of Hawaii became as corrupt as the politics and government of some large cities in the United States about that time.' [21]

Whatever the comparative state of corruption between Honolulu and New York or Philadelphia, however, the American residents in Hawaii set themselves firmly against these new influences. The sons of the missionaries, who now considered Hawaii their own country and had in so many instances 'chosen the way of Dives rather than the thorny path of Paul'; the merchants building up Pacific trade, and the sugar planters, were all prepared to resist any reactionary turn in Hawaiian affairs. And seeing little hope for the preservation of their liberties or for Hawaiian progress under the decadent native dynasty, they turned to annexation to the United States as the only possible solution of their problem. They took up this old issue and determined to press it to a conclusion.

The three chief factors in the situation as it had developed in 1891 were Queen Liliuokalani and the reactionaries, the American annexationists, and the United States minister in Honolulu, John L. Stevens. It was the interplay of these forces in Hawaiian politics which provided the drama of the next few years.

From the day of her accession to the throne the friction between Queen Liliuokalani and the American community was marked by a bitterness hitherto unknown in the islands. She defied the legislature, which was largely controlled by American planters, and relied wholly upon the advice of a small group of adventurers of whom the most notable was a Tahitian half-caste. Their influence was thrown on the side of reaction and corruption and the royal palace was reputed to be the scene of licentious revelries which served to shock the whole foreign community.

The Queen, however, had a definite purpose in mind. Strong, self-willed, imperious, she believed that she could counteract foreign influence, and, by restoring the old prerogatives of the Hawaiian monarchy, exorcise the danger of annexation to the United States and establish Hawaiian independence upon a new basis. She was an extreme reactionary, this unusual woman whose political activities contrast so strangely with her talent in music and poetry. She allowed herself to be made the tool of the unprincipled adventurers who surrounded her and played upon her vanity and pride. She was narrow-minded and short-sighted. Yet her goal was a patriotic one. It was her mistake that she was opposing a development which the history of her little kingdom should have shown her was inevitable, and her tragic misfortune that she could not realize that by fighting annexation she was creating a situation which brought it on all the sooner.[22]

To the Americans on the islands who had gradually won such a large measure of control over the government, there could be no turning back of the clock, while their feeling that the Queen's reactionary policies could in the final analysis be combated only by annexation found decisive support in an entirely different reason for closer union with the United States. The island sugar planters saw in the McKinley tariff's bounty system for American beet sugar growers a deathblow to the prosperity which they had so long enjoyed under reciprocity. It seemed to presage the entire loss of their American markets. They would have wanted annexation on economic grounds even if the local political situation had not forced the issue.

In this policy they had an open and faithful ally in the American minister, John L. Stevens. He was an appointee of James G. Blaine, now Harrison's Secretary of State, and though there is no record of any special instructions given to him, his intimate personal relationship with Blaine leaves little doubt that the course he pursued in Hawaii was approved in Washington. It was one of tacit if not open encouragement for the American planters upon every possible occasion, and from the day of his arrival in Honolulu he sent home such frank and outspoken pleas for annexation that the latitude allowed him by the State Department speaks for itself. It was apparent that Blaine felt that the time had at last come for that 'American solution' of the Hawaiian problem of which he had spoken in 1881.[23]

Stevens reported on the danger of a revolt against Queen Liliuokalani and on the necessity in that event of American intervention. He wrote long dispatches on the growing confusion in Hawaiian affairs and of the possibility that this might lead to British action should we hold aloof too long. He brought up the effect of the imposition of duties on Hawaiian sugar imports which meant disaster for the American interests in the islands unless new commercial arrangements were made at once. He injected what was still a comparatively new issue into the question by dwelling upon the effect on Hawaii of immigration from China and Japan. This development was becoming so important, he declared, that the United States would soon have to face the vital question of whether an American or an Asiatic civilization was to prevail in a country so close to its western coast.[24]

At first, Stevens contented himself with advising the immediate development of Pearl Harbor, which he considered more important to our naval interests than Samoa, and the conclusion of new agreements for absolute free trade between Hawaii and the United States. But he soon took up a more advanced position. 'Annexation must be the future remedy,' we find him writing on February 8, 1892, 'or else Great Britain will be furnished with circumstances and opportunity to get a hold on the islands, which will cause future embarrassment to the United States.' [25] Nine months later, after Blaine's retirement from the State Department, he sought instructions on what he should do should revolution break out and concluded an eloquent appeal for definite action by confidentially declaring that 'the golden hour is near at hand.' [26]

In this statement Stevens was, of course, entirely right. The deadlock between Queen Liliuokalani and the Hawaiian legislature was bound to lead to an open break, and it actually occurred in January, 1893. The Queen decided to proclaim a new constitution which would have restored the old prerogatives of the Crown and deprived the legislature of almost all its power, and she summoned the assembly on January 14 to hear the announcement of her new policy. But so great was the outcry against this proposed step and so evident the determination of the American party to resist by every means in its power what it considered an illegal act, that Liliuokalani hesitated. At the last moment she modified her attitude and, instead of announcing the new constitution for which the native Hawaiians were now vociferously clamoring, she declared that its promulgation would be postponed for a time.

This temporizing did not satisfy the Americans. They saw, in the Queen's attempt to override existing law and herself proclaim a new and reactionary constitution, positive evidence of her determination to restore the old royal autocracy. They felt that their position was now 'like living on a volcano,' and that they had to act at once to protect their interests. A committee of public safety was immediately appointed, and plans made for an appeal to the United States for protection and for the establishment of a Provisional Government. Then, on January 16, a mass meeting of some thirteen hundred foreign residents of Honolulu was held and a proclamation issued declaring that a state of emergency existed, while the committee of public safety hurriedly sought out Stevens to request his intervention to safeguard American interests, because 'we are unable to protect ourselves without aid, and, therefore, pray for the protection of the United States forces.' [27] The American minister had been away from Honolulu as these storm-clouds were gathering, but he had providentially returned on the U.S.S. *Boston* at the critical moment and promptly ordered the landing of one hundred and sixty marines and two guns for the preservation of law and order.

Events now moved quickly. On the next day the committee of public safety, on which there was not a single native representative, issued a proclamation abrogating the Hawaiian monarchy and establishing a Provisional Government 'to exist until terms of union with the United States of America have been negotiated and agreed upon.' [28] It then appointed an executive council of four Americans, and, after proceeding to take over the government buildings, asked the United States minister for *de facto* recognition of the new régime. Again the enthusiastic Stevens acted with that promptitude which was subsequently to become a burning issue in the United States and accorded the Provisional Government the recognition which it sought.

In the face of these rapid and concerted moves by her enemies, Queen Liliuokalani found herself powerless. The popular support she could muster among the natives availed her little in such a fast-moving crisis. But more important than anything else, she saw, in the prompt landing of American troops and the immediate recognition of the Provisional Government, the official hand of a nation which she could not possibly combat. Consequently, she yielded to the revolution under protest and surrendered her power. Recalling, perhaps, the act of one of her predecessors in the face of British aggression, her admission of defeat was accompanied by a proclamation in which she declared that she had yielded 'to the superior force of the United States of America, whose minister plenipotentiary, his excellency John L. Stevens, has caused United States troops to be landed at Honolulu and declared that he would support the said Provisional Government.' [29]

There were several aspects of this kaleidoscopic change of scene in Hawaii which were later to lead to widespread controversy in the United States. It was noted in the first place that the committee of public safety had called for help because of its inability to preserve order, but that within thirty hours it had been recognized by Stevens as the Provisional Government, thereby implying that it had won complete control of Hawaii. If a situation existed on Monday so dangerous to American interests as to demand the landing of marines, it was surprising, to say the least, that the *de facto* Government deserved recognition on Tuesday. Moreover, there was the question of whether the American minister's prompt extension of recognition, with complete disregard for the Government to which he was officially accredited, did not even precede the Provisional Government's seizure of those administration buildings which symbolized governmental control. What rôle did the American marines play in the revolution and how far was Queen Liliuokalani justified in her contention that she was compelled to surrender to 'the superior force of the United States'? But these questions we may leave for the moment, as the last act in this exciting drama is still to be recounted. Further speed records were to be established by the new Hawaiian Government.

The Queen had convoked her assembly on January 14, the committee of public safety had called for American aid on January 16, the Provisional Government had been proclaimed and recognized on January 17, and on the next day a special commission was appointed to negotiate a treaty of annexation and left immediately for the United States with the blessing of Minister Stevens. It took this commission fifteen days to reach Washington. Nevertheless, a treaty incorporating Hawaii into the United States as a Territory had been virtually agreed upon by February 11 and was formally concluded three days later.[30] Just thirty-two days after the first moves leading to the adoption of the scheme for annexation, as President Cleveland later pointed out, the United States had the treaty in its hands. For some sixty years the annexation movement had been slowly gathering headway, but it reached its climax with a sudden precipitancy which must have taken even the careful observers of Washington by complete surprise.

From the speed with which the annexation treaty was concluded and submitted to the Senate, however, it is evident that the project was received in Washington with an enthusiasm equal to that with which it had been initiated in Honolulu. If even President Cleveland in the previous Administration had referred to Hawaii as 'an outpost of American commerce and a stepping stone to the growing trade of the Pacific,' it is not surprising that a Republican Administration should do nothing to discourage Stevens's zeal. It had been willing only a few years before to sign a tripartite convention for the control of Samoa, and could hardly be expected to reject the overtures of a commission of the new Hawaiian Government which laid those islands upon America's doorstep.

In any event, the treaty negotiations were accompanied by dispatches to Stevens approving his conduct and instructing him to continue to support the Provisional Government while the treaty was pending. That enthusiastic envoy, however, did take one step which went a little too far even for the Washington expansionists. Assuming that annexation was now imminent, that the Hawaiian pear was ready to pluck, he gladly acceded to a request of the Provisional Government for the establishment of an American protectorate and raised the American flag over the government buildings in Honolulu. To Washington he reported that only his prompt action in taking this step had prevented the British and the Japanese from intervening in the situation, and he asked for the dispatch to Honolulu of the 'most powerful American ship available' to support the position he had assumed.[31]

Secretary of State John W. Foster, who had succeeded Blaine on the eve of the revolution, felt forced to disavow this last act, but there was no rebuke for Stevens.[32] His new instructions merely warned him against any infringement of Hawaiian independence or sovereignty, a somewhat belated move, and curiously enough the American flag continued to float over the Hawaiian capital so long as Stevens remained in Honolulu.

In submitting the treaty to the Senate both President Harrison and Secretary Foster were very careful in their accompanying reports to explain that events in Hawaii had left the United States with no other alternative than acceptance of the treaty which had been so expeditiously negotiated. It was made abundantly clear that the State Department had had no hand in the proceedings at Honolulu and that the annexation proposal brought to Washington by the special commission was a voluntary offering. It was also adequately set forth in a review of our past relations with Hawaii that annexation was the natural culmination of our Hawaiian policy and entirely consistent with our declared attitude toward the islands.

'This report shows,' wrote the Secretary of State, 'that from an early day the policy of the United States has been consistently and constantly declared against any foreign aggression in the Kingdom of Hawaii inimical to the necessarily paramount rights and interests of the American people there, and the uniform contemplation of their annexation as a contingent necessity. But beyond that it is shown that annexation has been on more than one occasion avowed as a policy and attempted as a fact.'[33]

President Harrison declared that under the existing circumstances a protectorate or annexation were the only courses open to the United States and that the latter was greatly to be preferred in the interests of both the United States and Hawaii. 'These interests are not wholly selfish,' he added. 'It is essential that none of the other great powers shall secure the islands. Such possession would not consist with our safety and the peace of the world.' [34] It was an exceedingly broad-minded view.

In the light of past policy and the apparently unassailable arguments in favor of annexation, senatorial approval of the Hawaiian treaty might appear a foregone conclusion. But unfortunately the Senate did not act with that promptitude with which the Administration, watching the sands of its term of office fast running out, had confidently expected. Before any action whatsoever was carried through, President Cleveland returned to Washington at the head of the triumphant Democracy and events then took a sudden and unexpected turn.

CHAPTER XI

Imperialism's First Fruit

PRESIDENT CLEVELAND for the second time took the presidential oath on March 4, 1893, and one of his first official acts was to withdraw the Hawaiian treaty which President Harrison had submitted to the Senate with so strong a plea for immediate ratification. It was an unusual if not entirely unprecedented step, but the President's liberal susceptibilities had been deeply offended by the rapidity with which the Provisional Hawaiian Government had been recognized and the equally hasty conclusion of the annexation treaty. He decided to send to Hawaii a special commissioner, James H. Blount, and on the basis of a thorough investigation determine the further policy of his Administration.

Public opinion had shown itself to be fairly divided on the course which President Harrison had pursued. There was a strong popular demand for Hawaii's annexation and a general recognition that it was the culmination of our traditional policy toward the islands. Republicans generally were prepared to accept Secretary Foster's explicit disclaimer of American intervention in the revolution which dethroned Queen Liliuokalani. On the other hand, Democrats supported Cleveland's position that the United States could not afford to allow annexation to be colored by the suspicion of unfair tactics or by a threat of force against the native régime.

Blount's instructions, sent him seven days after Cleveland's inauguration, gave him paramount authority in all matters concerning our relations with Hawaii and ordered a full report on the events leading up to the Queen's deposition. He was accredited to the President of the Provisional Government, Sanford B. Dole, the son of an American missionary and former judge of the Hawaiian Supreme Court, whom President Cleveland addressed as 'Great and Good Friend.' [1]

When the new minister took over Stevens's post in
Honolulu he at once hauled down the American flag, which
was still floating over that of Hawaii on all government
buildings as a sign of our protectorate, and reëmbarked on
the U.S.S. *Boston* the marines which his predecessor had
caused to be landed upon the request of the committee of
public safety. It was clearly evident that the policy of the
United States had changed, and the American and anti-
American groups in Hawaii prepared to act accordingly.
As Blount proceeded with his investigation, he found
himself swamped in a mass of annexation and anti-
annexation propaganda which made his task exceedingly
difficult. Unfortunately, he was not the best possible
appointee for an impartial investigation, carrying on his
inquiries in a rather high-handed style, and consequently
he found himself bitterly assailed by most of the Americans
in Honolulu for the methods he used in obtaining his
information.

After examination of all the obtainable data and inter-
views with countless witnesses, Blount submitted his
report to President Cleveland in July.[2] It tended to confirm the worst suspicions of the worthy Democrats. And
for all the bitter controversy which it provoked both in
Hawaii and in the United States, and for all the attacks
made upon it as a politically prejudiced document, the
factual background of its story of the revolution cannot
easily be disputed.

Blount declared in the first place that Minister Stevens
had agreed to support the revolution before it was begun
and that he promised to recognize the Provisional Government the moment it occupied the government buildings in
Honolulu. For this his actions rather than written documents were submitted as proof. No one could have acted
so promptly and efficiently in support of the revolutionaries' cause, according to the Blount thesis, without some
previous understanding with its leaders. Furthermore,
his report was able to cite the opinion of Admiral Skerrett
that the troops landed from the *Boston* were improperly
stationed in so far as the protection of American interests

was concerned, but very well located if their objective was support of the Provisional Government. This was vigorously denied by all concerned, but it was an accusation which gave great force to Queen Liliuokalani's contention that she was compelled to surrender her throne because overawed by the superior forces of the United States.

Blount also emphasized the rapidity with which a Government, forced to appeal for aid as unable to protect itself, had been judged capable of maintaining law and order throughout Hawaii, and attempted to show that in actual fact Stevens's recognition of the new régime did not take into consideration any question of its stability or authority. He produced evidence to show conclusively that the American minister had acted even before the Provisional Government was in control of administrative headquarters in Honolulu, another charge which lent support to the Queen's position that it was American recognition of her enemies rather than their own power which forced her capitulation.

In regard to public opinion in Hawaii, Blount reported that native sympathy was entirely with the Queen, and he was able to quote the opinion of the annexationists themselves that their cause would be overwhelmingly defeated in a popular vote. 'From a careful inquiry,' he wrote President Cleveland, 'I am satisfied that it would be defeated by a vote of at least two to one. If the votes of persons claiming allegiance to foreign countries were excluded, it would be defeated by more than five to one.' [3]

After receiving this report, the President sent out to supersede Blount, whose special mission was completed, a new minister, Albert S. Willis, with secret instructions. None knew on what course Cleveland had decided. In this country the controversy over annexation was greatly overshadowed by domestic questions growing out of the 1893 financial depression, but in Honolulu the conflicting aims and hopes of the annexationists and royalists created a dangerous state of unrest which the uncertainty over American policy did nothing to allay. The Provisional Government remained in power, but the supporters of the Queen actively hoped that further intervention on the part of the United States, which had formerly led to their downfall, might now somehow lead to their restoration to power. When Willis arrived in Honolulu in November, he found a situation even more disturbed than that which had confronted Blount.

As events were soon to prove, his secret instructions actually did aim at the Queen's restoration. Cleveland had consulted his cabinet upon the reception of the Blount report and adopted a plan first suggested by his Attorney-General, Richard Olney. It provided for a restoration of the *status quo ante* by peaceful measures. Guarantees were to be demanded of Liliuokalani as to her future course of action and she was then to be replaced upon the throne. In case forcible measures should prove necessary in carrying out this policy, Congress was to be consulted as to what action could be taken, but Cleveland hoped to settle the problem on executive responsibility.[4]

This scheme had the hearty support of Secretary of State Gresham. His wife has explained his zeal in the Queen's cause on the ground that 'a woman in trouble, my husband would certainly side with her against the power, greed and lust of man,'[5] and to a certain extent his attitude reflected the sentimental sympathy for Queen Liliuokalani which for a time swept the country. It was on a wave of moral indignation that the Cleveland Administration undertook its difficult task of undoing the harm which it believed the Harrison Administration had done unprotected Hawaii.

'Should not a great wrong done to a feeble but independent State by an abuse of the authority of the United States be undone by restoring the legitimate government?' Gresham asked in his report to the President. 'Anything short of that will not, I respectfully submit, satisfy the demands of justice.'[6]

On this theory Willis was instructed to arrange for the Queen's restoration, consequent upon her grant of an amnesty to the revolutionaries, and to advise the Provisional Government 'that they are expected to promptly relinquish to her her constitutional authority.'⁷ Subsequent instructions on December 3, when it occurred to Washington that the Provisional Government might not wholly approve of the presidential policy and resent the American program for upsetting a régime which it had just brought into power, carefully warned Willis that 'the President cannot use force without the authority of Congress.'⁸

Charged with this difficult mission, Willis's first move in Honolulu was to interview Queen Liliuokalani. After telling her of President Cleveland's desire to help her, he officially asked if she would grant a complete amnesty to the leaders of the January revolt. Apparently nothing was more unexpected than the possibility of a negative reply to this simple question, and it is not difficult to picture the consternation of the American minister when the indomitable Hawaiian emphatically answered: 'My decision would be, as the law directs, that such persons should be beheaded and their property confiscated to the Government.'⁹ Willis repeated his question and asked the Queen if she fully understood its import. She declared she understood it perfectly and that her answer was just exactly what she meant. The startled diplomat cabled for instructions.

In the meantime excitement was growing in Honolulu. It was not known just what President Cleveland intended to do, but when Willis's instructions for the restoration of the *status quo ante* became public knowledge, they created a furor. It was rumored and widely believed that the United States planned to reëstablish Queen Liliuokalani on the throne by force, and when an American warship arrived in the harbor during the height of the excitement, the annexationists' worst forebodings seemed to be confirmed. Nor did Minister Willis help matters when his only answer to a question from Provisional President Dole, as to whether the intentions of the United States were hostile, was the blunt statement that he could not divulge the American policy.

On further instructions from Washington, the American

envoy now approached the Queen again and found her, due to pressure from her foreign advisers, more amenable to the program which the United States was pursuing so assiduously. At first she promised only to rescind the death penalty and still insisted upon exile and property confiscation for her enemies, but at length she agreed to meet the terms of the United States in full. She promised a general amnesty for all concerned in the revolution.

With this royal concession, Willis felt his task almost completed. The agitation among the annexationists and the actual preparations for defense made by the Provisional Government were seemingly ignored in the belief that they would collapse with announcement of Cleveland's policy. But when the American minister officially asked President Dole if the Provisional Government was willing to abide by the decision of the American Government that the monarchy must be restored, he received an unequivocal refusal.

In an able statement of his Government's case, delivered on December 23, President Dole protested the United States' usurpation of authority in suggesting a restoration of the *status quo ante*, declared that the independence and sovereignty of his country could not be called into question, and finally requested Willis to inform President Cleveland that the Hawaiian Government 'respectfully and unhesitatingly declines to entertain the proposition of the President of the United States that it should surrender its authority to the ex-Queen.'[10]

Here was a new deadlock far more serious than the first, but already, unknown to Willis, the United States had given up its ill-advised attempt to restore the balance upset by intervention in behalf of the revolutionaries by a second intervention in behalf of the monarchists. The American minister's report on Liliuokalani's intransigency and her bloodthirsty sentiments as revealed in his first interview with her, had shown President Cleveland and his cabinet that the Hawaiian problem was not the simple question they had imagined it to be, even without the added evidence of the Provisional Government's determination to hold on to the power it had won. Consequently Cleveland virtually washed his hands of the whole affair by submitting it to Congress. The only word Willis received from Washington in reply to his latest dispatches was a brief and conclusive order: 'Consider that your special instructions upon this subject have been fully complied with.'[11]

So ended the Hawaiian phase of the 1893 annexation movement. It had been marked by blunders from its earliest inception. Unquestionably Stevens had exceeded his authority and interfered in the internal affairs of a friendly nation. Without the implied support of the American troops from the *Boston*, the revolutionaries might not have been able to depose Queen Liliuokalani with so little effort. But at the same time once the Provisional Government was recognized, it was that Government which represented Hawaii and we had no right to intervene a second time. Granted that the original policy as exemplified in the activities of Stevens was wrong, the perpetration of another wrong could not possibly right it.[12]

In the message in which President Cleveland surrendered to Congress the responsibility for determining our future policy, he did not hesitate to condemn in scathing terms the action of his predecessor. The ownership of the Hawaiian Islands, he declared, had been traduced without the sanction of either popular revolution or popular suffrage. The landing of United States marines was characterized as an act of war, since it had not been immediately necessary for the protection of American lives and property and had not been requested by the recognized Government of the islands. The President stated his firm conviction that the Provisional Government owed its existence to the armed invasion of the United States, and in handing over the problem of what should now be done 'to the broader authority and discretion of Congress,' he emphatically declared, despite the failure of his own policy, that 'our duty does not, in my opinion, end with refusing to consummate this questionable transaction.'[13]

Congress decided otherwise. It agreed with the President in his refusal to carry through the annexation program, but it saw nothing else which could be done. It was now all too obvious that only forcible intervention could restore Queen Liliuokalani to power and for such a policy there was no support whatsoever. Her arrogance, her bloodthirsty attitude toward her enemies, and various unsavory charges brought against her in the propaganda of the annexationists, had somewhat dampened the enthusiasm with which the cause of this abused native queen had at first been taken up.

In February, the House passed a resolution denouncing Stevens's interference with the domestic affairs of an independent nation, and declared its opposition to either annexation or a protectorate. Some months later, the Senate, after further investigation on its own part, voted unanimously to let Hawaii maintain its own government without further American interference.

The prevailing difference of opinion as to the wisdom of the course followed by President Cleveland is, however, well illustrated by the division within the Senate Foreign Relations Committee which reported on Hawaii in February, 1894. The majority report as submitted by Senator Morgan exonerated everyone concerned. It declared that Stevens's desire for annexation was not open to criticism and that the only irregularity which marked his conduct was the proclamation of an American protectorate after the organization of the Provisional Government. It saw no impropriety in the negotiation of the annexation treaty, and, somewhat paradoxically, also extended its benediction to the policy of President Cleveland which had been to undo that same instrument.

But Senator Morgan was the only man to accept all the conclusions of his report. The four other Democrats on the committee took occasion to dissent from the first section, censuring Stevens for overzeal and declaring that he had exceeded the proper limits of his authority; the four Republican members took exception to the second section and issued a statement of their own outlining

their position on the Cleveland policies. They termed
the appointment of Blount unconstitutional, declared he
had no right to exercise military power or to lower the
flag which Stevens had raised, and severely criticized the
whole policy of intervention after the Provisional Government had been formally recognized. Furthermore, it
was made clear in the report that the four Republicans
favored annexation, and even two of the Democrats declared their support for such a move if it was made under
the proper conditions.[14]

Criticism of the Government's course centered on the
one hand on Stevens's use of the armed forces of the
United States to overawe Queen Liliuokalani, and on the
other on Willis's secret tactics and implied threat of force
to overawe the Provisional Government. Both men had
bitter critics and violent partisans,[15] while the whole affair was so entangled in domestic politics that it is not
surprising that Congress's decision to drop it entirely
was accepted with universal relief. Consequently when
on July 4, 1894, the Provisional Government organized
itself on a permanent basis under the presidency of former
Judge Dole and made official declaration of the independence of the Hawaiian Republic, the United States promptly
extended recognition.

Annexationists both in Hawaii and in the United States,
however, did not fail to note the significance of the thirty-
second article of the new Hawaiian constitution. It expressly authorized the President of the Republic to conclude whenever possible a treaty of commercial or political union with the United States.[16]

Despite the failure of this annexation movement in
1893, the majority opinion of the Senate Foreign Relations
Committee in favor of acquisition of Hawaii if it could be
brought about under less questionable circumstances, and
the declared attitude of the new Hawaiian Government,
clearly indicated that, if annexation was for the time being
dropped, it would soon be brought up again. Nor was other
evidence lacking that if the withdrawn treaty was a false

start, it pointed the way in which our policy was headed.

The eighteen-nineties were an era in which the United States had revived its old interest in a national navy, and the big navy men of that day, less concerned than President Cleveland about the ethics of annexation, regretted the failure of 1893 and marshaled their forces to promote another attempt to secure what they regarded as a territory essential to the development of American naval power. Writing to the *Boston Herald*, Admiral George E. Belknap forcibly expressed the opinion of these naval circles and sounded a note of alarm as to Great Britain's possible seizure of Hawaii which carries us back half a century to the days when the acquisition of Oregon and California was demanded to prevent that same 'unconscionable power' from wresting from America the control of the Pacific.

'Let the British lion once get its paw on the group,' Admiral Belknap declared, 'and Honolulu would soon become one of the most important strongholds of Great Britain's power.' But he was unalterably opposed to a joint protectorate: 'We want none of that — no entangling alliances. We have had enough of such business at Samoa.' And then, in conclusion: 'Westward the star of empire takes its way. Let the Monroe doctrine stay not its hand until it holds Hawaii securely within its grasp.' [17]

More temperate and also far more influential were the articles of Captain Alfred Thayer Mahan. This noted exponent of the influence of sea power on history and subsequent member of the naval board of strategy made himself in the last decade of the nineteenth century the advance agent of American imperialism. His program was that which Commodore Perry had held forty years earlier, and he lost no opportunity to preach the need for acquiring naval bases in the Pacific. A recognized authority on his subject, there can be no question that his views carried great weight in Washington and with the public, and as he now came to the fore in the movement to secure Hawaii, so did he later exert all his influence for the acquisition of the Philippines.

As early as 1890 we find Captain Mahan writing upon
'The United States Looking Outward' and issuing a clar-
ion call for expansion. Noting the general restlessness
of the world at this period, the pressure of British activities in the Pacific, and our own need for commercial development, he challenged America to secure its own interests in the new world order. 'Whether they will or
no,' he wrote, 'Americans must now begin to look outward. The growing production of the country demands
it. An increasing volume of public sentiment demands
it.' [18]

The revolution in Hawaii three years later he accepted
as a Heaven-sent opportunity to put his policy to the
test. He stressed the islands' strategic position in the
Pacific and again brought up the danger of British rivalry.
'It is rarely that so important a factor in the attack or
defense of a coast-line — of a sea frontier — is concentrated in a single position,' he wrote; 'and the circumstances render it doubly imperative upon us to secure it,
if we righteously can.... The annexation, even, of Hawaii
would be no mere sporadic effort, irrational because dis-
connected from an adequate motive, but a first-fruit and a
token that the nation in its evolution has aroused itself
to the necessity of carrying its life — that has been the
happiness of those under its influence — beyond the borders which heretofore have sufficed for its activities.' [19]

Nor were these naval spokesmen voices crying in the
wilderness. Among the Republicans, if not among the
Democrats, there were many statesmen — or politicians —
who were convinced that we could not with impunity
fumble another opportunity to acquire the islands as we
had in 1893. 'It is, in my opinion,' former Secretary
Foster told the National Geographical Society, 'the plain
duty of the United States to annex them to its territory.' [20]
In the *Forum*, and then before the Senate, Henry Cabot
Lodge took up the cause of annexation with a rare enthusiasm. 'For the sake of our commercial supremacy in
the Pacific we should control the Hawaiian Islands and
maintain our influence in Samoa,' he wrote in the maga-

zine; to his fellow lawmakers in Congress he declared that
Hawaii was 'the one place where the hand of England has
not yet reached out, to throw away those islands is mad-
ness.' [21]

Here was the final and complete reversal of the old
rôles of the two American political parties. In 1844 it was
the Democrats who declared for a policy of annexation
and defied England with the slogan of 'Fifty-Four Forty
or Fight'; in 1896 the Republican platform announced
that 'the Hawaiian Islands should be controlled by the
United States and no foreign power should be permitted
to interfere with them.'

The election of the latter year brought the Republicans
back into power and they lost no time in pursuing their
policy of expansion. In fact, President McKinley took
up the Hawaiian question so promptly and so vigorously
that within a little more than three months of his inauguration a new annexation treaty had been signed. This time
there seemed little danger that the Democrats would be
able to block the Administration's program for very long.

There was now no question of the right of the Hawaiian
Government to decide the annexation question on its
own responsibility. For three years the little republic had
maintained its stability and succeeded in bringing to
Hawaii a measure of peace and prosperity which it had
never experienced before. An attempted counter-revolu-
tion on the part of the royalist faction had completely
failed, and in 1895 Queen Liliuokalani had at last accepted
the inevitable, relinquishing all her rights to the throne
and swearing allegiance to the new régime. If the leaders
of the Republic still sought annexation, it was impossible
to deny that they spoke for Hawaii even though their
control of the country marked the end of the native monarchy.

The treaty concluded by the American and Hawaiian
commissioners and submitted to the Senate by President
McKinley did not differ greatly from that of 1893. It
was no longer necessary to offer annuities to the members

of the royal family, but otherwise its terms were the same as those of the preceding treaty and provided for the incorporation of the islands into the American Union as a Territory.[22] In his accompanying message McKinley stated that this agreement represented no new scheme, but was the 'inevitable consequence of the relation so steadfastly maintained with that mid-Pacific domain for three quarters of a century.' He pointed out that the stability of the Hawaiian Republic for the past four years demonstrated beyond doubt that its citizens knew what they wanted, and that under the circumstances 'annexation is not a change; it is a consummation.' [23]

But the course of Hawaiian annexation was never to run altogether smooth. While the treaty was still pending in the Senate a new complication was encountered. Japan formally protested. Its Government declared that the maintenance of the *status quo* was essential to the peace of the Pacific and that the islands' annexation by the United States would seriously jeopardize the rights of Japanese subjects resident in Hawaii. [24]

Japan had made no protest in regard to the treaty of 1893, but that was before her successful war against China. She was now beginning to feel her strength and believed that she had a right to have a voice in any political developments in the Pacific. There had also been such an increase in Japanese emigration to Hawaii in recent years that the islands had assumed a new importance to Tokyo. In 1883 there were only 116 Japanese in Hawaii; in 1896 there were 24,407. This figure was but slightly below the total of the native population at this time and approximately equal to that of the combined total of American and European residents in the islands.

This situation, furthermore, had caused a sharp conflict between the Japanese and Hawaiian Governments which came to a head in 1897. Fearing the effect of such a heavy influx of Asiatics, the authorities of the Republic refused admittance to some 1174 immigrants. Japan immediately sent a war vessel to Honolulu; Hawaii appealed to the United States for protection.

The appeal was not made in vain. Secretary of State Sherman promptly instructed the United States minister in Honolulu to be prepared for any emergency. In the event that Japan should resort to force in an attempt to compel a recognition of its claims in the immigration dispute, his orders were explicit: 'Confer with the local authorities and Admiral, land suitable force, and announce provisional assumption of protectorate by the United States over Hawaii pending consummation of annexation treaty.'[25] Several times our ministers in Hawaii had taken it upon themselves to protect the islands from foreign aggression by establishing a protectorate, but this was the first occasion on which such a step had been officially authorized by Washington.

In the United States the protest of Japan against the treaty was coupled with reports from the islands of her aggressive attitude as an indication that Japan actually intended to dispute our control over Hawaii. Despite assertions to the contrary from the Japanese Government, the belief was widely held that the Japanese immigration was in reality a peaceful invasion stimulated by the Government with the purpose of undermining American influence in the islands. For a time a rather tense situation existed as protests and counter-protests were cabled back and forth between Washington and Tokyo. Many American statesmen professed to believe that Japan was about to snatch from our hands the prize which had been dangled before our eyes for so many, many years. 'We cannot let the Islands go to Japan,' President McKinley told Senator Hoar. 'Japan has her eye on them.... If something is not done, there will be before long another Revolution, and Japan will get control.'[26]

The controversy gradually moved toward a settlement despite these outbursts of nervous fear. Japan patched up her quarrel with the Hawaiian Government and withdrew her protest against annexation. It is indeed highly improbable that Tokyo ever meant to carry her opposition to our policy very far, while even her protest may have been the result of political pressure at home as much as

anything else. Certainly there was never any intention
of resorting to extreme measures. Japan could not help
realizing that at this late date the United States would
not under any circumstances tolerate foreign interference
with its declared program for Hawaii's annexation.

This issue out of the way, prompt action on the pending
treaty might have been expected from the Senate. The
Administration brought all its pressure to bear in favor of
ratification. But as history has shown so many times,
there is no power which can hurry the Senate. In this
instance there were enough reluctant Democrats to block
the necessary two-thirds majority and the Hawaiian debate seemed to drag on endlessly. When 1897 gave way
to 1898, however, and the threat of war with Spain which
had been hanging over the country for so long became a
certainty, President McKinley made up his mind he
would wait no longer on Democratic pleasure. Hawaii
had to be annexed.

In this contingency the Administration forces decided to
follow the precedent set in the annexation of Texas and
bring Hawaii into the Union by a joint resolution of
Congress. This measure was reported favorably in both
houses and in March, 1898, the annexation of Hawaii
entered upon another and final stage.

All the traditional arguments in favor of annexation
were brought up in the report submitted to the Senate.[27]
It cited the long list of American statesmen who had approved and worked for such a move, brought together
the evidence of naval officers from Admiral du Pont to
Captain Mahan, and with equal emphasis pointed out our
moral duty to the Hawaiians, the value of the islands to
the United States, and the imminent danger of their
seizure by some other Power. It was a typical expansionist document, as applicable on the whole to any of our
territorial acquisitions as it was to Hawaii.

For the usual charge of British designs to thwart our
policy, the committee was able to report a recent attempt
on England's part to secure from the Hawaiian Govern-

ment the exclusive right to a cable station on one of the
outlying islands in the archipelago. More important was
the 'silent but rapid invasion of the pagan races from
Asia.' Here in fact was a definite danger which more than
ever brought up the question posed by Minister Stevens
five years earlier as to whether an American or an Asiatic
civilization was to prevail upon territory so close to our
western coast. The immigration from Japan clearly proved
to the annexationists, and not without reason, that unless
the United States obtained the islands, it could not hope
indefinitely to prevent these Asiatics from dominating
Hawaii completely.

If the thought of such a development had its greatest
effect in summoning up a picture of a Japanese spearhead
pointed at California, it could also serve to emphasize
our moral obligation to come to the aid of independent
Hawaii. A helpless people had called upon us for assistance
and, regardless of strategic or commercial considerations,
which happily were not found in conflict with these higher
motives, our course was clear. We had only to obey the
summons of a duty which had its origin 'in the noblest
sentiments that inspire the love of a father for his children... or our Great Republic to a younger sister that
has established law, liberty and justice in a beautiful land
that a corrupt monarchy was defiling with fraud, harassing
with unjust exactions, and dragging down to barbarism.'[28]

Finally, the committee set down five specific reasons
for annexing Hawaii: to secure for the United States
strategic control of the Pacific, to prevent Hawaii from
drifting any further toward Japan, to increase and promote our commerce, to develop our shipping interests,
and to promote peace in the Pacific.[29] Along these familiar
lines the debate was now to be held in both houses of
Congress.

It opened on a minor key. But when the impending conflict between the United States and Spain broke out in this
exciting spring of 1898 and America found herself at war
in the Spanish colonies of both the Atlantic and the Pacific, it rose in a crescendo of patriotic fervor. It quickly

became apparent that in reality far more than the fate of Hawaii was at stake. It was our national destiny upon which impassioned speakers declaimed. The question was whether we should take a first step in a new assertion of American power, or deny the call to overseas expansion and draw back within ourselves. At times the debate reached unexpected heights of eloquence and passion; at times it sank to depths of petty political partisanship; but throughout it demonstrated a new conception of America's world position and bore witness to the bitter conflict of principle between those who felt that our expansion should recognize no limits and those who still clung to the tradition that the American Republic could have no colonies. [30]

If the expansionists favored the annexation of Hawaii as the first step in a program which was finally to bring us control of the Pacific, to the opponents of the new imperialism such a move merely foreshadowed more and more distant territorial acquisitions in the name of destiny and duty. The Democrats in the House rose in their wrath at this new evidence of the 'unconquerable Anglo-Saxon lust for land,' and in attacking Hawaii's annexation as an indication of a greedy policy of colonial expansion which could not be justified by historical precedents, they declared that 'the way to remain sober is resolutely to refuse the first drink.'

These were the phrases of Champ Clark, but he was ready to go much farther in pouring out his vitriolic scorn upon the imperialists. In his opinion 'manifest destiny' was 'the specious plea of every robber and freebooter since the world began, and will continue to be until the elements shall melt with fervent heat,' while he inelegantly characterized Hawaii as 'the fly which will make our whole pot of ointment stink in the nostrils of the civilized world.' [31]

In a more moderate but sterner tone Representative Dinsmore said that the establishment of a colonial empire would mean the disintegration of the Republic and 'no longer will our ancient peace abide with us.' Henry U. Johnson held out the prospect of a dazzling career of aggrandizement which the United States might follow, but pertinently asked, 'Will our people be the happier, the more prosperous, the more powerful, if they pursue it?'

In the Senate, George Frisbie Hoar valiantly tried to keep the debate confined to Hawaii. He set himself unflinchingly against the emotional fervor aroused by the war, declared his opposition to imperialism, and rejected emphatically the idea of acquiring any territory in the Orient. But he favored the annexation of Hawaii on the basis of those arguments advanced by the Committee on Foreign Relations and declared that the islands were really a part of the American system as a line drawn between the Aleutian Islands and Southern California would readily show. He felt they were necessary for the protection of the coast, and, aroused by the Japanese issue, he thought that our failure to take them would mean their eventual absorption by Japan. 'I believe that this is a contest,' he told the Senate, 'to be settled now peacefully or to be settled hereafter by force between America and Asia.'

His position was logical, but in 1898 entirely impractical. The annexation of Hawaii could not be separated from the possible annexation of the Spanish colonies which seemed about to fall into our hands. It could not be put in a water-tight compartment. The imperialists thought of it as an advance along a road which would lead the United States to a new and exalted position in international affairs as a colonial power; the anti-imperialists accepted this thesis and opposed annexation far more strenuously than would have been the case had they believed that we could stop with Hawaii. Senator Hoar was right in his position on the logic if not the necessity of taking over the island kingdom, but he was not justified in his confidence that annexation in one direction could be approved without making approval of other such moves in other directions almost foregone.

'If this be the first step in the acquisition of dominion over barbarous archipelagoes in distant seas,' he declared in a speech which must often have come back to plague

him when he was leading the fight against the annexation
of the Philippines; 'if we are to enter into competition
with the great powers of Europe in the plundering of
China... then let us resist this thing in the beginning, and
let us resist it to the death.... But, Mr. President, I am
satisfied, after hearing and weighing arguments and much
meditation on this thing, that the fear of imperialism is
needless alarm.' [32]

It is futile today to debate whether such valid arguments
for annexing Hawaii as the historical background for such
a step, the precedents found in previous acquisitions of
territory, the theory of establishing effective control over
the Pacific, would or would not have carried the day without the support of war hysteria. For the fact remains that
hysteria played an important rôle in the decision of Congress. The debates on Hawaii served as a curtain-raiser
for those on the Philippines. But we can consider them
here only as a climax to the long process of the islands'
absorption which goes back to the arrival of the whalers
and missionaries in Honolulu in 1820, leaving to subsequent chapters a more complete study of the imperialism of 1898. As the congressional oratory thundered on
to its inevitable close, we can only note that once America
had the taste of further expansion, even though it was
only little Hawaii, she began excitedly applying to herself
Kipling's call to his own country:

> We sailed wherever ship could sail;
>   We founded many a mighty state;
> Pray God our greatness may not fail
>   Through craven fear of being great.

As might be expected, the McKinley Administration
waited impatiently while these debates were being held.
Even though it could count with almost definite assurance
on passage of the annexation resolution, the delay seemed
inexcusable. The President was not interested in senatorial oratory. When Manila fell into American hands
in one of the first actions of the Spanish War, he felt that,
regardless of all other considerations, the control of the

Hawaiian Islands had become a military necessity. It is true that upon the outbreak of war the Hawaiian Government, anxious to facilitate annexation, had made no pretense of observing that neutrality which the law of nations imposes upon an independent country. It welcomed the transports carrying American troops to the Philippines with the greatest cordiality and showered attentions upon officers and men.[33] Nevertheless, the Administration declared it needed an even freer hand for possible operations in the Pacific in which Hawaii might prove useful as a base, and demanded with a new insistence that the islands be brought under American sovereignty.

At one time the President appeared to be ready to annex Hawaii by executive decree as a war measure. He grew more and more impatient. He worried over possible action by Japan. 'We need Hawaii just as much and a good deal more than we did California. It is manifest destiny,' he told his secretary. [34] But all these problems were soon to be solved. Congress was finally prepared to act. Both houses at last passed the annexation resolution and on July 7 it received presidential approval. A month later, August 12, the Hawaiian Islands were at long last formally transferred to the United States.[35]

The fruit was ripe; it had fallen into our hands. From former President Cleveland, however, came low growls of dissatisfaction. 'Hawaii is ours,' he wrote to his former Attorney-General. 'As I look back upon the first steps in this miserable business and as I contemplate the means used to complete the outrage, I am ashamed of the whole affair.' [36]

He was exaggerating. He was misreading history. The Republicans were merely doing what the Democrats had done half a century earlier. Whether they were the dominant party because they favored expansion, or whether as the dominant party they forced the country to adopt an expansionist policy, the fact remains that in 1898 as in 1848 'manifest destiny' was in the saddle and its force could not be withstood by its political foes.

How powerful this imperialist movement really was

cannot be fully realized from the annexation of Hawaii alone. For whatever the influence of the war fever, this event was fundamentally the culmination of a long and gradual process as natural as our acquisition of Oregon and California. How 'duty' and 'destiny' led us in that same year much farther afield will be seen in the history of the Philippines.

CHAPTER XII

Dewey Captures Manila

UNLIKE the history of the annexation of Hawaii, that of the acquisition of the Philippines covers the briefest possible interval of time. It was within nine months and a few days of Dewey's startling victory in Manila Bay that the Senate ratified a treaty which made the islands a part of the domain of the United States. Few Americans knew where the Philippines were or had the haziest conception of their resources or value to the United States when the first cable message flashed halfway round the world the news of the sinking of the Spanish fleet. It dawned unexpectedly upon the country what this victory might mean. But in the course of those nine months before ratification of the treaty, the disposition of the Philippines was so widely and so critically debated, in and out of Congress, that no step in our expansion in the Pacific was taken with a more deliberate consciousness of just what we were doing.

We had had commercial contacts with Manila for over a century, but instead of developing an interest in the Philippines, these tenuous ties had on the whole become weakened rather than strengthened during the passage of time. The islands were far better known at the close of the eighteenth century, when the China traders called regularly at Manila and Rufus King actually suggested that we should seek trade concessions there from Spain,[1] than they were at the end of the nineteenth century.

The first merchantman to display the American flag in the Spanish colony was the *Enterprise*, Captain Adam Babcock, which put into the harbor of Manila in 1792. Four years later a direct trade with Salem in sugar, hemp, and indigo was opened by the *Astrea*, Captain Henry Prince. Before the beginning of the nineteenth century, at least one American was a resident of Manila; soon thereafter the firm of Russell, Sturgis and Company had estab-

lished an office, and in 1817 an American consul was appointed. Even though this early trade was never more
than an adjunct to that with Canton, twenty-three American vessels touched at the Philippines in 1819 and in 1835
a high mark was set when 13,876 tons of United States
shipping were in Manila Harbor.[2]

These early American visitors found Manila an imposing
walled city with heavily guarded ramparts manned by
twelve thousand native troops. Its houses were largely
made of stone, its streets were spacious, well paved, and
lighted at night. The chief public building was the governor's palace, 'very elegant and extensive,' and there were
also innumerable churches and monasteries.[3] For two
centuries Spain had controlled the islands, and they could
boast a moderate foreign trade, largely with the mother
country; a stable, though despotic and inefficient, government, and a degree of peace and prosperity from which
the Spanish rather than the natives derived the most
benefit. The Church had followed in the wake of conquest
and the Filipinos had been almost wholly converted to
Christianity.

The Yankee traders were welcomed cordially. Even
though the Philippines, in common with all other Spanish
colonies, had regulations against trade with foreigners,
they seem to have been largely ignored in this early period.
It was noted by one visitor, however, an officer aboard the
U.S.S. *Congress* which touched at Manila in 1820, that the
Spanish officials held themselves rather aloof from the
Americans. 'They pay us little or no attention,' he wrote,
'even in their own houses, where we often go to visit the
ladies, whose polite attention amply compensates for the
rudeness of the men.'[4]

Of the natives one enthusiastic mariner said that almost
every one was 'a suitable model for a Venus or an Apollo';
but a more modified opinion of Filipino virtues was that
of Nathaniel Bowditch, the famous author of the 'Practical
Navigator.' He found their honesty somewhat open to
question as a result of thefts from his vessel. Another
cause of complaint was the slow sale of his vessel's cargo

of Madeira because there were not 'above three thousand Europeans in the city and suburbs who made use of liquor.'[5]

When in 1842 the port was visited by Commodore Wilkes, this naval officer severely criticized the stringency of the Spanish Government and stated his belief that a more liberal policy would lead to a great development of the islands because of their valuable resources and fertile soil. He stated emphatically that the Philippines were one of the most favored parts of the globe and expressed a grave doubt as to how long Spain's iron rule could continue.[6]

Here was a vague conjecture of possible change in the Philippines which was to be repeated and linked more directly with the United States in the writings of another foreign observer and of a Filipino leader. Feodor Jagor, a German traveler, predicted in 1860 that the United States would some day fall heir to the Spanish Empire through its expansion in the Pacific. 'The influence of North America in the Spanish provinces beyond the seas,' he wrote, 'will make itself felt, and especially in the Philippines, as the commerce of its western coast develops.'[7] Thirty years later, the Filipino patriot, José Rizal, expressed his fear that, if ever the islands broke away from Spanish rule, the United States would advance upon them from Samoa.[8]

Beyond these rather insignificant contacts there is little to relate of early American influence in the Philippines. With our trade at Manila falling off, and with the reports of Commodore Wilkes and Feodor Jagor long since forgotten if, indeed, they had ever been noted, the islands were an unknown quantity at the end of the nineteenth century. After all they were thousands of miles from our western coast and apparently far beyond any conceivable American sphere of interest. What few dispatches the consul at Manila might send home excited little interest, and not since 1876 had the Navy Department received any report on local conditions. There is no evidence that, before the series of dramatic events to which we now come, either the American Government or the American people had given the slightest thought to our future possession in the Far East.

Closely involved in the first steps which led to our un-expected appearance in the Philippines in 1898 was that young newcomer to American politics, Theodore Roosevelt. In his aggressiveness, his energy, his impatient desire to see the United States playing a major rôle in world affairs, he typified more than his contemporaries could well realize the new mood which had come over the United States in the last decade of the nineteenth century. As our attitude toward Hawaii had already shown, we had reached in this period a stage in our national development where we were looking about for new worlds to conquer. The filling-up of those great reaches of open country, over which the first pioneers on the Pacific Coast had crossed without halt, no longer absorbed our energies. The United States was an industrial nation driven by an irresistible urge to expand still further by its pressing need of new markets and new fields for the investment of capital. It demanded an aggressive foreign policy which would make its weight felt in a highly competitive world.⁹

In 1897 this restlessness and this impatience to assert ourselves found expression in a growing absorption in the affairs of Cuba. To whatever extent it was motivated by a feeling that this island, for so long an object of desire by American expansionists, was a logical field for American penetration, or to what extent it sprang from moral indignation over Spanish misrule and the tragic plight of the Cuban revolutionaries, the fact remains that the American people began to believe that intervention in Cuba was a necessity.

As it became more and more apparent that this could only mean war, Roosevelt was perhaps the first American official to remember that Spain also had colonies in the Pacific. He represented that element in our national life which looked upon the impending conflict more as an opportunity for building up American power than as a self-denying mission to help the Cubans. If circumstances were to prevent our reaping the rewards of war in the Caribbean, he saw nothing to compel an equally generous policy in the Pacific. He realized, with a vision in which the wish was at least partly father to the thought, that the moment war broke out we should have to strike at Spanish power wherever we could and that in this event there were the Philippines. Whether in 1897 he already considered these islands a potential American colony cannot be definitely stated, but he was convinced we should have to capture them if the expected war materialized.

In September, seven months before war actually did break out, he was discussing these ideas with President McKinley and Secretary of the Navy Long. A month later, he was pulling all the strings available to an Assistant Secretary of the Navy to be sure that our Asiatic squadron should have a commander fully alive to both his responsibilities and his opportunities.[10] In this situation he turned to Commodore George Dewey, an officer whose record gave him every reason for confidence. Moreover, whether or not it was known to Roosevelt, Dewey had already contemplated the capture of Manila. At the time of the *Virginius* affair in 1873, he tells us in his autobiography, he was in command of the sloop-of-war *Narragansett* off California and at the prospect of war with Spain in those critical days his officers complained that they would be out of it. 'On the contrary,' Dewey reports himself as telling his men, 'we shall be very much in it. If war with Spain is declared, the *Narragansett* will take Manila.'[11]

Dewey's appointment to the command of our naval forces in the Far East, which propitiously fell open at this time, was involved in some difficulties. Secretary Long, who was not as alive as his forceful assistant to the necessity for a man of action in the Pacific, favored the routine promotion of another man. Roosevelt thereupon urged Dewey to exert what political pressure he could in favor of his own appointment and the naval officer somewhat reluctantly sought the aid of Senator Proctor of Vermont. The latter's prompt intercession with President McKinley carried the day and Dewey received the orders appointing him to his new command on October 21, 1897.[12]

In these orders no mention was made of the Philippines other than a vague reference to rumors of rebellion against Spanish rule, with the explicit statement that there was 'no information of any sort that shows American interests to be affected.'[13] But Dewey on his own initiative began studying everything he could about the islands and soon after he took over his post on January 3, 1898, he moved his squadron to Hongkong and quietly began preparations for possible action against the Spanish fleet at Manila.

War was still more than three months in the future, but Dewey wanted to be ready for all eventualities. It is not probable that he had any idea that he was actually to be the instrument through which the policy of a long line of naval officers beginning with Commodore Perry was at last to be realized. There is no record that he was thinking of Pacific naval bases. But as Roosevelt had known when he sponsored his appointment, Dewey was a man of action.

Before he had been in Hongkong very long, an order from the Navy Department confirmed the policy for which he was getting ready on his own initiative. In the event of hostilities with Spain, he was instructed on February 25, his duty would be 'to see that the Spanish squadron does not leave the Asiatic coast, and then offensive operations in Philippine Islands.'[14] It had been sent by Roosevelt. Impatient for war to break out, anxious that Dewey should have authorization for prompt action, the Assistant Secretary of the Navy had seized the opportunity of his chief's temporary absence from his office to carry preparations for war a good step farther than might have seemed justified by an Administration still working for peace. Furthermore, in the last phrase of this remarkable order, Roosevelt had enjoined upon Dewey a policy of which the country was entirely ignorant, but one which was to have the most far-reaching results. Secretary Long rebuked his zealous subordinate for assuming so much upon his own responsibility, but the order stood.

Dewey now redoubled his efforts to be prepared for the
emergency. His ships were overhauled, all necessary supplies obtained, and communications opened with the American consul at Manila in order to obtain all possible information on conditions in the Philippines. Consequently,
he was fully prepared when on April 25 he received his
final orders: 'War has commenced between the United
States and Spain. Proceed at once to the Philippine Islands.
Commence operations at once, particularly against the
Spanish fleet. You must capture vessels or destroy. Use
utmost endeavors.' [15]

The battle of Manila Bay remains one of the most
dramatic events in our national history. In the rapidity
and completeness with which Dewey acted there was an
epic quality which will continue to stir American imagination long after the controversy over the place his victory
should hold in the world's naval annals has been forgotten.
With one telling stroke he revived a tradition of American
seamanship which had sadly languished since the days
when our ships were able to outsail those of any other
nation, and served notice upon the world that the navy
of the United States could not be ignored. That the
Spanish fleet which he destroyed was impotent to stand
up against any determined enemy attack, cannot alter
the fact that Dewey's success signalized a new balance of
power in the Pacific.

He left Hongkong on the day his orders were received
and after a brief wait in the Chinese harbor of Mirs Bay
sailed for Manila with four protected cruisers, two gunboats, and a revenue cutter. The Spanish fleet he was
prepared to challenge consisted of two protected cruisers,
five unprotected cruisers, and some few gunboats under
the command of Admiral Montojo. American superiority
in both guns and ships was marked, but there were thirty-
nine heavy guns in the Spanish land batteries. Also there
was some question as to whether the harbor was mined.
It is interesting today to note that the British naval officers
at Hongkong, perhaps giving more importance to these

land armaments than events justified, wished the American fleet a lugubrious Godspeed and declared they never expected to see their American friends again.

Far more important than any difference in guns or armaments, however, was the contrast in the spirit of the two opposing fleets. The Americans were thirsting for battle and their commander superbly confident of the outcome; the Spanish forces in Manila waited resignedly for what they regarded as their inevitable destruction. America knew it was a rising power in 1898; Spain knew it was a dying one.

The Spanish governor-general in Manila issued a defiant address to his countrymen. 'The North American people, made up of all social excrescences, have exhausted our patience and have provoked a war by their perfidious machinations,' he declared eloquently. 'The struggle will be short and decisive. The God of victories will grant unto us one that is brilliant and complete, as reason and the justice of our cause demand....' [16] But this was hyperbole. Admiral Montojo had no such illusions. He was ready to do the best he could, to uphold Spanish honor at all costs, but he did not apparently consider for a moment the possible chance of a Spanish victory. Never was there a contest in which the confidence of one side and the defeatism of the other so surely foretold the outcome of a battle.

It was on May 1 that Dewey brought his squadron into Manila Bay and deployed in front of the Spanish fleet anchored off the batteries at Cavite. Five times his flagship led a grim procession of American vessels across the line of enemy ships pouring a withering gunfire into them at a steadily decreasing range. Then so dense were the black clouds of smoke from this bombardment that Dewey withdrew. He was unable to tell the effect of his attack, a report which later proved to be mistaken said his ammunition was running low, and he felt that under the circumstances it was wise to reconsider his position.

As the air cleared, the Americans suddenly realized that their fire had been far more effective than they had even dared to hope. The Spanish vessels were riddled with shots. The flagship was sinking; another vessel already sunk, and a third was on fire. The enemy fleet was so broken that the end was already in sight. At the same time reports to the flagship showed that little damage had been done to the American ships except for the smashing of crockery from the concussion of their own guns, while there was a total of nine casualties, the most serious a man with a fractured leg who had fallen on deck. As the American consul from Manila later reported, the crews of the American vessels were hoarse from cheering 'and while we suffer for cough drops and throat doctors, we have no use for liniments or surgeons.'

It did not take long for Commodore Dewey to mop up what was left of the Spanish fleet. The vessels still afloat, which had moved into a new position, were abandoned soon after the Americans returned to the attack and Admiral Montojo was forced to strike his colors. The action had opened at 5:41 A.M.; the order to cease firing was given at 12:30 P.M.[17]

In those dramatic seven hours the United States had acquired the Philippines even though neither Dewey nor his superiors in Washington realized it. It was undoubtedly true, as President McKinley later insisted and as the Republican platform of 1900 declared, that Dewey sank the Spanish vessels at Manila, not to capture the Philippines, but to destroy the enemy fleet, but a reading of the history of our activities in the Pacific would have shown the strong improbability of our being able to stop at that point. The young man in the Navy Department who had sent the order for 'offensive operations in the Philippines' certainly must have realized this. Within three weeks of the battle of Manila Bay he was writing to his friend Henry Cabot Lodge opposing any move toward peace with Spain 'until we get Porto Rico, while Cuba is made independent and the Philippines at any rate taken from the Spaniards.'[18] Nor were most of his Republican confrères, who had never dreamed of American possession of the Philippines because they hardly knew the islands existed, very far behind him when they were confronted with the possibilities opened up by Dewey's victory.

The destruction of the Spanish fleet did not by itself, however, mean control of the Philippines. There were still the fortified city of Manila, and, as subsequent events were to prove, the Filipinos themselves. It would, of course, have been possible for Dewey to have sailed away now that his objective was attained, thereby leaving Spain in undisputed possession of her colony. There are many Americans who devoutly wish he had. But naval strategy seemed to demand otherwise. Without holding Manila as a base, there was no port in the Far East where the fleet could assemble and Dewey would have been compelled to sail for home. The situation in China, even more than any question relating to the war with Spain, made it appear necessary for American influence and prestige in Asia that we maintain the position in the Pacific which the defeat of the Spanish fleet had given us.

In any event, Washington had taken the first steps toward organizing a military expedition for the Philippines even before Dewey cabled that he could capture the city of Manila at any time, but needed five thousand men for its occupation.[19] There was not yet any definite evidence that the Administration contemplated a permanent hold on the islands. It was wholly preoccupied with assuring the safety of Dewey's position. But President McKinley's instructions to the troops assembling at San Francisco had one of those ambiguous phrases which were to become so characteristic of orders relating to the Philippines. If the first objective of the military expedition was the complete reduction of Spanish power in the East, the second was the enforcement of order and security in the Philippines 'while in the possession of the United States.'[20]

Before the arrival of the troops dispatched by the War Department, a new problem was injected into the situation in Manila involving the relations between the American naval forces and the Filipinos. Dewey's original orders had made some slight reference to revolutionary activities in the islands and before he reached Manila they had been brought very much to his attention. They were to continue to plague him and his military successors in Manila for a good many years.

Rebellion had been chronic in the Philippines for some years. In 1897, however, a temporary truce had been patched up through the treaty of Biacnabató. According to its terms the leaders of the native revolt, in return for a grant of money and some vague promises of reform, agreed to retire from the islands. They had gone no farther than Hongkong and there established a Filipino junta which watched with growing restlessness the failure of the Spanish to carry out their terms of the contract. As early as November, 1897, learning of America's growing friction with Spain, representatives of the rebels had proposed an offensive-defensive alliance between the United States and the Filipino people,[21] and it would in any case have been very surprising if the Hongkong exiles had not seized the opportunity presented by Dewey's attack upon Manila to renew the struggle against Spanish authority.

The initiative for this move, to the subsequent embarrassment of the United States, came from the American side. Some time after Dewey's arrival in Hongkong the leading Filipino revolutionist, Emilio Aguinaldo, was in Singapore. He was there interviewed on April 24 by the American consul-general, E. Spencer Pratt, who endeavored on his own responsibility to arrange for insurgent coöperation with the American forces in any attack upon Spanish power in the Philippines. He won Aguinaldo's consent to such a policy and cabled Dewey to this effect. The latter's brief reply to this announcement was to tell Aguinaldo to come to Hongkong as soon as possible.[22]

In after years a furious controversy was to rage as to just what Pratt and Aguinaldo said to each other. In his reports to Washington and in later testimony, the American consul specifically stated that he went no farther than to arrange for immediate coöperation between the Americans and the Filipinos and declined to discuss the future policy of the United States. But Aguinaldo was to claim that Pratt gave him a promise of American recognition for the insurgents. Certainly the evidence would seem to show that the consul did not mind letting the Filipino leader get the impression that he favored the independence of the Philippines even though he may have refrained carefully from making the specific promises with which Aguinaldo was later to tax him.[23]

Commodore Dewey, on the other hand, does not appear at this time to have set as high a value upon Filipino co-operation as did Pratt. He did not delay his departure for Manila to wait for Aguinaldo and treated somewhat cavalierly other members of the Filipino junta who promised to raise the natives in revolt. He was ready to hear their plans, but he did not take them very seriously. 'They were bothering me,' he was later to tell a Senate investigation. 'I was very busy getting my squadron ready for battle, and these little men were coming on board my ship at Hongkong and taking a good deal of my time, and I did not attach the slightest importance to anything that they could do, and they did nothing.'[24]

Nevertheless, after the battle of Manila Bay the Commodore sent for Aguinaldo. Upon his arrival, Dewey persuaded the Filipino that it was his duty to lead a new revolt against Spanish rule. Aguinaldo agreed to this program with some reluctance, but finally set up his headquarters at Cavite under American protection and obtained from the fleet some rifles and a smoothbore gun. Dewey was subsequently to deny that he had entered into any agreement with the Filipinos or given them any encouragement to expect American recognition, but that Aguinaldo and the other native leaders interpreted his support for their cause as a tacit promise of such recognition is clearly apparent.[25]

In his first proclamation, on May 24, Aguinaldo made very clear what he expected from the United States and no one disabused him of his ideas. 'The great North American nation,' he declared, 'the cradle of genuine liberty, and therefore the friend of our people, oppressed and enslaved by the tyranny and despotism of its rulers, has come to us manifesting a protection as decisive as it is undoubtedly disinterested toward our inhabitants, considering us as sufficiently civilized and capable of governing for ourselves our unfortunate country.' [26]

Even though the American officials may not have definitely committed themselves on this point, both their attitude and the official attitude of the United States as demonstrated in the declared objectives of the war with Spain were a sufficient warranty for his belief in our disinterestedness. Since we had promised Cuba her freedom, there was every reason to believe that we would not infringe upon the liberties of a colony so far distant and of such slight importance to us. In fact, this was probably in all sincerity the view of the Americans in Manila until the tenor of their instructions from Washington indicated that other ideas were being evolved in the nation's higher councils.

At first Washington quite clearly did not understand what was happening in regard to the Filipinos. From the American consul at Singapore it first heard of somewhat mysterious negotiations with Aguinaldo coupled with vague talk of Philippine independence.[27] The consul in Hongkong reported, on the other hand, that the insurgents were fighting for annexation to the United States and spoke of a proclamation issued by Aguinaldo which 'I had outlined for him.'[28] From the consul at Manila, who was imbued with the imperialist fever which so often colored the activities of our consular officials in Samoa and Hawaii, came glowing dispatches on the necessity for America to acquire an island archipelago 'many times more extensive, more populous, and more valuable than Cuba.'[29] And finally Commodore Dewey cabled that Aguinaldo was in Manila and might 'render assistance that will be valuable.'[30]

In the face of these confused reports the Government was content to leave everything in Dewey's hands. Secretary Long, it is true, warned him on May 26 that it was not desirable to have any political relations with the insurgents which would incur future liabilities, but this statement was modified by the prefix 'as far as possible, and consistent for your success and safety.' [31] In other words, the Administration still had no Philippine policy, was chiefly concerned about Dewey's position which it did not very well understand, and apparently would not have hesitated to enter into any agreement with the Filipinos which Dewey might have thought dictated by the needs of his squadron.

Soon, however, more emphatic orders against any alliance with the Filipinos were forthcoming and both the naval and consular officials were expressly instructed to 'avoid unauthorized negotiations with the Filipino insurgents.' [32] Washington was catching glimpses of the future and became a little fearful that its *carte blanche* to Dewey might have carried him too far. But Dewey was able to reply that both in word and spirit he had carefully observed the warning against entangling alliances, that he regarded the Filipinos only as friends fighting a common enemy, and that he was in no way committed to render any assistance to Aguinaldo. As an interesting addendum to this dispatch he stated his opinion that 'these people are far superior in their intelligence and more capable of self-government than the natives of Cuba, and I am familiar with both races.' [33]

In the meantime Dewey faced two other problems while his ships lay in Manila Bay waiting for the assembly of the land forces which would enable him to capture and hold the city itself. There were vague reports of a new and powerful Spanish fleet setting out for the Philippines; there were the strange and disturbing actions of the ships of another Power unduly interested in what happened at Manila.

It is easy today to point out the futility of Spain's entirely impractical gesture of dispatching a squadron to the Philippines by way of the Suez Canal. Events proved that it could not possibly make the long voyage, that it was ill-equipped, unseaworthy, and powerless, and that the slightest movement on our part toward a naval expedition directed against the coast of Spain would necessitate its immediate recall. But it is as well to remember that neither Dewey nor the Navy Department could appreciate all this in the feverish, exciting days of 1898. After all the American fleet was six thousand miles from a friendly port, in helpless dependence upon a naval base which it did not wholly command. The anxiety of the victor of Manila Bay was not as absurd as it is often said to have been.

In any event, as the reports came from our consuls *en route* that Admiral Camara, in command of a squadron including two powerful armed cruisers superior in tonnage and guns to any of Dewey's ships, had passed through the Suez Canal, the American officer keenly felt the dangers of his isolated position. He feared the two Spanish cruisers would be 'an equal antagonist for my squadron,' and he urged in his cables to Washington that an American fleet be sent against Spain in order to draw Camara back to guard his own coast. For his protection in case this scheme could not be carried through, Dewey planned to leave Manila, meet the reënforcements being sent him from San Francisco, and then return with them to challenge the Spanish commander.[34]

Neither of these operations proved necessary. Meeting difficulties in obtaining supplies through the refusal of the Egyptian Government to allow him to coal in that country, Camara was forced to give up the Philippine expedition and on July 8 he was ordered to return to Spanish waters.

Almost as quickly dissipated was the apparent threat of foreign intervention which arose from the presence in Manila Bay of five German war vessels. This was a squadron equal to that of the United States and commanded by an officer superior in rank to Dewey even though he had now been made a rear admiral. We know today both that the Kaiser was fishing in troubled waters, prepared to do anything he could to secure the Philippines should they be thrown upon the international market either through our overthrow of Spanish rule or through the Filipino revolt, and also that despite these ambitions Germany had no idea of challenging our fleet.   Her squadron was in Manila Bay to be ready for anything that might happen, but not to threaten or coerce the United States.

But again hindsight is better than foresight, and in 1898 Germany's intentions could not be so easily analyzed. Nor has there ever been offered an adequate explanation for the boorish, interfering, arrogant attitude of the German commander, Vice Admiral von Diedrichs.   He acted as if he were doing his best to invite a quarrel and cause one of those 'incidents' which so easily lead to open hostilities.   By ignoring the American blockade regulations and virtually insulting the American commander, he made himself thoroughly objectionable.   In this situation it was more than fortunate that Dewey kept his head so admirably, and, while vigorously upholding American rights, refused to allow the Germans to ruffle his temper.   In his dispatches to Washington he reported the presence of the German squadron without comment and in his autobiography he has minimized his difficulties with von Diedrichs, yet the situation in Manila Bay was for a time fully as delicate as that which prevailed ten years earlier in Samoa. [35]

Friction came to a head over an episode in Subig Bay. When a band of Filipino insurgents attempted in an armed vessel to capture the Spanish garrison at this point, the German cruiser *Irene* unexpectedly appeared upon the scene and prevented the Filipinos from carrying out their attack.   Dewey refused to allow such wanton interference with the operations of his nominal allies and promptly dispatched to Subig Bay two American cruisers.   Whatever Admiral von Diedrichs's intentions may have been, he now changed his policy.   The *Irene* disappeared as the American vessels came into sight.   Dewey had made it unmistakably clear that no foreign Power had the right to intervene in the Philippines in any way whatsoever while he was in command of the situation.

At home the report of this incident, together with other accounts of the Germans' disregard of American blockade regulations, awoke a storm of protest which played its part in convincing public opinion that there was a grave danger of Germany stepping in to seize the spoils of war. In Manila it helped to clear the air by showing the German commander that Dewey could not be imposed upon, and soon afterwards he gave up his obstructive and interfering tactics. It is an interesting sidelight on this situation, however, that General Merritt, in command of the military expedition to the Philippines, at one time sought instructions as to what he should do in the event of foreign interference with the landing of his troops. When asked to explain just what he meant, he replied that he referred to Germany, but 'it perhaps is not important.'[36] Fortunately it wasn't.

The troops dispatched to the Philippines under the command of General Merritt reached Manila in three contingents during July and totaled some ten thousand officers and men. *En route* the first contingent made a call at Guam. It had been ordered to capture this little mid-Pacific colony of Spain.

On approaching the island the expedition's convoy ship fired a few shots at its antiquated fort. There was no reply. Presently, however, a boat put off from the shore and two Spanish officials were soon clambering aboard the American ship. They brought profuse apologies for being unable to return the visitors' salute because the Spanish garrison had no ammunition. They had heard no word of the outbreak of war between the United States and Spain. It was to their utter consternation that they now learned that what they had taken for a salute was a tentative bombardment and that the American ships, whose arrival had seemed such a welcome break in the dreary monotony of their lonely and isolated existence, came to demand their surrender. A hurried consultation was held on shore, but the Spanish officers had no recourse other than to submit to superior force, and on June 21, Guam saw the American flag run up over its public buildings.[37] The United States had given its first indication that it might have designs upon Spanish territory in the Pacific and was ready to seize its opportunity to acquire at least a few naval bases.

Hurrying on to the Philippines after this brief but significant episode, the American troops reached Manila to find relations with the Filipino insurgents rather critical. Aguinaldo had by now established a revolutionary government of which he was dictator-president and was soon to issue a formal declaration of independence together with an appeal to the Powers for recognition. Moreover, he was beginning to question the policy of the United States in sending to the Philippines such a large occupation force. Despite the protestations of friendliness on the part of the Americans, and their repeated assurance that our policy meant the safeguarding of Filipino rights, his suspicions were aroused as to how long American occupation of the islands might last.

General Anderson, in charge of the first contingent of the troops, was quick to recognize the dangers in this embarrassing situation. He reported to Washington on July 9 that Aguinaldo was 'very suspicious and not at all friendly,' and nine days later he frankly stated in his dispatches that 'the establishment of a provisional government on our part will probably bring us in conflict with the insurgents.' [38] He was apparently convinced that the Filipinos would regard our failure to support their independence movement as a betrayal and felt that they had good grounds for such an attitude. 'Every American citizen who came in contact with the Filipinos at the inception of the Spanish War or at any time within a few months after hostilities began,' he was later to write, 'probably told those he talked with... that we intended to free them from Spanish oppression.' [39] Even though this may not have been wholly true, there is no question that we raised Filipino expectations very high before dashing them to the ground in the gradual unfolding of our own policy.

Even Anderson himself contributed to this misunderstanding. Military necessity demanded that he maintain as friendly relations as possible with the insurgents. They were proving very useful and their operations against the

Spanish had been of material importance, as Dewey was to write in his autobiography, 'in isolating our marine force at Cavite from Spanish attack and in preparing a foothold for our troops when they should arrive.' [40] Consequently, Anderson sought Aguinaldo's further coöperation and tactfully answered the Filipino's request for recognition by the United States of Philippine independence by asserting his lack of authority to deal with such questions.[41]

This was, of course, technically correct and as Washington had not even yet definitely decided upon its Philippine policy, neither the naval nor army officers in Manila could be expected to know what the United States' intentions really were. But if there were any doubts in their own minds on the ultimate purpose of sending so large an occupation force to the Philippines, they were not quite frank in their dealings with Aguinaldo. Their policy was to obtain the maximum of Filipino coöperation with the minimum of American obligation. To the insurgents' repeated demands for a clarification of the American program, the inevitable answer was that the United States were in the islands for the benefit of the Filipinos and 'to give good government to the whole people.'

When General Merritt arrived at the end of July to take over control of these matters from General Anderson, there was a perceptible change in the policy of the Americans. For by now there were enough troops to relieve the occupation force of any dependence on the Filipino insurgents. Their assistance was no longer needed and as the American commander intended to take Manila (which the Spanish still held, although closely invested by the Filipinos) without insurgent coöperation, he felt free to adopt a sterner attitude toward them. Washington was not ready for a break with our quondam allies, and on August 10, General Merritt was instructed: 'No rupture with insurgents. This is imperative.'[42] But at Manila it was more clearly realized that the ambiguity of our relations with the Filipinos could not be continued indefinitely.

General Merritt met this situation for a time by refusing to have any direct communications with Aguinaldo. As he later explained his policy, he did not wish to treat with the Filipino leader until Manila had been captured because not until then would he be in a position to issue a proclamation and enforce his authority in case Aguinaldo's 'pretensions should clash with my designs.' [43]

The preparations for the final assault on the Philippine capital were completed early in August. They had largely taken the form, oddly enough, of secret negotiations between Dewey and the commander of the Spanish garrison. Through the medium of the Belgian consul a curious arrangement was reached whereby the city would not be shelled by the American fleet if the Spanish land batteries were not fired, and that at the onset of the attack by the United States troops the Spaniards would raise a white flag as a signal of immediate surrender. In other words, Spanish honor was to be upheld by a feint at resistance, but no real attempt would be made to defend Manila in frank recognition of the hopelessness of the Spanish cause. This agreement was communicated to General Merritt, but the army as a whole was not informed upon the extent to which the assault for which it had come so many thousand miles was in reality a sham battle. [44]

The day set for the attack was August 13. Everything ran true to form. While Dewey's squadron trained its guns on the city and the troops advanced along the shore, with some desultory firing at retreating Spaniards, the white flag duly appeared. The order to cease firing was enforced as soon as the confused mix-up of Spaniards, Filipinos, and Americans allowed, and before the rank and file of the two armies quite knew what it was all about, their commanders had agreed upon the terms of Manila's capitulation. So easily and after such a long delay did the Philippine capital actually fall into the hands of the United States.

If there was any difficulty with this operation, it was with the unlucky insurgents. They had invested Manila for over three months, made possible the quick action of the American troops, and quite naturally wanted to take part in the city's final capture. But it was just this the Americans were determined to prevent. Washington had made it clear that there could be no divided responsibility in this decisive operation and the complicated arrangements with the Spaniards for surrender to the American forces had been made with this policy in view. Consequently, when the Filipinos endeavored to share in Manila's occupation, the Spanish and American troops coöperated to keep them out.

If there was some warrant for this program in the Filipinos' possible misunderstanding of the rules of civilized warfare, and a doubt as to what they might do should they win control of Manila, its real motive was to be found in our slowly formulated policy of holding on for ourselves to whatever we could capture. It can at least be said that in the uncertainty which still prevailed in the United States as to the eventual disposition of the Philippines, there was no intention of burning our bridges behind us by handing Manila over to the insurgents.

The President made this immediately clear. When Dewey and Merritt cabled for instructions as to how far they should go in making the insurgents submit to American authority, the emphatic reply was that under no circumstances could there be a joint occupation of the Philippine capital. 'Use any means in your judgment necessary to this end,' was McKinley's unequivocal order.[45] We had abandoned our policy of temporizing with the insurgents, avoiding a rupture at all costs. We were ready to employ force to keep them in their place.

This meant a showdown with Aguinaldo, and the disappointed Filipino leader found himself confronted with an ultimatum demanding the immediate withdrawal of all his troops from about Manila. It was coupled with a vaguely worded promise that in the event of the United States' retirement from the Philippines, he would be left 'in as good condition as he was found by the forces of the Government,' but this must have been a slight solace.[46] With the best grace he could muster, Aguinaldo now submitted to an order dictated by superior force. While his hopes of Philippine independence under the protection of 'the great North American Nation, the cradle of genuine liberty,' went glimmering, he drew back his troops and awaited the next step of this invading power which still proposed, by what means he did not know, to protect the Filipinos 'in their homes, in their employment, and in their personal and religious rights.' [47]

It was only now, three days after Manila's capture but too late to prevent that final act in the military drama of our war with Spain, that word reached the Philippines that, on the very eve of the assault on the island capital, there had been signed at Washington a protocol suspending hostilities between the United States and Spain. But that even the news of peace would not have greatly changed the situation in the Philippines was clearly apparent in this protocol's third article: 'The United States will occupy and hold the city, bay and harbor of Manila...' [48]

So far had we come on the road toward imperialism, and events were to prove that we had not yet reached the end of the path.

CHAPTER XIII

McKinley's Sense of Duty

THE news of Dewey's victory in Manila had been received at home with an enthusiasm which the country had seldom experienced in all its history. It was so dramatic, so complete, so absolutely glorious. It struck a responsive chord in our national consciousness that awoke new and alluring dreams of conquest and expansion. Forgotten was the immediate problem of what we should do in Cuba in the happy realization that we had dealt so decisive a blow at Spain in the Pacific. Once again statesmen and editorial writers polished their phrases on 'manifest destiny.' The country was again in the mood of 1846 and a new era of imperialism was upon us. There was an instinctive and entirely natural reawakening of old ambitions for power in the Pacific which had been simmering beneath the surface for half a century, sedulously kept alive by those forward-looking statesmen who were responsible for drawing within the orbit of American control Alaska, Samoa, and Hawaii.

Moreover, behind this emotional outburst there was a solid basis for increased interest in the Pacific. It was not only the victory of Manila Bay which turned our attention to the opportunities open to us in the Far East. They were already well recognized in 1898. In the search for new markets for our surplus goods and new fields of investment for our surplus capital, the Pacific area appeared more than ever to be the natural field for expansion. A series of articles in the *North American Review* during the early months of 1898 had graphically called attention to 'Our Future in the Pacific,' 'America's Interest in China,' and 'America's Opportunity in Asia.' 'The markets of the Orient,' wrote Charles Denby, Jr., a secretary of legation at Peking, in the latter of these articles, 'are the heritage of her [America's] merchants, and the time will inevitably come when the voice of the Republic will be heard in

Oriental courts with the same accent of authority as in the commonwealths of South America.'[1]

But what particularly awakened the United States to the necessity for strengthening its position in the Pacific were the activities of the other Powers. The year 1898 brought to a climax a movement which appeared to mark the final partition of China. Great Britain established its sphere of influence in the Yangtze Valley and took over Kowloon and Weihaiwei, France obtained Kwangchowwan, Japan was winning its hold over Fukien, Russia seized Kwangtung, and Germany took over Kiaochow.[2] Our rivals were establishing footholds in Asia which threatened to shut us out from the rich markets of China. We had always felt that they were the heritage of our merchants, and here we were being blocked from any possible fulfillment of our ambitions at a time when we most needed new markets and new fields for investment. In commercial circles it seemed self-evident that we had to have some equivalent for the territory which the Powers were squeezing out of helpless China.

Under such circumstances the victory at Manila Bay appeared to provide a Heaven-sent opportunity to redress the secondary position into which we were being forced in the Pacific. The Philippines would be our Hongkong, our Kwangtung, our Kiaochow. A strongly entrenched minority would have none of this new idea of territory off the shore of Asia, but the new imperialists had on their side the tradition of our expansion and of our particular interest in the Pacific, the positivist philosophy of an aggressive spirit which, thank God, would not hesitate for fear of being great, and that rare combination of emotional and practical arguments which pointed so definitely toward empire in the Western Ocean.

'Popular passion for territorial aggrandizement is irresistible,' Seward had written many years before. 'Prudence, justice, cowardice, may check it for a season; but it will gain strength by its subjugation. It behooves us to qualify ourselves for our mission. We must dare our destiny.'[3] In 1898 we were ready to answer this challenge.

The demand for retaining the Philippines was voiced almost simultaneously with the report of Dewey's victory. Roosevelt and Lodge began working zealously for this objective at once, and envisioned a broad policy of expansion as a result of the war with Spain. Soon they had reason to believe that the Administration was ready to accept their program. Replying to Roosevelt's plea in the latter part of May that the Philippines should be freed from Spanish rule, Lodge wrote encouragingly that in his opinion the Administration was now 'fully committed to the larger policy that we both desire.'⁴ A few weeks later, he was again assuring him, in response to Roosevelt's statement that 'you must prevent any talk of peace until we get both Porto Rico and the Philippines as well as secure the independence of Cuba,' that 'the whole policy of annexation is growing rapidly under the irresistible pressure of events.'⁵

This was in July demonstrated in Congress's action upon Hawaii. The passage of the resolution annexing the islands revealed the new national temper. Senator Sulzer's eloquent declaration that the booming guns of Dewey's battleships had sounded a new note on the Pacific, proclaiming to all the world that 'we are there to stay, and that we are there to protect our rights, promote our interests, and get our share of the trade and commerce of the opulent Orient,'⁶ was not an isolated instance but a typical expression of the emotional fervor which swept through the congressional halls.

Nor was the press one whit behind the imperialistic politicians in Washington. It awoke at once to the new opportunities before us. Some papers, it is true, felt that our ownership of a group of islands off the coast of Asia would be as foreign to our policy as to our geography, but few could resist the dazzling prospect of acquiring a territory which would so strengthen our position in the Pacific. Complete ignorance of conditions in the Philippines did not affect their views in any way whatsoever. We had long needed naval bases and here was one ready to hand and well worth keeping. 'It is fairly clear,' wrote the independently Democratic Philadelphia *Record*, 'that our war in aid of Cuba has assumed dimensions undreamed of by those who forced the country into the conflict. Our international relations have become as complicated as are those of Great Britain. Willy nilly we have entered upon our career as a world power.' [7]

The most moderate opinion was inclined to go as far as Senator Morgan of the Senate Foreign Relations Committee. 'There is a proper and necessary reservation, to be made at the proper time,' he wrote in the June issue of the *North American Review*, 'of limited areas that will include certain bays and harbors that are best adapted to the purposes of military outposts, and for coaling stations and places of refuge for our warships and other national vessels.' [8]

When the reports of the unusual tactics of the German fleet at Manila and of the Subig Bay incident were received, our possessive instincts received a new impetus. It was universally felt that we should do what we wanted with the Philippines and that there should be no foreign interference in our program. If Germany wanted them, it made them seem all the more desirable for the United States. 'This is the most accommodating country on earth when it is fairly treated,' the Philadelphia *Press* wrote; 'but we take no crowding, and any signs in that direction put us in the middle of the road, and the road generally proves only broad enough for one.' [9] The New York *Times* noted that opinion on our position in the Philippines was divided, but declared that 'should any power attempt to define those rights or to limit their exercise, then, indeed, we should become one in mind — and in action.' [10]

There is no question that with the public, and also in administration circles, this feeling that Germany was attempting to crowd us off the center of the road to Pacific power was a decisive influence in formulating our Philippine policy. It acted upon popular opinion in the same way that supposed British designs upon California and Japanese designs upon Hawaii had in those examples of

national expansion. Furthermore, there was in the case
of our suspicions of Germany's policy very real justification.

In 1898, Germany's interest in the Pacific was at its
zenith. Inspired by the seizure of Kiaochow, the colonial
party was determined to make every possible effort to
acquire at least some part of those Spanish possessions
which might become available either through our action
or through Spain's realization that her empire was doomed.
'His Majesty the Emperor,' declared a classic dispatch to
the German ambassador in Washington which would have
aroused our imperialists even more than they were had they
known its contents, 'deems it a principal object of German
policy to leave unused no opportunity which may arise
from the Spanish-American war to obtain maritime *fulcra*
in East Asia.' **ⁱⁱ**

On this theory Germany sought an understanding with
Spain which would have allowed her to fall heir to Spanish
holdings in the Pacific, negotiated with the other Powers
over various schemes for dividing the spoils of a war in
which she was not a participant, and dispatched Admiral
von Diedrichs to Manila to safeguard German interests
and be ready for all eventualities. No stone was left unturned in her efforts to reap some benefit from the clash
between Spain and the United States.

In so far as her sympathies were concerned, Germany
was entirely on Spain's side during the war and the ill-
feeling between Germany and the United States, which
had never completely subsided since the Samoa incident
some ten years earlier, was naturally intensified. The
American ambassador in Berlin, Andrew D. White, found
his position very awkward, but as he was a Cleveland
Democrat, very much out of sympathy with the new mood
of imperialism, he endeavored to counteract Germany's
antagonism to the United States with assurances that we
had no intention of annexing any Spanish colonies. Told
that Germany wanted Samoa, the Carolines, and one or
two positions in the Philippines, he saw no objections. On
one occasion he even went so far as to suggest a conference

between the United States and Germany upon the disposition of these Pacific islands. [12]

His ideas were not shared by our ambassador in London. When word of Germany's intrigues reached John Hay, he unburdened his soul to Senator Lodge with a frankness he did not confide to his official dispatches. 'They want the Philippines, the Carolines, and Samoa,' he wrote on July 27; 'they want to get into our markets and keep us out of theirs. They have been flirting and intriguing with Spain ever since the war began and now they are trying to put the Devil into the head of Aguinaldo. I do not think they want to fight. In fact they frankly tell us they can't. Hatzfeldt said the other day, "We cannot remove our fleet from German waters." But they want, by pressure, by threats, and by sulking and wheedling in turn to get something out of us and Spain. There is, to the German mind, something monstrous in the thought that a war should take place anywhere and they not profit by it. This is awfully indiscreet, but I get sick of indiscretion once in a while. Don't file me.' [13]

It would be unnatural not to expect Senator Lodge to pass on this interesting information, but in any event Washington knew enough of Germany's policy to be very much on its guard. Its attitude on annexation was undoubtedly stiffened. But the blow to Germany's hopes of gathering up Spain's possessions was struck by England rather than by the United States. The Kaiser's program could find no support in that quarter and the growing rivalry between England and Germany made the issue one of vital importance to European politics. London openly rebuffed Berlin's quiet overtures and let it be known that it hoped the United States would hold the Philippines for itself. On the day after his letter to Lodge, Hay cabled the Secretary of State that the 'British Government prefer to have us retain the Philippine Islands, or failing that, insist on option in case of future sale.' [14]

Germany's plans were thus forestalled by opposition on the part of both Anglo-Saxon nations, for she could hardly afford to arouse the ill-will of England and the United

States at the same time. Nevertheless she continued to seek some concession from Spain and concluded a secret agreement, dependent upon the Spanish-American peace terms, whereby she would receive some of the islands in the Caroline group and 'favorable consideration in any future disposal of Spanish insular possessions.' [15] This was followed by a second treaty, after the peace terms were known, which actually resulted in the purchase for $4,200,-000 of the Carolines, the Pelews, and, with the exception of Guam, the Mariannes. With this rather inadequate compensation for America's acquisition of the Philippines, the Kaiser had to be content.

Nothing could have run truer to the usual form of imperialism than this interplay of American and German ambitions in the Pacific. If the Kaiser, through political alliances in Europe, had been in a stronger position for the conquest of 'maritime *fulcra* in East Asia,' the consequences of Germany's intrigues might have been more serious. As it was, combined with rumors that Japan would not be averse to taking over the Philippines, they supplied the imperialists with the important incentive of a national necessity to protect American interests against foreign attack.

The burden of determining our Philippine policy during these hectic days of public clamor and German intrigue rested chiefly upon the shoulders of President McKinley. His final decision we know, but when and how it came to be made constitutes a fascinating study. Under the slow pressure of imperialistic counsel, of public opinion, and of events beyond his control, he gradually convinced himself that national interests and national duty combined to make the Philippines a necessary acquisition. Unquestionably his policy was in the final analysis founded upon what he considered our commercial needs. That was the keynote of his Administration. Perhaps the basic idea behind his program was expressed with a frankness he could never himself command in a statement made by Mark Hanna after the die had been cast. 'If it is commercialism to want the possession of a strategic point giving the American people an opportunity to maintain a foothold in the markets of that great Eastern country [China],' McKinley's mentor declared, 'for God's sake let us have commercialism.' [16]

One is immediately struck by the sharp contrast between McKinley and that other President who headed the Government during a period of great expansion in the Pacific. Polk came into office with a definite program for the accession of both Oregon and California. He was an imperialist by conviction, a determined leader, and an outspoken realist. McKinley, on the other hand, had no policy on which he was prepared to stand or fall. He became an imperialist only as the tide of imperialism made such a course safe and practical, he was the amiable servant of his party rather than its leader, and it was impossible for him to admit unpleasant realities. The one entered upon a war of aggression with slight hesitation and was ready to defy the Powers of Christendom should they endeavor to keep from him the spoils of that war; the other allowed himself to be pushed into a war which was to be waged only with the highest motives and in which there were to be no spoils. Yet the only difference between the results of the Mexican War and those of the Spanish War was that Polk seized California without hesitation, while McKinley took over the Philippines only after long communion with God, as he himself has recorded, had convinced him that it was his duty.

At the beginning of the war, McKinley certainly had no idea of where our intervention in Cuba would eventually lead us. There is no reason to doubt the essential sincerity of his declaration that 'forcible annexation... cannot be thought of. That, by our code of morality, would be criminal aggression.' [17] But the idea of acquiring at least naval bases in the Pacific must have occurred to the Administration very early. Such action had been urged for so long by naval strategists. Moreover, the President was fully alive to the needs of our trade in the Far East, he was a strong advocate of the annexation of Hawaii, and he upheld our policy in Samoa. As he must have himself known very well, the moment he authorized a military expedition to the Philippines, he laid the way open for further Pacific expansion. [18]

It is also significant that the decision to capture and hold Manila was reached even before authentic word had been received in Washington of Dewey's victory. [19] This would appear to demonstrate a desire to win a foothold in the islands entirely apart from the declared objectives of the war with Spain, a theory still further emphasized in the tenor of the army expedition's instructions. Had we had no intention of retaining any Spanish territory neither a military government for the Philippines nor the seizure of Guam would have been necessary.

By June 3, within a month of Dewey's victory, definite evidence is available of the line along which the President's policy was developing. On that date Secretary of State Day cabled Ambassador Hay in London that the President, 'speaking for himself,' would be ready to grant Spain terms of peace which would provide for the cession of Porto Rico and an island in the Ladrones, together with a port and necessary appurtenances in the Philippines which the United States would itself select. [20] We had not yet captured Manila, we were still coöperating with the Filipino insurgents, but regardless of local conditions in the islands, the retention of some part of them was deemed necessary by the President. Then eleven days after this first cable, Hay was informed that peace terms in regard to the Philippines would probably have to be modified because the insurgents had become an important factor in the situation 'and must have just consideration in any terms of settlement.' [21]

Did this mean that McKinley was now considering a more friendly policy toward the Filipinos? It is not likely. We have the testimony of Lodge's letter to Roosevelt on June 15 that 'the whole policy of annexation is growing rapidly under the irresistible pressure of events,' [22] and a few weeks later this indefatigable statesman was again writing that, while the President seemed worried over the

Philippines, 'he wants to keep them evidently, but is a little timid about it.' [23] Then in still another of these interesting letters, on July 23, Lodge wrote that McKinley's imagination 'is touched by the situation' and the only question seemed to be how much to take. [24] Certainly the President's strictures on forcible annexation had by now been conveniently forgotten.

It is his biographer's opinion that McKinley at first felt 'a natural revulsion' against the acquisition of a vast unknown territory thousands of miles away. 'He did not want the islands,' writes Charles S. Olcott, 'but, once in our possession, he felt that the people would never be satisfied if they were given back to Spain.' [25] It is not a very convincing statement. If the President felt so strong a revulsion against holding the Philippines, it becomes difficult to explain why he followed a policy which so definitely saw to it that they came into our possession, and was then so very careful that we should take no step and make no promise which would prejudice our complete freedom of action.

As the war drew to a close, it is clear that McKinley had convinced himself that we must have at least a naval base in the Philippines and that he was playing with the idea of retaining a good deal more. If he still hesitated in openly espousing the 'larger policy' which was being so strongly advocated on all sides, it was because of his ignorance of actual conditions in the islands and his natural dislike of adopting any line of action until fully convinced that it was supported by public opinion throughout the country. At this point Mark Hanna was also a little undecided. It was a problem which would have to be worked out for the best interests of the country, the New York *Times* quoted him as saying on July 31, but 'we at least want a foothold on those islands.' [26]

In the cabinet's discussion of possible peace terms — for on July 22 Spain had suggested an armistice after the rapid fall of her defenses in Cuba — a division of opinion developed which also reflected the indecision in the President's own mind. At least three cabinet members wanted

to take over all the Philippines, and three favored a naval
base only. In this situation it was McKinley's own ingen-
ious proposal which carried the day. He suggested that
the United States hold on to Manila and await developments. A final decision on our policy would be postponed. [27]

On the basis of this understanding, the President demanded in his note to Spain the cession of Porto Rico
and one of the Ladrones, as he had outlined his policy
to Hay some two months earlier, but instead of any definite
arrangement in regard to the Philippines he stipulated
that 'the United States is entitled to occupy, and will
hold the city, bay and harbor of Manilla pending the conclusion of a treaty of peace which shall determine the control, disposition and government of the Philippines.' [28]
Spain protested this clause and accurately pointed out
that 'the Spanish standard waves over the city,' but the
third article of the peace protocol signed on August 12
contained the stipulation in regard to Manila as the President had decreed it should be. [29]

Two further incidents at this time, in addition to testimony from both Senator Lodge and Whitelaw Reid, prove
conclusively that McKinley had very definitely advanced
from his first position, in favor of a naval base only, to one
of broader and still indefinite implications. If in June,
hard upon the news of Dewey's victory, he would have been
content with a single Philippine port, he now wanted an
island if not the whole archipelago. His appetite was
growing.

Following the cabinet meeting at which the armistice
terms had been agreed upon, Secretary Day remonstrated
that the President had not put to a vote his motion for
the retention of just a naval base. '"No, Judge," was
the answer with a twinkle of the eye,' as the story is told
by McKinley's biographer, '"I was afraid it would be
carried."' [30] Then on the day after signature of the protocol, Admiral Dewey was instructed to report upon the
resources, value, etc., of the Philippines and to give his
opinion, for the information of the President, as to which
island would be most valuable to the United States from
a naval and commercial point of view. [31]

With the announcement through the terms of the protocol that the United States would hold Manila pending
conclusion of a treaty determining the future disposition
of the whole island archipelago, the imperialist campaign
for retaining all the Philippines gathered a new momentum.
It is true that an anti-imperialist movement had by now
been born and was gathering into its fold all those who
questioned colonial ventures so far afield, but Senator
Lodge could still offhandedly dismiss it as a 'comic incident' in view of the apparently overwhelming drift
of public opinion in the other direction. [32] So, too, did Congressman Dingley, writing in the New York *Tribune*,
speak enthusiastically of the growth of annexation sentiment throughout the country and completely ignore any
signs of opposition. [33]

In so far as the press reflected public opinion, these
advocates of expansion seemed to be entirely justified.
For when the *Literary Digest* conducted a newspaper poll
on our Philippine policy, it was able to report on September 10 that of one hundred and ninety-two replies to its
questionnaire, eighty-four favored American possession
of the entire Philippine group and sixty-three wanted a
naval base. Among the others were fourteen in favor of an
American protectorate, four with the suggestion of retaining the islands and then selling them, and only half a dozen
which wanted the United States to clear out altogether.
Not a single newspaper favored returning the Philippines
to Spain. [34]

Naval, commercial, and moral considerations were the
three leading motives advanced for keeping us in the
islands. The need to acquire those bases which naval
strategists had been so long demanding as necessary for
our position in the Pacific dovetailed neatly with the
desire of the country's commercial interests for a foothold
in the Far East, and the whole was then crowned by a new
conception of our duty to the Filipinos and to humanity.

It might have been pointed out by critics of naval expansion, though there were few in 1898, that certain of
the arguments of the naval base school were somewhat

ingenuous. With Dewey in Manila they had urged the annexation of Hawaii in order to secure a basis of support for his fleet; now that we had taken that archipelago, they declared that we had to have the Philippines to protect Hawaii. This line of reasoning was overlooked, however, in the enthusiasm of the moment. Naval bases we had to have at a time when the navy had so signally proved its value to the country. Captain Mahan, eagerly developing at Washington the policy of which he had made himself such an ardent champion, found an audience which accepted everything he said. [35]

The business interests of the country had support for their theories on all sides, from Senator Lodge who declared that Manila 'is the great prize, and the thing which will give us the Eastern trade,' [36] to Frank A. Vanderlip, Assistant Secretary of the Treasury, who significantly stated in an article in the *Century* that the Philippines were the key to the Orient and Manila the natural rival of Hongkong. [37] The American consul-general in Shanghai sent home impressive dispatches on the necessity of taking over the Philippines, the Carolines, and the Ladrones in order to counteract the territorial bases which the Powers were carving out for themselves in China.[38] Nor could imperialism hope to find anywhere a more enthusiastic spokesman than our only State Department representative in Manila itself. Consul Williams could hardly wait for the United States to 'write in living letters a page of history that this magnificent insular empire has become a part and parcel of the United States of America.' [39]

He had looked upon the Philippines and found them desirable from every point of view. 'I hope for an influx this year,' he wrote Washington, 'of 10,000 ambitious Americans, and all can live well, become enriched, and patriotically assist your representatives in the establishment and maintenance of a republican government on these rich islands so extensive in area as to form an insular empire.' Also there was a postscript to this dispatch, an interesting commentary on the motives which so often influenced imperialists in the field. Consul Williams hoped for promotion. He suggested that he might be appointed Philippine commissioner of customs, lighthouse inspector, commissioner of agriculture, or, as an afterthought, super-intendent of public instruction.[40]

Closely reflecting the attitude of men actually in the East, the chambers of commerce of the Pacific Coast and other organizations actively interested in Asiatic trade bombarded Washington with resolutions favoring retention of the islands. The *Journal of Commerce* declared that the question was not one of academic interest and that no halfway measures were possible. The promotion of foreign commerce by whatever means were possible had become an immediate necessity if the United States was to find an outlet for its surplus products. Once again it was the China trade, that same trade which had played so impor-tant a rôle in our acquisition of Oregon and California, in the development of our close ties with Hawaii, even in the purchase of Alaska, which was inviting us to new ventures in Pacific expansion.

'It is from no general policy of "annexation" or "colon-ization," or "imperialism" — which, in spite of the decep-tive use of those terms, we neither seek nor need — that the acquisition of the Archipelago is to be urged,' wrote the *Journal of Commerce's* editor. 'The one all-controlling reason is that we have an imperative need for an impregna-ble defensive position in the Pacific, and that we have no other way of getting it than by keeping these Islands, and cannot calculate upon another opportunity if this be neglected.'[41]

To these combined naval and commercial arguments for remaining in the Philippines, Congressman Dingley had added the third when he noted that the Protestant Church was practically a unit in favor of annexation of the islands. Missionaries had gone to Oregon to save the Indians and remained to save the Columbia Valley for the United States, the sons of missionaries had brought Hawaii into the fold, and while the Church could not exactly repeat this process in the Philippines, it was ready to play its part. It gladly recognized the duty of Protestantism toward a people who might be Christians, but unfortunately were of the Roman faith.

The religious press was almost unanimous in its opinion. It stressed the moral necessity of doing what we could for the Filipinos, of action forced by the dictates of humanity, of our obligation to hold the islands for Christianity. It pictured in glowing terms the beneficent effect of extending our laws and institutions to the down-trodden and suffering natives. It saw the United States in a new and godly rôle.

The *Churchman*, almost alone, viewed the question in a coldly realistic light and called attention to the startling growth of the irreducible mimimum of the demands we proposed to make upon Spain. 'It began a coaling station,' this religious organ pointed out succinctly. 'It grew to be a bay and suitable territory. It expanded to Manila and its district, as the protocol laid down. It is now Manila and Luzon. The minimum may yet embrace all the Philippines.'[42]

It was on the whole a startling development of public opinion and nowhere has the essential irony of our imperialism been more aptly expressed than in one of Mr. Dooley's pointed comments:

'I know what I'd do if I was Mack,' said Mr. Hennessy, 'I'd hist a flag over the Ph'lippeens, an' I'd take in th' whole lot iv' thim.'

'An' yet,' said Mr. Dooley, ''tis not more thin two months since ye larned whether they were islands or canned goods.'

Nevertheless, the President seemed to be slowly making up his mind to take the advice of the naval strategists, the chambers of commerce, the religious press, and Mr. Hennessy. He was keeping his ear very close to the ground. In his appointment of peace commissioners he conventionally chose three members of the Senate's Foreign Relations Committee, including one Democrat, and his Secretary of State, but the fifth appointee might have been taken as more indicative of his own policy. It was Whitelaw Reid, editor of the New York *Tribune*, and as staunch an im-

perialist as the country could boast. As early as June he
had written an article for the French press, with a frankness which contrasted strangely with the idealistic attitude so common in the United States, declaring in regard
to the Philippines that 'what we seize we shall certainly
hold, so long as it serves our purpose, and so far as the
responsibility in destroying the existing government may
carry us.' [43]

In his instructions to this peace commission, McKinley
definitely took the third step in his laborious progress
toward the final policy of annexation. A naval base had
led to a demand for a suitable port with the necessary appurtenances, as crystallized in the protocol provision for
retaining the city, bay, and harbor of Manila, and this
now led in turn to the demand for the cession of an entire
island. In addition, it was clearly stated that this represented an irreducible minimum. The avenue to further
cessions was not blocked. The President was just feeling
his way. How his mind worked, how he fortified himself
in each advance upon the road to imperialism, is graphically
revealed in the remarkable document given to the commissioners on September 16 as they were about to sail
for the peace conference in Paris.

'The Philippines stand upon a different basis,' McKinley
wrote after outlining the American position in regard to
Cuba, which we had pledged ourselves not to take, and
Porto Rico and Guam, which we intended to annex without any beating about the bush. 'It is none the less true,
however, that, without any original thought of complete
or even partial acquisition, the presence and success of
our arms at Manila imposes upon us obligations which we
cannot disregard. The march of events rules and over-
rules human action. Avowing unreservedly the purpose
which has animated all our effort, and still solicitous to
adhere to it, we cannot be unmindful that, without any
desire or design on our part, the war has brought us new
duties and responsibilities which we must meet and dis-
charge as becomes a great nation on whose growth and
career from the beginning the Ruler of Nations has plainly

written the high command and pledge of civilization.

'Incidental to our tenure in the Philippines is the commercial opportunity to which American statesmanship cannot be indifferent. It is just to use every legitimate means for the enlargement of American trade; but we seek no advantages in the Orient which are not common to all....

'In view of what has been stated, the United States cannot accept less than the cession in full right and sovereignty of the island of Luzon....' [44]

If in this statement there appears to be a rather abrupt and unexpected transition from duty of a great nation 'on whose growth and career the Ruler of Nations has plainly written the high command and pledge of civilization' to commercial opportunities and foreign trade, it was nevertheless admirably suited to assuage the American conscience.

The scene now shifts to Paris where on October 1 the conference opened which was to decide the terms of peace. The only real question before the commissioners was that of the Philippines. Little difficulty was experienced in working out such other problems as arose, and while the somewhat protracted negotiations went on concerning such matters as the Cuban debt, the American envoys had occasion to consult a number of witnesses from Manila as to actual conditions in the islands. It soon developed that the President's program for the cession of Luzon did not represent a practical solution for the Philippines' future.

General Merritt had been ordered to report to Paris and he gave his considered opinion that the United States would find it far easier to retain the entire archipelago than a single island. Even more emphatic was General Greene. He flatly declared that should the United States evacuate the islands, 'anarchy and civil war will immediately ensue and lead to foreign intervention.' From Admiral Dewey, still in Manila, came less definite advice, but he believed Manila could be made one of the finest ports of the world and urgently asked settlement of the question and establishment of a strong government. His representative in Paris, Commander R. B. Bradford, gave his opinion that to have Manila we had to have Luzon, and to have Luzon we really needed the entire island group.[45]

These views of the men on the ground emphasized an aspect of the problem which had been only dimly appreciated in Washington. The imperialists had given little thought to the Filipino insurgents except in so far as their discontent with Spanish rule supplied an argument for placing them under the more kindly control of the United States, but it was brought home to the commissioners in Paris that their revolt was a factor of the first importance which could not be ignored. It would be impossible to take Luzon without giving full consideration to what might be expected to happen on the other islands, and the more this was looked into, the more impossible it appeared to be to stop with a single island. If there is little justification for the theory that events forced us, whether we would or no, to hold the Philippines, it was undoubtedly true that we had to take all or none. It was not to prove possible, as the New York *World* advocated, to take 'the juice of the orange without the rind and pulp.'

For what were the alternatives as presented at Paris? We had broken down Spanish rule and nowhere was there any confidence in Spain's ability to regain her authority. Nor was there warrant to believe that the Filipinos themselves could establish and maintain a stable government without aid of some sort. Consequently, should the United States withdraw from all or a part of the islands, temporary anarchy would be assured wherever the Filipinos were left to themselves. Under such circumstances foreign intervention would be inevitable. We had definite evidence of the willingness with which Germany would seize an opportunity to assume the burden of any part of the Philippines in the interests of good government and general welfare; there were rumors that Japan might feel it her duty to accept such a mission. Would the island of Luzon be of any value to the United States as a naval and commercial base with such close and powerful neighbors?

Nor did there appear to be any way in which we could meet the dangers of such a situation except by annexing the entire archipelago. If we withdrew from the Philippines in whole or in part with the idea of allowing the Filipinos to work out their own destiny, we would be under an obligation to safeguard them from the designs of less altruistic nations. This implied a protectorate with all the disadvantages of annexation and none of its advantages. It was a clear case of annexation and all which that implied, or of withdrawing from the field, surrendering the position we had newly won in the Pacific, and allowing our commercial rivals to reap where we had sowed.

Of the five commissioners in Paris, three accepted the implications of this new presentation of conditions in the Philippines without hesitation. Senators Davis and Frye, together with Whitelaw Reid, were convinced that the islands could not be separated and that divided control under any form was impossible. Reporting to Washington on October 25, in a joint statement which laid special stress upon the danger to American interests in holding Luzon alone, the commercial advantages in retaining all the islands, and our moral obligation not to return the Filipinos to Spanish rule, they sought wider powers for their negotiations with the Spanish envoys.[46]

Somewhat less certain of the advisability of such a policy, but going almost as far in his own proposals, was former Secretary Day, who had resigned his post to come to Paris as a peace commissioner. He suggested the retention of the islands of Luzon, Mindoro, and Palawan, together with an agreement whereby Spain would be constrained from alienating any of the other islands without our consent. 'This gives us practical control of the situation,' Day contended, 'with a base for the navy and commerce in the East.' [47]

Only Senator Gray, the Democratic member of the peace delegation, was flatly and unequivocally opposed to any imperialistic venture. He looked at the question from the point of view of the principles and ideals upon which the

United States had been founded, and regardless of all other considerations categorically declared that there was 'no place for colonial administration or government of subject people in the American system.' [48] On this principle he was fully prepared, if need be, to sacrifice our ambition for Pacific power.

When these reports reached President McKinley, they found him in a signally receptive mood. He was influenced not so much by international considerations, however, as by a growing conviction that the American people had made up their minds, however ignorant they might be of actual conditions in the islands, that the Philippines had to be ours. In a tour of the country early in October he had been gently playing upon the imperialistic theme and the result had been more than gratifying. To what extent he carried the country with him along what now appears to have been the inevitable path of Pacific expansion, or to what extent the country led him, is less important than the fact that the President and the majority of his fellow citizens were in full harmony. 'My countrymen,' he had declared in sonorous periods at Chicago, 'the currents of destiny flow through the heart of the people. Who will check them? Who will direct them? Who will stop them?' [49] Certainly not President McKinley when the currents of destiny coincided so clearly with his own ideas.

In any event, on the same day on which the peace commissioners were cabling for new instructions, the President was writing to former Secretary Day that the general feeling in the country favored the establishment of a strong foothold in the Philippines and that the interdependence of the islands made the future of those we might not take a grave problem. 'It is my judgement,' he wrote, 'that the well-considered opinion of the majority would be that duty requires we should take the archipelago. I will be ready to give instructions when you reach that point.' [50] Still a little hesitant, though his mind must have been definitely made up. It was only that this final step in the evolution of his program, the jump from retention of Luzon to holding all the islands, required excessive caution.

But the line of least resistance was growing apparent. Were not Republican conventions throughout the country declaring that where the American flag had once been raised, it could never be lowered?

So it was that on the day after his letter to Day, more specific instructions were sent to Paris in answer to the commissioners' request for greater authority. Secretary Hay, newly back from London whence he had been called to take Day's place at the State Department, cabled that the President was convinced that the cession of Luzon alone 'cannot be justified on political, commercial or humanitarian grounds.' It had become a question, as the developments in Paris had shown, of all or none. 'The latter,' McKinley was reported as believing, 'is wholly inadmissible, and the former must therefore be required.' [51]

How had the President finally made up his mind to take this final plunge? Was it the pressure of that public opinion to which he was always so responsive, the influence of the imperialistic statesmen who surrounded him,·his own recognition of our destiny in the Pacific? He has himself left an explanation of his momentous decision which ascribes it to none of these causes.

To a delegation of clergymen which visited him over a year later, he carefully explained that he had thought at first of taking Manila, then of taking Luzon, then of taking other islands. But he could not make up his mind. He sought counsel on all sides, but could get little help.

'I walked the floor of the White House night after night until midnight,' the President then continued; 'and I am not ashamed to tell you, gentlemen, that I went down on my knees and prayed Almighty God for light and guidance more than one night. And one night late it came to me this way — I don't know how it was, but it came: (1) That we could not give them back to Spain — that would be cowardly and dishonorable; (2) that we could not turn them over to France or Germany — our commercial rivals in the Orient — that would be bad business and discreditable; (3) that we could not leave them to themselves — they were unfit for self-government — and they would

soon have anarchy and misrule over there worse than
Spain's was; and (4) that there was nothing left for us to do
but to take them all, and to educate the Filipinos, and up-
lift and civilize and Christianize them, and by God's
grace do the very best we could by them, as our fellow
men for whom Christ also died. And then I went to bed
and went to sleep and slept soundly.'[52]

And well he might after so satisfying a revelation of
Divine Will. Yet we are probably not justified in doubt-
ing McKinley's sincerity. He was a conscientious and
deeply religious man. It was not within his power to
recognize to how great an extent his insistence upon
America's moral responsibility toward the Filipinos was a
cloak thrown over the very real and very definite advantages which were believed to accrue to the United States
from the islands' acquisition. Nor could either the President or the country appreciate how very closely his outline
of the reasons why we should assume the burden of an
Asiatic colony approximated the traditional formula of
territorial expansion as it has always been practiced. As
Parker T. Moon has observed, the President's statement
touched 'almost every string in the familiar harmony of
imperialism' in stressing as it did, so unconsciously but
so significantly, national honor, economic nationalism,
racial superiority and altruism.[53]

If we are to seek beneath the pious phraseology of
McKinley's explanation of how he reached his decision,
so unlike President Polk's frank acceptance of the spoils
of his war, for the chief motive behind his policy, it is
probably to be found in a natural desire to promote our
traditional interest in the Pacific reënforced by the challenge to our power in the activities of our rivals in China.
The Philippines and the European concession race on the
Asiatic mainland were more closely connected than it is
generally realized. McKinley did not really need Divine
guidance; the approval of the Ruler of Nations was an
afterthought. There is the interesting testimony of a
memorandum found among his papers: 'While we are
conducting war and until its conclusion we must keep all

we can get; when the war is over we must keep what we want.'[54]

However, the decision was now made. Two days after Secretary Hay informed the peace commission that the President's mind was made up, final and conclusive instructions were sent to Paris. With a renewed insistence upon duty and humanity — 'territorial expansion should be our least concern, that we shall not shirk the moral obligation of our victory is of the greatest' — went the order to insist upon Spain's cession of the entire Philippine archipelago.[55]

There were still many difficulties to be ironed out by the peace commissioners. Curiously enough, Spain did not welcome the idea of surrendering her Pacific possessions and was not fully in sympathy with the United States' moral obligation to relieve her of the burden of Philippine administration. Such intricate questions were involved as the status of our 'conquest' of the islands, and our surrender of all indemnity for the war except Porto Rico and Guam. The commissioners found their demand for the Philippines rejected, and the conference might well have been wrecked on this issue had it not occurred to Senator Frye that we might be willing to pay Spain something in compensation for her sacrifice.

This proposal found the American envoys divided in their opinions and for a time met a cool reception in Washington, but after further discussions and correspondence a program was adopted representing a measure of generosity which had not been originally contemplated. It was decided to offer Spain twenty million dollars. We were willing, if necessary, to pay for our moral obligation. When this final demand was presented to the Spanish envoys, a virtual ultimatum, they gave up their fruitless attempt to soften the terms of a victor so obsessed by 'questions of duty and humanity,' as the President was still characterizing our colonial expansion in his last instructions to Paris. They accepted the American proposal.

It was on December 10, 1898, that the treaty was finally signed bringing to an end the Spanish-American War.

Spain had been forced to relinquish its control over Cuba and the United States had attained the objective for which it took up arms. Both Porto Rico and Guam were to remain under the flag of their conquerors. And, finally, it was written into the treaty: 'Spain cedes to the United States the archipelago known as the Philippine Islands....'[56]

CHAPTER XIV

Imperialism Triumphant

DURING the course of the negotiations at Paris public discussion on the disposition of the Philippines had not let up, and the conclusion of the treaty awarding the islands to the United States added new fuel to the fires of nation-wide controversy. There was little question that majority opinion, carefully maneuvered by the administration forces, supported President McKinley's policy, yet at the same time the anti-imperialist movement, which Senator Lodge had so casually dismissed in June as a 'comic incident,' could no longer be ignored. Its adherents were not limited to Democrats opposed to a Republican-made peace. They included men of both parties who felt that the issue of imperialism was one of the most important which the country had ever been called upon to face, and that the United States should not under any circumstances embark upon a colonial policy. With a two-thirds majority in the Senate necessary for the treaty's ratification, the anti-imperialists' hope that they might be able to muster enough strength to repudiate the cession of the Philippines was far from vain.

According to the position assumed by the anti-imperialists, this move to acquire the Philippines, regardless of all previous examples of American expansion, represented an absolutely new departure in our policy which was foreign to every principle of our national life. Never before had we taken over territory which definitely fell into the category of a colony and meant the exercise of American authority over a large alien population which could never be absorbed into the United States. They flatly denied their opponents' claim that in our prolonged advance in the Pacific there was precedent for the annexation of the Philippines. Oregon and California were destined to be settled by Americans whatever the Government might have done, Alaska had had no appreciable native population, Samoa was little more than a naval station, Hawaii was largely controlled by American residents and was also within the natural orbit of our influence. But the Philippines were on the other side of the world, were a territory not suited to American settlement, and over and above everything else were inhabited by a people who had no desire for American rule, but sought their independence, and, by every principle of nationality and democracy, were entitled to enjoy it.

The anti-imperialists had no adequate answer to the imperialist doctrine that from every naval and commercial consideration ownership of the Philippines was essential to American power and influence in the Pacific. They did not concern themselves with our moral obligation to the Filipinos or with the theory that to withdraw from the islands and leave them derelict would be to promote war and not peace in the Far East. They felt a more important principle at stake. They took the stand assumed by Senator Gray in Paris that there was 'no place for colonial administration or government of subject people in the American system.'

To promote their cause, they had in June, a month after Dewey's victory, founded an anti-imperialist league. It undertook to educate public opinion upon the issues involved in the controversy and hundreds of thousands of pamphlets were distributed throughout the country, speakers sent to every State in the Union, and meetings to protest against imperialism organized in every large city. If the Democrats formed the rank and file of this organization, as their policy since the Civil War so clearly dictated, there were many influential Republicans who did not hesitate to sacrifice party to principle. Senator Hoar, Speaker Reed, Carl Schurz, and Charles Francis Adams were among the powerful voices raised in denunciation of what they considered the abandonment of the fundamental principles of our government and of our foreign policy.

The propaganda of the anti-imperialist league emphasized the distance of the Philippines from the United States, questioned the value to this country of commitments so far afield, stressed the difficulty of holding the islands should our title be confirmed. The imperialists answered that these points had been raised in every other case of expansion and had been that very year rebutted with success in the debates on Hawaii. The league declared that we had encouraged the Filipinos to expect independence and our moral obligation to them was to satisfy their aspirations. The imperialists replied with a denial that we had given the Filipinos any grounds for expecting independence and declared that, as they were unable to govern themselves, and if left alone would be subject to foreign aggression, our moral obligation was to take them under American protection. So the controversy raged, and beneath all these arguments there remained the fundamental difference between the point of view of those who clung to the tradition of self-government which made American imperialism a denial of our heritage, and the thesis of their opponents, no less strongly fortified by the tradition of expansion, who believed that the United States had been summoned to play a larger part upon the world's stage.[1]

It was a struggle between two forces in our national life, influenced, it goes without saying, by political considerations, but nevertheless fighting for what were considered basic principles. Had it not been for the enthusiasm, the hysteria, the reckless ambitions awakened by war, the question might conceivably have been decided differently. As it was, the anti-imperialists were fighting against a current which in the mood of 1898 they were powerless to block.

Former President Cleveland, who still stood firmly by those principles which had led him to urge our withdrawal from Samoa and to oppose the annexation of Hawaii, vainly tried to stem the tide. In a notable address at the Founder's Day ceremonies at Lawrenceville School, he pleaded eloquently for an uncompromising moral courage in dealing with the problems raised by war 'which, unmoved by clamor and undisturbed by the excitement of triumph, will demand the things that true American citizenship desires to be right and just and safe.'² But to ask that the public remain uninfluenced by the emotions engendered by war was to ask the impossible.

In the Senate the anti-imperialist campaign reached a first climax on the very day on which the treaty of peace was signed in Paris. Senator George G. Vest brought up a resolution that the United States could not acquire or hold foreign colonies. He took the stand that on constitutional grounds we were legally barred from governing without the consent of the governed, and that in every other acquisition of territory we had provided for the citizenship of the inhabitants and for statehood as soon as possible. Since this was out of the question with the seven million Filipinos, there was no way in which we could hold the Philippines.

To his support came the venerable Senator Hoar, now sadly aware of how vain had been the confidence with which he had dismissed the possibility of further adventures in imperialism at the time of the debates upon Hawaii. He considered the Philippine question the most important since the origin of the country. 'Have we the right, as doubtless we have the physical power,' he sternly asked, 'to enter upon the government of ten or twelve million subject people without constitutional restraint?' He did not think so. It would mean, he told the Senate, 'descending from the ancient path of republican liberty which the fathers trod down into this modern swamp and cesspool of imperialism.'³

His fellow senators either did not agree with him or had no horror of the swamp and cesspool of imperialism. The Vest resolution was defeated. Nor was a second bill against government without the consent of the governed, introduced by William E. Mason, any more successful. And finally the Bacon resolution, providing for the transference of the government and control of the islands to a stable and independent Philippine Government, also went down in defeat. The anti-imperialists could not command a majority, yet so close was the division of opinion in the Senate on the ultimate fate of the Philippines that a later amendment to the treaty promising the Filipinos their independence was rejected, 30 to 29, by the casting vote of the Vice-President.

To these attempts to provide for the eventual independence of the Philippines, even though we might temporarily accept the islands through ratification of the peace treaty, the imperialist spokesmen were resolutely opposed. They tried to satisfy the doubts of their opponents by vague affirmations of faith in America's determination to treat the Filipinos fairly, but they would make no definite promise for a future which they were willing to let take care of itself.

Senator Lodge, projecting himself vigorously into this debate, now made the question one of immediate expediency — acceptance or rejection of the peace treaty. He was confident, he declared on January 24, that the United States would fulfill its obligations and so carry out 'a great, a difficult and a noble task.' John C. Spooner maintained that the future could not be decided at this time, but that 'no one can well doubt that the purpose of the United States in accepting this cession is one of benevolence and good will to that people.' He affirmed that any subsequent arrangement for the Philippines 'will religiously maintain the best ideals of the Republic, and will be in harmony with justice, generosity, and the highest civilization.'[4]

Many of the anti-imperialists in the Senate were prepared to vote for the treaty in the interests of peace with Spain if its supporters would transcribe these worthy sentiments in definite and specific pledges. Acceptance of a reservation declaring it to be the intention of the United States to grant the Filipinos their freedom when they had given proof of their ability to govern themselves would have given the treaty an overwhelming majority. Furthermore, it would have entirely changed the situation in the Philippines themselves. There is good ground for believing that a promise of eventual independence, such as we made in later years, would have prevented the outbreak of the anti-American revolt so soon to be launched by Aguinaldo and spared the United States the humiliating experience of its Philippine war of subjection. But the refusal of the imperialists to support the Vest and Bacon resolutions could be interpreted in no other way than as an indication that in taking over the islands they really hoped to hold them permanently.

Unable to command a majority, but apparently able to control the votes necessary to defeat a treaty requiring a two-thirds majority, the anti-imperialistic forces did not abandon their campaign. But before the issue came to a vote there appeared upon the scene William Jennings Bryan, standard-bearer of the Democracy and staunch anti-imperialist. To the consternation of his followers the message he brought to Washington was to vote for the treaty.

It was Bryan's theory that the problem of imperialism should not be settled by the Senate, where a minority could decide the issue, but by the people as a whole. Political leaders generally welcome settlement of a question under circumstances which allow a minority to decide it in their favor, and consequently Bryan's decision to approve the treaty in the interests of peace and leave the future of the Philippines as an issue for the next presidential election stands suspect. Undoubtedly he misinterpreted the spirit of the day and believed that on an anti-imperialist platform a triumphant Democracy would carry him to the White House. The complete failure of his program has consequently left upon his shoulders a large measure of responsibility for the action which we finally took. 'One word from Mr. Bryan,' later wrote Andrew Carnegie, one of the foremost opponents of the acquisition of the Philippines, 'would have saved the country from disaster. I could not be cordial to him for years afterward. He had seemed to me a man who was willing to sacrifice his country and his personal convictions for party advantage.'[5]

Perhaps as in the case of President McKinley, with whom a sense of duty and party advantage had so comfortably coincided, Bryan really believed that we should first have peace and then determine our policy toward the Philippines. He had announced his program before submission of the treaty to the Senate, and it was then widely approved by both Democrats and independent Republicans.[6] He can no more be judged wholly insincere than can McKinley. Moreover, it was undoubtedly true that defeat of the treaty would not by itself have settled the issue. By this time President McKinley, leaving no stone unturned to carry through his policy, had blithely gone ahead without waiting for the Senate's action and had established a Provisional Government over the Philippines. 'The actual occupation and administration of the entire group of the Philippine Islands,' he wrote on December 21, 1898, with very doubtful authority, 'becomes immediately necessary.'[7] Under such circumstances we were already in *de facto* occupation of our new colony and approval of the treaty meant acknowledgment of an accomplished fact.

If the treaty had been rejected, this fact of occupation would still have had to be faced. We would have been unable to withdraw from the islands until a new treaty had been negotiated with Spain and new arrangements made for the Philippines. A confused situation would have been worse confounded. Bryan might have chosen to embarrass the President by emphasizing this aspect of the problem and accused the Administration of attempting to coerce the Senate, but he preferred to save the issue for the election of 1900.

Regardless of these considerations, however, the fate of the treaty was still in doubt. It now had the support of the imperialists, of many wavering senators who felt that peace was more important than our colonial policy, and of seventeen Democrats and Populists cajoled and dragooned into approving it by Bryan's powerful influence.[8] Was this enough? 'It was the closest, hardest fight I have ever known,' Lodge was later to write,[9] and none knew better than this zealous worker in the imperialist vineyard just what the situation was.

On Saturday, February 4, 1899, the junior senator from Massachusetts was able to count on fifty-eight votes for ratification with four still doubtful. Two of these four had to be won over to secure a two-thirds majority. Then on Sunday came a cable from the Philippines that the restive and discontented Filipinos, despairing of the course of events in Washington, had precipitated a general engagement with the American troops in Manila. Was this final indication of how deeply implicated we already were in the islands the motive which swung the doubtful votes into the column for ratification? Senator Lodge has denied it. But in any event three of the waverers voted for the treaty, and on February 6 it was approved by a vote of 57 to 27.[10]

The war with Spain was over; another had started in the Philippines.

The situation in Manila which had led to the Filipino attack upon the American troops was a culmination of insurgent resentment against the policy of a nation whose intervention had at first been so warmly welcomed as promising the Philippines' deliverance from Spanish oppression. From the day when an ultimatum from the American commander had forced Aguinaldo to withdraw his troops from about Manila, friction between the American and Filipino forces had steadily increased. As suspicion of our intention to hold the islands as an American colony gave way to certainty, some such clash as the tragic attack of February 5 was clearly foreshadowed.

General Otis replaced General Merritt in command of the American forces in the Philippines when the latter was summoned to the peace conference in Paris, and throughout November and December of 1898 his reports on the attitude of the insurgents reflected the uncertainties and confusion of the situation in the islands. At one time he would state that the attitude of the Filipinos was friendly and that a considerable element in the native population actually favored annexation to the United States; at another he would report that their attitude was unfriendly and even threatening.[11] But beneath these surface indications of wavering sentiment, it soon became all too apparent that the Filipinos had lost none of their desire for complete independence and were no more anxious to accept the overlordship of the United States than they had been satisfied to remain under that of Spain. The goal toward which Aguinaldo and his companions had set their faces when, under Dewey's protection, they had taken up the struggle against Spain, was complete liberty, and nothing had occurred to change their objective.

Aguinaldo had set up a republican government, organized an army whose efficiency and discipline the American army officers did not hesitate to praise, and throughout the islands was gradually winning over from the Spanish troops left in the Philippines more and more territory. On the day when President McKinley made up his mind to retain the islands for the United States, the Filipino insurgents controlled not only Luzon, with the exception of the zone about Manila occupied by the Americans, but the islands of Negros, Cebu, and most of Panay. It was an anomalous situation. Simultaneously the United States was negotiating at Paris for the cession of the archipelago, a few scattered Spanish garrisons were holding out against insurgent attack in order to be able to deliver control of their posts to the Philippines' prospective rulers, and Aguinaldo was proclaiming the islands' independence and seeking recognition of the Philippine Republic.

To Admiral Dewey, cabling to Paris for a quick decision on the disposition of the islands in order that proper steps might be taken for the maintenance of order, and to General Otis, reporting the need of twenty-five thousand additional troops if he was to be in a position to hold the islands, the dangers in this situation were not long overlooked. They realized that it was not a question of giving the islands back to Spain or of quietly accepting their cession. The attitude of the insurgents convinced them that, if the United States were to hold the Philippines, they would have to be won by conquest. It became increasingly clear as 1898 gave way to 1899 that Aguinaldo was ready to fight for his liberties, and that his followers were fully as determined to defy the power of the United States as they were that of Spain.

Yet neither in Washington nor in Paris was this fully understood. 'The delegates in Paris,' Dewey later wrote, 'scarcely comprehended that a rebellion was included with the purchase.'[12] It was impossible for the United States, even though its independence had been won by a revolt against the mother country, to realize how deeply the Filipinos resented the idea of a substitution of American control for that of Spain. It is true the anti-imperialists and their spokesmen in Congress made what capital they could out of the reports that the Filipinos were ready to fight for their liberty, but even they did not appreciate how formidable the opposition to American rule was really becoming.

With the defeat in the Senate of the resolutions introduced to assure the Philippines their eventual independence, Aguinaldo could only draw the obvious conclusion that we intended to annex his country. President McKinley's orders, dated December 21, for the United States' occupation and administration of the entire archipelago then further confirmed his conviction of the hopelessness of any American concessions to Filipino aspirations. In fact so drastic and imperialistic were the President's orders for 'benevolent assimilation,' that General Otis felt constrained to tone them down in order to prevent an immediate Filipino outbreak against the American army of occupation.[13]

From other sources, however, the real tenor of the new instructions became known and a fresh momentum was given to the insurgent movement. In vain might President McKinley order the troops to avoid a clash at all costs and assure the Filipinos in his fulsome phraseology that the United States was actuated only by the loftiest motives and had accepted the Philippines 'from high duty in the interests of their inhabitants and for humanity and civilization.'¹⁴ The Filipinos were not interested in his conception of duty, humanity, civilization. They were interested in the independence of their country and they now knew that they could expect no aid from the American President.

Aguinaldo early in January issued a proclamation of his own in which in bitter terms he assailed our policy and accused the United States of betraying the promises made by its representatives to support Philippine independence. He declared that Manila would never have fallen to American arms had it not been invested by his troops, protested the orders which had forced his withdrawal from the city, and in rejecting the proclamation asserting American sovereignty over the islands, poured out his scorn upon the President's statement that 'we come, not as invaders or conquerors, but as friends.' He made it unmistakably clear that his people were ready to resist by force any attempt upon the part of the United States to subjugate them.¹⁵

Nevertheless, no effective effort was made to avert the hostilities so definitely threatened. A few futile conferences were held in Manila, but they could accomplish nothing. On the one side was the American Senate moving toward a transfer of the Philippines from Spain to the United States which took no account whatsoever of the wishes of the Filipinos; on the other was Aguinaldo putting into effect a formal constitution and striving to win foreign recognition of his republic. There was no middle ground. The tension in the islands approached the breaking point. In their opposing lines the American troops and the insurgents waited for the inevitable 'incident' which sooner or later always serves as a spark to ignite situations of such inflammability.

The spark in this case was the shot of an American sentry who fired upon a Filipino patrol which refused to obey his order to halt. The insurgents opened an attack. There is no reason to believe that it was premeditated. It was simply inevitable one day or another. And so it was that on February 5, 1899, the day before the Senate finally

approved the peace treaty, the naval and military authorities in Manila were cabling Washington that the Filipinos
had attacked the American lines and been repulsed with
heavy losses.[16]

The long-drawn-out, costly, tragic struggle which followed this outbreak of hostilities constitutes one of the
sorriest chapters in American history. It is hardly necessary to stress the bitter irony of a fate which found us
supplementing a war for Cuban liberty by a war to conquer
the Philippines, and employing against our hostile subjects
those very measures which, when used by Spain in Cuba,
we had attacked so vigorously. It was a heartrending
situation. Within ten months of that day when Aguinaldo
had called upon his countrymen to flock to the banner of
the great nation which had come to bring them their
liberty, he was assailing America in wild and bitter terms
which, for all their extravagance, reflected the frantic
indignation which most of the Filipinos now felt.

'This is the nation of unrestrained liberty!' read his
proclamation of February 24. 'This is the nation which
does not know how to teach women to become mothers!
This is the nation where honor is yet unknown, in a word,
is a nation hated by all other nations! A nation which
knows not honor, has not an atom of feeling! Are these
our protectors? Better death than be related to a people
whose evil is inborn! Away with the wretches! Destruction to the Americans! Down with the United States!'[17]

It may be said that we had given the Filipinos no promise of liberty. But our representatives had allowed them
to believe that we came to free them from the yoke of Spain
and that we sympathized with their aspirations for freedom. It may be said that the course of events had forced
us into the rôle of aggressors and that for the sake of the
Filipinos, adrift in a hostile world, we had to take them
over from Spain and establish law and order, if necessary
by force. But this did not mean that we had to take the
islands as a permanent possession. Our tragic mistake in
1898–99 was that we refused to give the Filipinos any

definite pledge of eventual independence and on this basis hold out the hand of friendly coöperation. All our protestations of acting in the interests of humanity and civilization crashed on the rock of this blunt refusal to announce a policy which was subsequently to be proclaimed and reiterated by each of President McKinley's successors. To the Filipinos in 1899 no other interpretation of our program was possible than that we accepted the Philippines as a permanent foreign colony and were ready to conquer the islands by whatever military measures proved necessary in order to bring them under the beneficent influence of that share of our laws and institutions which we condescended to extend to them.

For almost three years the insurgents under Aguinaldo endeavored to resist the fate we were powerful enough to force upon them. With courage, sometimes with unprincipled ferocity, they fought the new invaders. And the American troops retaliated in kind. It was a war stained by acts of cruelty on both sides. Beaten back by the triumph of American arms in regular warfare, the Filipinos opened a ruthless guerrilla campaign which sometimes invited reprisals in the execution and even torture of prisoners. Such reversions to barbarism may have occurred only in scattered and isolated instances, but nevertheless they contrasted sardonically with our protestations that we were acting in the interests of peace and civilization.

After the first Filipino attack, General Otis refused to accept Aguinaldo's suggestion for a truce on the ground that the United States could consider nothing except the complete submission of the insurgents to American rule. [18] This was the uncompromising attitude adopted by the military authorities and thereafter we refused to recognize the insurgents. Their answer was an order for the extermination of all foreigners and an attempt to burn Manila. Whereupon the Americans, with reënforcements bringing their total strength to twenty-four thousand, pushed northward in a campaign which drove the enemy before them in slow retreat. The insurgent capital at

Malolos was captured and the republican government driven into hiding; the Tagalog provinces, fount and head of the insurrectionary movement, were gradually occupied, and one by one the other islands fell under American control.

But the casualties mounted, more reënforcements had to be sent from the United States, and, driven into hiding, the Filipinos continued their furtive attacks upon the American troops and gave no signs of submission. After the first series of successes, the military reports of this period are a long recital of indecisive engagements, casualties, questions regarding the reënlistment of volunteers whose terms of service were running out, military censorship and anti-imperialism propaganda, dysentery, the need for more mules, such grievous problems as whether the troops should be supplied with mattresses, Spanish prisoners of war, rations, and dozens of other problems, relevant and irrelevant. It is all dreary reading. [19]

At home an alarmed Administration did not know quite what to do. It could no longer deny the fact that we had a real war on our hands. President McKinley had dispatched a special mission, headed by Jacob Gould Schurman, to investigate the situation early in 1899. It promptly issued a proclamation decrying the hostilities and declaring that, if the Filipinos wanted their liberty, which after all was rather obvious, the 'United States is not only willing, but anxious to establish in the Philippine Islands an enlightened system of government under which the Philippine people may enjoy the largest measure of home rule and the amplest liberty consistent with the supreme ends of government and compatible with those obligations which the United States has assumed toward the civilized nations of the world.' It went so far as to outline eleven points on which definite concessions would be made. But this conciliatory pronouncement was headed by the statement: 'The supremacy of the United States must and will be enforced throughout every part of the Archipelago.' [20] And the Filipinos were fighting for independence.

The war dragged on endlessly, now wholly degenerated

into guerrilla warfare in which little quarter was given by either side, and with a year of hostilities behind him the President appointed a second Philippine commission to attempt to substitute civil control of the islands for that of the military. It was headed by William Howard Taft. It has been said that when first consulted upon his appointment Taft told McKinley, somewhat as Schurman had before him, that he did not approve of his policy and did not want the Philippines. 'Neither do I,' the President replied, 'but that isn't the question. We've got them.' [21] Certainly the war had brought home to both the Administration and the American public a new realization of what we had committed ourselves to in accepting the islands.

To the anti-imperialists events in the Philippines had confirmed all their fears. The spectacle of the United States in the rôle of dictator subjecting a helpless people to the control of iron-handed military pro-consuls exceeded their most ominous warnings. They renewed their attack upon President McKinley's policy with a virulence and bitterness which American politics has seldom known. Bad as actual conditions were, the anti-imperialists contended they were even worse, and there was a wild extravagance in their views hardly justified by the facts.

'I have carefully and laboriously studied what has happened in all its details and bearings,' Carl Schurz wrote Charles Francis Adams, 'and that study has profoundly convinced me that the story of our attempted conquest of the Philippines is a story of deceit, false pretences, brutal treachery to friends, unconstitutional assumption of power, betrayal of the fundamental principles of our democracy, wanton sacrifice of our soldiers for an unjust cause, cruel slaughter of innocent people and thus of horrible blood guiltiness without parallel in the history of politics; and that such a policy is bound to bring upon the republic danger, demoralization, dishonor and disaster.' [22] It was an extravagant indictment, but perhaps Schurz went to such lengths because he could not resist the temptation of alliteration.

Even more telling was Senator Hoar's declaration in the Senate that, assuming the Declaration of Independence to be a part of the Republican creed, there was not a supporter of the war who if he himself were a Filipino would not be fighting for his liberty just as the insurgents were. It recalled an earlier attack on imperialism when the United States was invading another country to wrest control of a territory which it wished to add to the national domain. Half a century before in this same legislative body Senator Corwin had flung out a challenge which Senator Hoar might well have applied to the Philippines: 'If I were a Mexican I would tell you: "Have you not room in your own country?... If you come into mine, we will greet you with bloody hands and welcome you to hospitable graves."'

Yet for all the opposition to the course upon which the new imperialism seemed to be leading us, the country did not repudiate President McKinley's policy as Bryan had so hopefully thought it would. The Republican ranks were closed. There was no trafficking with the proposals of such mavericks as Senator Hoar, who would have had us strive for peace on the basis of recognition of Filipino independence and friendly aid in establishing self-government. The Republican platform declared that it had become 'the high duty of the Government to maintain its authority, to put down the armed insurrection, and to confer the blessings of liberty and civilization upon all the rescued people.' The Roosevelts, the Beveridges, the Platts, the Lodges, the Reids carried the day with a triumphant reassertion of 'manifest destiny.' We had to have our Pacific empire even if we had to have war along with it.

This, at least, was the verdict of the country as expressed at the polls in the autumn of 1900. President McKinley was reëlected and Bryan's forlorn hope went down in crushing defeat. Still under the influence of the ambitious dreams inspired by the fever of war, the American people could not reject the imperialism which the Republican orators had made so popular. There could be no turning back. We were committed to go on fighting the Filipinos until we had beaten them into submission.

While the Democrats sarcastically spoke of 'civilizing 'em with a Krag' and the Republicans hugged to their breasts Rudyard Kipling's kindly approval of our assumption of the 'White Man's Burden,' [23] the war went on. But the Filipino ranks were breaking under the relentless pressure of our arms and the winter of 1900 and the spring of 1901 saw the end approaching. When Aguinaldo was finally captured on March 23 of the latter year by General Funston, through a questionable exercise of military strategy which pleased the anti-imperialists no more than such aspects of the American campaign as the famous water cure and the orders of certain officers to take no prisoners, it was virtually all over.[24]

Commissioner Taft had begun setting up a civil administration to take over control of the islands from the military authorities in 1900, and in July of the next year a formal government was inaugurated to which the defeated Filipinos gradually pledged support. The last vestiges of revolt were slowly liquidated. A beaten people accepted the terms we offered them, and 1902 saw the situation sufficiently stable to allow the relief of the commander of the American troops from his duties as a military administrator.

At long last, after a second war which had cost thousands of lives and millions of dollars, the Philippines were really ours. President McKinley had not lived to see the final consummation of his plans, but they had been brought to complete success. We were the World Power which he had envisaged; we had attained a position in the Pacific which would assure us an influential voice in the determination of the international policies of the Far East.

As the peace which made us a continental empire in 1848 had awakened dreams of further expansion, so did the peace half a century later create a new conception of America's future greatness. We had adopted an imperialistic policy to which the triumphant Republicans would set no limits in the flush of their victory over the forces attempting to recall us from our Philippine adventure. As Anglo-Saxons, the chosen people of the Ruler of Nations, it was 'our manifest destiny to go forth as a world conqueror.' In the bright days of the opening of a new century, still more distant horizons opened up before the ambitious gaze of a nation which believed it had at last found itself.

By no one was the spirit of the times more clearly reflected than by Senator Albert J. Beveridge. On January 9, 1900, he delivered a speech which was carried beneath flaming headlines to the entire country and accepted by all but the anti-imperialists as an expression of America's destiny no less true than eloquent.

'The Philippines are ours forever,' declared the young senator from Indiana. ' ... And just beyond the Philippines are China's illimitable markets. We will not retreat from either. We will not repudiate our duty in the archipelago. We will not abandon our duty in the Orient. We will not renounce our part in the mission of our race, trustee, under God, of the civilization of the world.... This island empire is the last land left in all the oceans. If it should prove a mistake to abandon it, the blunder once made would be irretrievable. If it proves a mistake to hold it, the error can be corrected when we will. Every other progressive nation stands ready to relieve us. But to hold it will be no mistake. Our largest trade henceforth must be with Asia. The Pacific is our ocean.... And the Pacific is the ocean of the commerce of the future. Most future wars will be conflicts for commerce. The Power that rules the Pacific, therefore, is the Power that rules the world. And, with the Philippines, that Power is and will forever be the American Republic.' [25]

Here was a proud assertion of the attainment of that goal toward which so many forward-looking American statesmen had set their faces ever since the Republic was established. It was the consummation of the ambitions of those early expansionists who urged us on to the settlement of Oregon and California in order to win our share of the China trade and challenge England in the Pacific; it was the fulfillment of the dreams of Seward and Perry; it was the final triumph of the policy which had brought us Alaska, Samoa, and Hawaii as progressive steps toward mastery of the Western Ocean.

Nevertheless, there were voices raised to question this new interpretation of 'manifest destiny' which substituted for 'the development of the great experiment of liberty and federated self-government entrusted to us' a trusteeship over subject races whose right to independence we denied. Senator Hoar took up the challenge.

'Yet, Mr. President,' he answered Senator Beveridge's resounding speech, 'as I heard his eloquent description of wealth and glory and commerce and trade, I listened in vain for those words which the American people have been wont to take upon their lips in every solemn crisis of their history. I heard much calculated to excite the imagination of the youth seeking wealth or the youth charmed by the dream of empire. But the words Right, Justice, Duty, Freedom, were absent, my young friend must permit me to say, from that eloquent speech.' [26]

This was the other side of the picture. It was largely forgotten in 1900. But time was to have a sobering influence. For while further tentative advances were to be made along the road of imperialism, the difficulties in the Philippines brought home a realization of the responsibilities we had undertaken, and the national ardor for further expansion sensibly abated. Instead of the opponents of imperialism becoming reconciled to the gospel according to Senator Beveridge, the wisdom of our attempted absorption of alien peoples was more and more questioned.

The acquisition of the Philippines marked a new departure in our policy. That cannot be gainsaid. If it conformed with the tradition that had steadily led us westward to an assertion of power and empire in the Pacific, it none the less clearly broke with the tradition that the United States was a nation in which self-government, democracy, and equal rights were the basic principles of national life. It meant that at least temporarily we had forsaken our own established ways to follow the familiar path by which the empires of the past had risen to greatness, and then collapsed as ambition overreached itself, the path along which the modern empires of Europe were struggling in jealous rivalry.

In no other instance of our expansion could this charge be sustained. It was only in the Philippines, with their alien millions demanding independence and increasingly resentful of the domination of the distant Power which was the United States, that America had denied her heritage. It may well have been that under the circumstances, for which we were largely responsible, any other course would have provoked a conflict in the Far East. There is no doubt that many Americans sincerely felt that regardless of national interests it was our duty to hold the islands. But basically we took them for trade and empire.

It was perhaps inevitable, given the background of our expansion, the restless urge for national aggrandizement which characterized the whole world at the close of the nineteenth century, and the natural ambitions of a young and aggressive nation, that in 1898 we should have temporarily ignored the traditions with which these forces were in conflict. But they have since been recalled. We stand pledged to grant the Philippines their independence. We stand committed to a new division of power in the Pacific based upon a twentieth-century program of international coöperation. None the less it was our century of striving to attain the mastery of the Western Ocean through a policy of expansion which today gives America such an influential rôle in the future destiny of the Pacific area.

THE END

BIBLIOGRAPHICAL NOTES

BIBLIOGRAPHICAL NOTES

THE material for this study of American expansion in the Pacific is so scattered that it has appeared advisable to cite the general sources for each chapter under the appropriate heading in the following bibliographical notes. No attempt has been made to compile a complete bibliography and special works to which only incidental reference is made are listed only in the notes themselves. In the earlier chapters reliance has at times been placed upon recognized secondary sources, but in the more detailed studies of Alaska, Samoa, Hawaii, and the Philippines, the basic material is taken from official government publications and other primary sources.

CHAPTER I

General secondary sources applying to the book as a whole which might be cited under this introductory chapter include: *The American Secretaries of State and their Diplomacy,* 10 vols., New York, 1927–29; Callahan, James Morton, *American Relations in the Pacific and the Far East, 1784–1900,* Johns Hopkins University Studies in History and Political Science, Series 19, Baltimore, 1901; Dennett, Tyler, *Americans in Eastern Asia,* New York, 1922; Fish, Carl Russell, *American Diplomacy,* New York, 1923; Dennis, Alfred L. P., *Adventures in American Diplomacy,* New York, 1928; Foster, John W., *American Diplomacy in the Orient,* Boston, 1904; Hart, Albert Bushnell, *The Foundations of American Diplomacy,* New York, 1901; Henderson, John B., *American Diplomatic Questions,* New York, 1901; Johnson, Willis Fletcher, *America's Foreign Relations,* 2 vols., New York, 1921; Johnson, Willis Fletcher, *A Century of Expansion,* New York, 1903; Latané, John H., *A History of American Foreign Policy,* New York, 1927; Moore, John Bassett, *Digest of International Law,* vol. 1, Washington, 1906; Moore, John Bassett, *Four Phases of American Development,* Baltimore, 1912; Paullin, Charles Oscar, *Diplomatic Negotiations of American Naval Officers,* Baltimore, 1912; Snow, Freeman, *Treaties and Topics in American Diplomacy,* Boston, 1894.

1. Senator Sulzer, quoted in Miller, Marion M., *Great Debates in American History,* 14 vols., New York, 1913, III, 211.

2. Senator Allen, *Congressional Globe*, 29th Congress, 1st session, February 10, 1846.
3. Turner, Frederick Jackson, *The Rise of the New West*, New York, 1906, 113.
4. John L. O'Sullivan, of the *Democratic Review* and New York *Morning News*, quoted in Pratt, J. W., 'The Origin of Manifest Destiny,' *American Historical Review*, vol. 32, 1927, 796.
5. Seward, William H., *Works of*, edited by George E. Baker, 5 vols., Boston, 1884, III, 409.
6. *Senate Executive Document 34*, 33d Congress, 2d session, 81.
7. From article in *The Nineteenth Century*, quoted by Dodsworth, W., *Our Industrial Position and Our Policy in the Pacific*, New York, 1898, 13–14.
8. See Moon, Parker T., *Imperialism and World Politics* (1926), New York, 1930, 524.

CHAPTER II

General Sources for the Northwest: Bancroft, Hubert Howe, *History of the Pacific States of North America*, vols. 13–19 (*California*), and 22–25 (*The Northwest Coast*), San Francisco, 1882–1890; Cleland, Robert Glass, *Asiatic Trade and the American Occupation of the Pacific Coast*, Annual Report of the American Historical Society, 1914, vol. 1, Washington, 1916; Fuller, George W., *A History of the Pacific Northwest*, New York, 1931; Schafer, Joseph, *A History of the Pacific Northwest*, New York, 1905.

For Oregon: Barrows, William, *Oregon, the Struggle for Possession*, Boston, 1884; Carey, Charles Henry, *History of Oregon*, Chicago-Portland, 1922; Gray, W. H., *A History of Oregon*, Portland, 1870; Greenhow, Robert, *The History of Oregon and California*, Boston, 1844; Lyman, Horace S., *History of Oregon*, 4 vols., New York, 1903; Meany, Edward S., *History of the State of Washington*, New York, 1909; *Quarterly* of Oregon Historical Society; *Washington Historical Quarterly*.

For California: Cleland, Robert Glass, *A History of California: the American Period*, New York, 1922; Hittell, Theodore H., *History of California*, 4 vols., San Francisco, 1885; Richman, Irving B., *California under Spain and Mexico*, Boston, 1911.

1. Ledyard, John A., *A Journal of Captain Cook's Last Voyage to the Pacific Ocean*, Hartford, 1783. See also Sparks, Jared, *The Life of John Ledyard*, Cambridge, 1828.

2. Thwaites, Reuben Gold, *Original Journals of the Lewis and Clark Expedition*, 8 vols., New York, 1904, I, xx.
3. Sparks, *The Life of John Ledyard*, 228.
4. *Writings of Thomas Jefferson*, edited by Paul Leicester Ford, 10 vols., New York, 1892–99, IV, 447.
5. Manning, W. R., *The Nootka Sound Controversy*, Annual Report of American Historical Association, 1904, 279–478.
6. Quoted in Carey, *The History of Oregon*, 112–13 n.
7. Morison, Samuel Eliot, *Maritime History of Massachusetts*, Boston, 1921, chap. 5; Dulles, Foster Rhea, *The Old China Trade*, Boston, 1930, chap. 4.
8. Quoted from correspondence in the State Department by Dennett, *Americans in Eastern Asia*, 40.
9. Bancroft, *History of the Pacific States*, XXII, 254 n. and 298 n.; also Dennett, *Americans in Eastern Asia*, 39.
10. Vancouver, Captain George, *A Voyage of Discovery to the North Pacific Ocean*, 3 vols., London, 1798, I, 209–10.
11. Greenhow, *The History of Oregon and California*, 434 (Appendix).
12. Quoted in Morison, *Maritime History of Massachusetts*, 51.
13. Fuller, *A History of the Pacific Northwest*, 75–76.
14. Journal of William Gale, quoted in Bancroft, *History of the Pacific States*, XXIII, 134.
15. *Solid Men of Boston* (MS.), 70, quoted in Morison, *Maritime History of Massachusetts*, 58.
16. Letter to John Quincy Adams, quoted in Greenhow, *The History of Oregon and California*, 439.
17. *Writings of Thomas Jefferson*, IX, 351.
18. Among the sources for the settlement of Astoria are: Irving, Washington, *Astoria*, 3 vols., London, 1836; Franchère, Gabriel, *Narrative of a Voyage to the Northwest Coast of America*, New York, 1854; Cox, Ross, *Adventures on the Columbia River*, New York, 1832; Ross, Alexander, *Adventures of the First Settlers on the Oregon or Columbia River*, London, 1849.
19. *American State Papers, Foreign Relations*, III, 731.
20. Schafer, Joseph, 'British Attitude Toward the Oregon Question,' *American Historical Review*, vol. 16, 1911, 286.
21. *American State Papers, Foreign Relations*, IV, 381.
22. Cleland, *A History of California*, 4.
23. *Ibid.*, 20. See also Cleveland, Richard J., *A Narrative of Voyages and Commercial Enterprises*, 2 vols., Cambridge,

1842; Cleveland, H. W. S., *Voyages of a Merchant Navigator*, New York, 1886.

24. Cleland, *A History of California*, 45.
25. Shaler, William, *Journal of a Voyage Between China and the North-Western Coast of America*, American Register, vol. 3, Philadelphia, 1808.
26. Dana, Richard H., Jr., *Two Years Before the Mast*, New York, 1869.
27. Quoted in Richman, *California under Spain and Mexico*, 300.
28. Cleland, *A History of California*, 27.
29. *Ibid.*, 29–30.
30. Adams, John Quincy, *Memoirs of*, 12 vols., Philadelphia, 1874–77, IV, 275.
31. Quoted in *The American Secretaries of State and their Diplomacy*, vol. 4 (Adams by Dexter Perkins), New York, 1928, 95.

Chapter III

In addition to works mentioned in the notes for Chapter II, the general sources for this chapter include: Bell, James Christy, Jr., *Opening a Highway to the Pacific*, Studies in History, Economics and Public Law, Columbia University, vol. 96, New York, 1921; Bourne, Edward Gaylord, *Aspects of Oregon History before 1840*, *Quarterly* of the Oregon Historical Society, vol. 6, 1905; Branch, Edward Douglas, *Westward*, New York, 1930; Chittenden, Hiram Martin, *The American Fur Trade of the Far West*, 3 vols., New York, 1902; Garrison, George Pierce, *Westward Extension*, New York, 1906; Ghent, W. J., *The Road to Oregon*, New York, 1929; McMaster, John B., *A History of the American People*, 8 vols., New York, 1886–1913, V–VII; Parkman, Francis, *The Oregon Trail*, Boston, 1875; Paxson, Frederic L., *History of the American Frontier*, Boston, 1924; Turner, Frederick Jackson, *The Frontier in American History*, New York, 1921; Turner, Frederick Jackson, *The Rise of the New West*, New York, 1906.

1. For Oregon debates of this period see *Annals of Congress*, 17th Congress, 2d session, and Benton, Thomas Hart, *Abridgement of the Debates of Congress, from 1789 to 1856*, 16 vols., New York, 1857–61, VII, 78–79, 394–405, VIII, 207–13. They are also discussed in detail in Benton, Thomas Hart, *Thirty Years' View*, 2 vols., New York, 1861–62; McMaster, V, Bancroft, XXIV, and Bourne, *Aspects of Oregon History*

before 1840. For Floyd's original report on Oregon see *Annals of Congress*, 16th Congress, 2d session, 946–58.

2. Quoted in McMaster, V, 27.
3. *Annals of Congress*, 17–2, 598.
4. *Ibid.*, 409.
5. Benton, *Abridgement of Debates*, VIII, 197. See also Roosevelt, Theodore, *Thomas Hart Benton*, Boston, 1886, 55.
6. *Annals of Congress*, 17–2, 398.
7. *Ibid.*, 417.
8. *Ibid.*, 251.
9. *Ibid.*, 408.
10. Quoted in McMaster, V, 481.
11. Benton, *Abridgement of Debates*, VIII, 186.
12. *Annals of Congress*, 17–2, 682.
13. Adams, John Quincy, *Memoirs*, 12 vols., Philadelphia, 1874–77, V, 252.
14. See Merck, Frederick, *Oregon Pioneers and the Boundary*, American Historical Review, XXIX, 1924, 696.
15. Quoted in Carey, *History of Oregon*, 477.
16. Cleland, *Early Sentiment for Annexation of California*, 15–17; *History of California*, 143.
17. Thwaites, Reuben Gold, *Original Journals of the Lewis and Clark Expedition*, 8 vols., New York, 1904, III, 210.
18. Irving, Washington, *The Adventures of Captain Bonneville*, 2 vols., Philadelphia, 1837, I, 27.
19. Kelly, Hall J., *A Geographical Sketch of that Part of North America called Oregon*, Boston, 1831, reprinted in *The Magazine of History*, XVII, 86. See also McMaster, VI, 109.
20. Report of Senator J. Semple, April 20, 1846, *Senate Document 306*, 29th Congress, 1st session, as quoted in Bell, *Opening a Highway to the Pacific*, 129–30 n.
21. *Letters of Sir George Simpson, 1841–43*, American Historical Review, XIV, 79.
22. Quoted in Lyman, *History of Oregon*, III, 304. See also McMaster, VI, 447–453.
23. *Letters of Sir George Simpson*, 89.
24. Daniel Webster, *Writings and Speeches of* (National Edition), 18 vols., Boston, 1903, XIII, 314.
25. Quoted in Tyler, Lyon G., *The Letters and Times of the Tylers*, 2 vols., Richmond, 1844, II, 264.
26. Manuscript letter, Thompson to Webster, April 29, 1842, quoted in Reeves, Jesse S., *American Diplomacy under Tyler and Polk*, Baltimore, 1907, 101.

27. *Senate Executive Document 166*, 27th Congress, 3d session, V, 69–86. See also McMaster, VII, 308–11.

28. Webster, Daniel, *Writings and Speeches of,* XVI, 394–95. See also Fuess, Claude Moore, *Daniel Webster*, 2 vols., Boston, 1930, II, 125–28.

29. Tyler, *The Letters and Times of the Tylers*, II, 448.

Chapter IV

In addition to histories of Oregon and California given in the notes for Chapter II, general sources for this chapter include: *American Secretaries of State and their Diplomacy*, vol. 5 (Buchanan by St. G. L. Sioussat), New York, 1928; Commager, Henry Steele, 'England and the Oregon Treaty of 1846,' *Quarterly of the Oregon Historical Society*, vol. 28, 1927, 18–38; Gallatin, Albert, *The Oregon Question*, New York, 1846; Garrison, George Pierce, *Westward Extension*, New York, 1906; Merck, Frederick, 'Oregon Pioneers and the Boundary,' *American Historical Review*, vol. 29, 1924; McCormac, Eugene I., *James K. Polk*, Berkeley, 1922; McMaster, John B., *A History of the American People*, vol. 7, New York, 1913; Polk, James K., *Diary*, 4 vols., Chicago, 1910; Reeves, Jesse S., *American Diplomacy under Tyler and Polk*, Baltimore, 1907; Schafer, Joseph, 'British Attitude Toward the Oregon Question,' *American Historical Review*, vol. 16, 1911; Schuyler, R. L., 'Polk and the Oregon Compromise of 1846,' *Political Science Quarterly*, vol. 26, 1911; Smith, Justin H., *The War with Mexico*, 2 vols., New York, 1919.

1. *Congressional Globe*, 27th Congress, 3d session, 198–200; McMaster, VII, 292–93; Benton, *Thirty Years' View*, II, 471.

2. Quoted in Cleland, *Asiatic Trade and the American Occupation of the Pacific Coast*, 286.

3. *Congressional Globe*, 29th Congress, 1st session; McMaster, VII, 291.

4. Among sources of propaganda at this time Greenhow, Robert, *The History of Oregon and California*, Boston, 1844, should be cited.

5. See McMaster, VII, 294–98.

6. Richardson, James D., *Messages of the Presidents*, 10 vols., Washington, 1896–99, IV, 381.

7. Cleland, *Asiatic Trade and the American Occupation of the Pacific Coast*, 288.

8. See Polk, *Diary*, I, 1–9; McCormac, *James K. Polk*, chap. 21; *American Secretaries of State*, V, chap. 3 (Buchanan).
9. Richardson, *Messages*, IV, 399.
10. Polk, *Diary*, I, 1–9; and letter of Webster to Fletcher Webster, January 14, 1846, in Webster, *Writings and Speeches of*, XVI, 440.
11. See Commager, *England and the Oregon Treaty*.
12. For treaty text see *Treaties, Conventions, etc., 1776–1909*, compiled by William M. Malloy, 2 vols., Washington, 1910, I, 656.
13. Roosevelt, Theodore, *Thomas Hart Benton*, Boston, 1886, 268.
14. Lowell, James Russell, *Biglow Papers*, in *Writings*, VIII, Cambridge, 1892, 46.
15. See Adams, Ephraim D., *British Interests and Activities in Texas, 1838–46*, Baltimore, 1910.
16. Buchanan to Slidell, November 10, 1845, quoted in Reeves, *American Diplomacy under Tyler and Polk*, 272. See also *Senate Executive Document 52*, 30th Congress, 1st session, 71, and Buchanan, James K., *Works of*, 12 vols., Philadelphia, 1908–11, VI, 294–306.
17. Smith, *The War with Mexico*, I, chap. 16.
18. Buchanan to Larkin, Oct. 17, 1845, Buchanan, *Works*, VI, 275–78.
19. *Ibid.*, 363–65; see also McCormac, *James K. Polk*, 394.
20. Smith, *The War with Mexico*, I, 155, and, for summation of American grievances against Mexico, 136.
21. Quoted in Reeves, *American Diplomacy under Tyler and Polk*, 284.
22. Polk, *Diary*, I, 397–98.
23. Cleland, *A History of California*, 200.
24. Smith, *The War with Mexico*, I, 335; see also chap. 17, and Nevins, Allan, *Frémont*, 2 vols., New York, 1928, I, chaps. 19 and 20.
25. Nevins, *Frémont*, I, 322.
26. For text of treaty, see *Treaties, Conventions, etc.*, I, 1107–21.

CHAPTER V

The chief primary sources for this chapter are *Senate Executive Document 34*, 33d Congress, 2d session, and the supplementary report, Hawks, Francis L., *Narrative of the Expedition of an American Squadron to the China Seas and Japan*, New York,

1856, for the Perry Expedition; and *Senate Executive Document 22*, part 2, 35th Congress, 2d session (China correspondence), for the Parker episode.   Supplementary sources include Spalding, J. W., *Japan and Around the World*, New York, 1855; Taylor, Bayard, *India, China and Japan*, New York, 1862; Williams, S. Wells, *A Journal of the Perry Expedition to Japan*, Transactions of the Asiatic Society of Japan, vol. 73, 1910.

Interesting secondary sources are Dennett, Tyler, *Americans in Eastern Asia*, New York, 1922; Griffin, William Elliot, *Matthew Calbraith Perry*, Boston, 1890; Rossiter, William S., 'The First American Imperialist,' *North American Review*, vol. 182, 1906.

1. Adams, John Quincy, *Memoirs*, VII, 247.
2. Seward, William H., *Works of*, 5 vols., Boston, 1884, III, 409.
3. Richardson, *Messages*, V, 198.
4. Seward, *Works*, II, 109.
5. *Ibid.*, I, 250; see also Dennett, Tyler, 'Seward's Far Eastern Policy,' *American Historical Review*, vol. 28, 1922.
6. Clark, Arthur H., *The Clipper Ship Era*, New York, 1912, 178.
7. Dennett, *Seward's Far Eastern Policy*, 45; Dennett, *Americans in Eastern Asia*, 270–72.
8. *Senate Executive Document 34*, 5.
9. *Ibid.*, 13.
10. *Ibid.*, 14.
11. See Griffin, *Matthew Calbraith Perry*, 41ff.
12. Spalding, *Japan and Around the World*, 129.
13. Taylor, *India, China and Japan*, 395.
14. *Senate Executive Document 34*, 31–32.
15. Cholmondeley, Lionel B., *The History of the Bonin Islands*, London, 1915, 11–22 and 91.
16. *Ibid.*, 107–08.
17. *Senate Executive Document 34*, 39, 44.
18. *Ibid.*, 43, 57.
19. *Ibid.*, 85.
20. *Ibid.*, 81.
21. *Ibid.*, 81.
22. *Ibid.*, 113.
23. *Senate Executive Document 22*, part 2, 35th Congress, 2d session, 1083.
24. *Ibid.*, 1184.

25. *Senate Executive Document 22*, part 2, 35th Congress, 2d session, 1214.
26. *Ibid.*, 1204.
27. *Ibid.*, 1208.
28. *Ibid.*, 1247–49.
29. *Ibid.*, 1211.
30. *Senate Executive Document 30*, 36th Congress, 1st session, 8.
31. See Dennett, *Americans in Eastern Asia*, 349.
32. Frelinghuysen *in re* Hayti, 1884, cited in Moore, *Digest of International Law*, I, 432.
33. Jefferson, Thomas, *Works*, V, 443.

CHAPTER VI

The two chief primary sources for this chapter are *House Executive Document 177*, 40th Congress, 2d session (361 pages) and *Proceedings of Alaska Boundary Tribunal*, 7 vols., Washington, 1904.

Other sources include: Bancroft, Hubert Howe, *Alaska* (vol. 28 of *The History of the Pacific States*), San Francisco, 1886; Barrett Willoughby, *Sitka, Portal to Romance*, Boston, 1930; Callahan, James Morton, *The Alaska Purchase*, West Virginia University Studies, Series 1, No. 2, 1908; Clark, Henry W., *History of Alaska*, New York, 1930; Davis, Mary Lee, *Uncle Sam's Attic*, Boston, 1930; Dunning, William A., 'Paying for Alaska,' *Political Science Quarterly*, vol. 27, 1912; Farrar, Victor J., 'The Background of the Purchase of Alaska,' *Washington Historical Quarterly*, vol. 13, 1922; Golder, Frank A., 'The Purchase of Alaska,' *American Historical Review*, vol. 25, 1920; Platt, Thomas Benjamin, *Russo-American Relations, 1816–1867*, Johns Hopkins University Studies in History and Political Science, vol. 48, No. 2, 1930; Schafer, Joseph, *The Pacific Slope and Alaska*, Philadelphia, 1904; Scidmore, Eliza R., *Alaska*, Boston, 1885.

1. Bancroft, Frederic, *The Life of William H. Seward*, 2 vols., New York, 1900, II, 472.
2. Quoted in Seward, Frederick W., *Seward at Washington as Senator and Secretary of State*, New York, 1891, 383.
3. See Callahan, *The Alaska Purchase*, 2–3.
4. Farrar, *The Background of the Purchase of Alaska*, 101–02.
5. Golder, *The Purchase of Alaska*, 411–12.
6. *Ibid.*, 413–18.
7. See Dennett, Tyler, *Seward's Far Eastern Policy*, 60.
8. Clark, *History of Alaska*, 71.

9. Farrar, Victor J., 'Joseph Lane McDonald and the Purchase of Alaska,' *Washington Historical Quarterly*, vol. 12, 1921, 87–89.

10. *House Executive Document 177*, 40–42.

11. Seward, *Seward at Washington*, 348.

12. For text see *House Executive Document 177*, 5–10.

13. Seward, *Seward at Washington*, 368.

14. Blaine, James G., *Twenty Years of Congress*, 2 vols., Norwich, 1884, II, 334.

15. Seward, *Seward at Washington*, 369.

16. See Sumner, Charles, *Prophetic Voices Concerning America*, Boston, 1874.

17. Pierce, Edward L., *Memoir and Letters of Charles Sumner*, 4 vols., Boston, 1877–1893, IV, 318–19.

18. Sumner, Charles, *On the Cession of Russian America*, Washington, 1867, 16.

19. *Ibid.*, 12.

20. Golder, *The Purchase of Alaska*, 423 n.

21. Seward, *Seward at Washington*, 392.

22. Golder, *The Purchase of Alaska*, 423–24. See also Dunning, *Paying for Alaska* and Farrar, *The Background of the Purchase of Alaska*.

23. Dunning, *Paying for Alaska*, 386.

24. *House Executive Document 177*, 12.

25. Walker, R. J., *Letter on the Purchase of Alaska, St. Thomas and St. John*, from *Washington Daily Morning Chronicle*, Jan. 28, 1868, (pamphlet) i.

26. *Congressional Globe*, 40th Congress, 2d session, Part 5, Appendix, 377–403, for this and following extracts from House debate of July 1, 1868. See also Binger, Hermann, *The Louisiana Purchase*, Washington, 1898.

27. Binger, *The Louisiana Purchase*, 53–54.

28. Dennett, *Seward's Far Eastern Policy*, 60.

CHAPTER VII

The chief primary sources used for this and the following chapter are the Senate and House executive documents as hereafter noted together with the volumes of *Papers Relating to the Foreign Relations of the United States* for the years concerned. Also Moore, *Digest of International Law*, I, 536–54.

Secondary sources dealing with Samoa include Foster, John W., *American Diplomacy in the Orient* (chap. 12), Boston, 1903; Henderson, John B., *American Diplomatic Questions* (chap. 3),

New York, 1901; Keim, Jeannette, *Forty Years of German American Political Relations* (chap. 5), University of Pennsylvania, 1919; Snow, Freeman, *Treaties and Topics in American Diplomacy*, Boston, 1894; Stevenson, Robert Louis, *A Footnote to History*, New York, 1892; Watson, Robert M., *History of Samoa*, London, 1918.

1. See Dulles, *The Old China Trade*, chap. 7.
2. See Porter, Captain David, *Journal of a Cruise Made to the Pacific Ocean*, 2 vols., New York, 1822.
3. *Ibid.*, II, 58–59.
4. *Ibid.*, II, 79.
5. Paulding, Lieut. Hiram, *Journal of a Cruise of the United States Schooner Dolphin*, New York, 1831.
6. Callahan, James Morton, *American Relations in the Pacific and the Far East*, Baltimore, 1901, 69–70.
7. Turner, Rev. George, *Nineteen Years in Polynesia*, London, 1861, and Russell, Rt. Rev. Michael, *Polynesia*, Edinburgh, 1843.
8. Wilkes, Charles, *Narrative of the United States Exploring Expedition*, 5 vols., New York, 1850, II, 80.
9. *Report of Captain E. Wakeman to W. H. Webb on the Islands of the Samoan Group* (pamphlet), New York, 1872.
10. Paullin, Charles Oscar, *Diplomatic Negotiations of American Naval Officers*, Baltimore, 1912, 350; also Townsend, Mary Evelyn, *The Rise and Fall of Germany's Colonial Empire*, New York, 1930, 65.
11. *House Executive Document 161*, 44th Congress, 1st session, 6.
12. *Ibid.*, 5.
13. *Ibid.*, 76.
14. *Ibid.*, 125.
15. Seward, Frederick W., *Reminiscences of a War-Time Statesman and Diplomat*, New York, 1916, 439.
16. *Ibid.*, 439.
17. For treaty see Malloy, *Treaties, Conventions, etc.*, II, 1574–76.
18. Paullin, *Diplomatic Negotiations of American Naval Officers*, 302.
19. *House Executive Document 238*, 50th Congress, 1st session, 150. See also Stevenson, *A Footnote to History*.
20. *House Executive Document 238*, 16–26.
21. Churchward, William B., *My Consulate in Samoa*, London, 1887, 379.

22. *House Executive Document 238*, 10.
23. Townsend, *The Rise and Fall of Germany's Colonial Empire*, 75.
24. Rees, William L. and L., *The Life and Times of Sir George Grey*, 2 vols., London, 1892, II, 603.
25. *Foreign Relations, 1889*, 276.
26. Protocols of conference of 1887 may be found in *Senate Executive Document 102*, 50th Congress, 2d session.
27. For these events see *House Executive Document 238*; *Senate Executive Documents 31, 68, 102*, 50th Congress, 2d session, and Stevenson, *A Footnote to History*.
28. *Senate Executive Document 31*, 50th Congress, 2d session, 125.
29. *Senate Executive Document 68*, 50th Congress, 2d session, 17.
30. See *House Executive Document 118, 119*, 50th Congress, 2d session.

Chapter VIII

For sources see note under Chapter VII

1. *House Executive Document 238*, 50th Congress, 1st session, 90.
2. *Ibid.*, 97–98.
3. *Ibid.*, 109–21.
4. *Congressional Record*, 50th Congress, 2d session, vol. 20, Part 2, 1889, 1283–91, 1325–37, 1372–75.
5. *The Nation*, vol. 28, 1889, 84.
6. *Senate Executive Document 102*, 50th Congress, 2d session, 3.
7. McElroy, Robert, *Grover Cleveland*, 2 vols., New York, 1923, I, 259.
8. Stevenson, *A Footnote to History*, 267.
9. *Ibid.*, chap. 10; also Woodruff, J. Lyon, 'The Story of the Samoan Disaster,' *Cosmopolitan*, vol. 20, 1895.
10. *Foreign Relations, 1889*, 195–204.
11. Tyler, Alice Felt, *The Foreign Policy of James G. Blaine*, Minneapolis, 1927, 218–53, bases account of conference on manuscript sources of commission's dispatches. See also Hamilton, Gail, *Biography of James G. Blaine*, Norwich, 1895, 659. For views of Bates see Bates, George H., 'Some Aspects of the Samoan Question, *Century*, vol. 37, 1889, and 'Our Relations to Samoa,' *ibid.*
12. *Foreign Relations, 1889*, 353–64; Malloy, *Treaties, Conventions, etc.*, II, 1576–89; *Senate Miscellaneous Document 81*, 51st Congress, 1st session.

13. *Foreign Relations, 1894,* Appendix 1; Stevenson, *A Footnote to History,* chap. 11.
14. *Foreign Relations, 1894,* Appendix 1, 504–13.
15. Richardson, *Messages of the Presidents,* IX, 531.
16. Ide, Henry C., 'Our Interest in Samoa,' *North American Review,* vol. 165, 1897, and 'The Imbroglio in Samoa,' *ibid.,* 168, 1899.
17. For settlement of claims see *Senate Executive Document 85,* 59th Congress, 1st session.
18. *Foreign Relations, 1899,* 615.
19. *Ibid.,* 626. For readable account of Tripp's mission see Tripp, Bartlett, *My Trip to Samoa,* Cedar Rapids, 1911.
20. *Foreign Relations, 1899,* 659.
21. *Ibid.,* 662–63.
22. Undated memorandum in State Department archives quoted in Dennis, Alfred L. P., *Adventures in American Diplomacy,* New York, 1908, 114.
23. *Foreign Relations, 1899,* xxvii.
24. Townsend, *The Rise and Fall of Germany's Colonial Empire,* 199–201.
25. *Foreign Relations, 1899,* 667–69; Malloy, *Treaties, Conventions, etc.,* II, 1595–97.
26. *Congressional Record,* 56th Congress, 1st session, vol. 332, 1295.
27. Thayer, William Roscoe, *The Life and Letters of John Hay,* 2 vols., New York, 1915, II, 282–83.
28. Lefébure, Paul, 'The Division of Samoa,' *Annales des Sciences Politiques,* vol. 15, 1900.
29. *Tutuila,* Memorandum of Navy Department, 1902, 24.
30. *America Samoa. A General Report by the Governor* (H. F. Bryan), Washington, 1927.

CHAPTER IX

For the study of Hawaiian relations in this and the next two chapters the basic sources are *Foreign Relations, 1894,* Appendix 2; *Senate Report 222,* 53d Congress, 2d session; *Senate Report 681,* 55th Congress, 2d session. They are supplemented by a large number of contemporary records by foreign residents in Hawaii.

Among such records in book form, in whole or in part serving as primary sources, are Anderson, Rufus, *The Hawaiian Islands,* Boston, 1865; Bingham, Hiram, *A Residence of Twenty-One*

Years in the Hawaiian Islands, Canandaigua (N.Y.), 1855; De Varigny, C., *Quatorze Ans aux Iles Sandwich*, Paris, 1874; Dibble, Sheldon, *History of the Sandwich Islands*, Hawaii, 1843; Gillis, J. A., *The Hawaiian Incident*, Boston, 1897; Hopkins, Manley, *Hawaii*, London, 1866; Jarves, James Jackson, *History of the Hawaiian or Sandwich Islands*, London, 1843; Judd, Laura Fish, *Honolulu*, New York, 1880; Simpson, Alexander, *The Sandwich Islands: Progress of Events*, London, 1843; Stewart, C. S., *A Residence in the Sandwich Islands*, Boston, 1839; Young, Lucien, *The Real Hawaii*, New York, 1899.

Other more general sources include Alexander, W. D., *A Brief History of the Hawaiian People*, New York, 1891; Alexander, W. D., *History of Later Years of the Hawaiian Monarchy*, Honolulu, 1896 (which has valuable first-hand material); Carpenter, Edmund Janes, *America in Hawaii*, Boston, 1899; Kuykendall, Ralph S., *A History of Hawaii*, New York, 1926. General reference should also be made to sections on Hawaii in Moore, John Bassett, *Digest of International Law*, I, 475–520; Papers of the Hawaiian Historical Society, and Publications of the Archives of Hawaii.

1. See Dulles, *The Old China Trade*, chap. 5.
2. Boit, John, *Remarks on the Ship Columbia's Voyage from Boston*, Proceedings Massachusetts Historical Society, vol. 53, 1919–20, 262.
3. Townsend, Ebenezer, Jr., *Extract from the Diary of*, Hawaiian Historical Society Reprints, no. 4, 31.
4. Cleveland, Richard J., *A Narrative of Voyages and Commercial Enterprises*, 2 vols., Cambridge, 1842.
5. See Gowen, Herbert H., *The Napoleon of the Pacific*, New York, 1919.
6. Ingraham, Capt. Joseph, *The Log of the Brig Hope*, Hawaiian Historical Society Reprints, no. 3, 25.
7. Townsend, *Extract from Diary of*, 6.
8. Reynolds, J. N., *Voyage of the U.S. Frigate Potomac*, New York, 1835.
9. Hopkins, *Hawaii*, 195.
10. *Ibid.*, 355–56.
11. Morison, Samuel Eliot, 'Boston Traders in Hawaiian Islands, 1789–1823,' *Washington Historical Quarterly*, vol. 12, 1921, 166–201.
12. Simpson, *The Sandwich Islands*, 40.
13. See Paulding, Hiram, *The Cruise of the Dolphin*, New York,

1831; also Foster, *American Diplomacy in the Orient*, 116–17, citing report of Court of Inquiry, Naval Archives.

14. Reynolds, *Voyage of the U.S. Frigate Potomac*, 422.
15. Simpson, Sir George, 'Letters of, 1841–43,' *American Historical Review*, vol. 14, 1908–09, 70–94.
16. Report quoted in Jarves, *History of the Hawaiian or Sandwich Islands*, 266.
17. Hopkins, *Hawaii*, chap. 24. For full exposition of missionary side see report of J. Q. Adams to House of Representatives in 1843 as cited hereafter; article by Richard H. Dana (1860) quoted in Foster, 107–08; and Bingham, Dibble, Jarves.
18. Morison, *Boston Traders in Hawaiian Islands*.
19. Simpson, Sir George, *Letters of*, 90; Simpson, Sir George, *An Overland Journey*, Philadelphia, 1847, 51–52.
20. Jarves, *History of the Hawaiian or Sandwich Islands*, 332; Simpson, Alexander, *The Sandwich Islands*, 108–09, *Foreign Relations, 1894*, Appendix 2, 44.
21. Howay, Judge F. W., *Early Relations with the Pacific Northwest*, Publication of the Archives of Hawaii, no. 5, 38.
22. Simpson, Alexander, *The Sandwich Islands*, 108–09; Wilkes, Charles, *Narrative of the United States Exploring Expedition*, 5 vols., New York, 1831, III, 376.
23. Wilkes, III, 376.
24. Warriner, Francis, *Cruise of the U.S. Frigate Potomac*, 1835, 224, quoted in Morison, *Maritime History of Massachusetts*, 264.
25. Morison, 264.
26. Vancouver, Capt. George, *A Voyage of Discovery to the North Pacific Ocean*, 3 vols., London, 1798, III, 55–57.
27. Alexander, W. D., *The Proceedings of the Russians on Kauai, 1814–1816*, Papers of the Hawaiian Historical Society, no. 6; Golder, Frank A., *Russian Occupation of the Hawaiian Islands*, Publication of the Archives of Hawaii, no. 5; 'Letter of Kamehameha to Alexander I of Russia,' *American Historical Review*, vol. 20, 1914–15, 831–33.
28. Quoted in Blue, George Verne, *The Policy of France Toward the Hawaiian Islands*, Publication of the Archives of Hawaii, no. 5.
29. Jarves, *History of the Hawaiian or Sandwich Islands*, 333.
30. *Foreign Relations, 1894*, Appendix 2, 244.
31. Paullin, Charles Oscar, *Diplomatic Negotiations of American Naval Officers*, Baltimore, 1912, 337–44; for visit of *Vin-*

cennes see Stewart, C. S., *A Visit to the South Seas*, 2 vols., London, 1832, II, 123–36.

32. *Foreign Relations, 1894*, Appendix 2, 44.
33. *Ibid.*, 39.
34. *House Report 93*, 27th Congress, 3d session, 2.
35. *Foreign Relations, 1894*, Appendix 2, 51.
36. *Ibid.*, 113.
37. *Ibid.*, 113.
38. *Ibid.*, 79–85. For treaty text see Malloy, *Treaties, Conventions, etc.*, I, 908–15.
39. *Foreign Relations, 1894*, Appendix 2, 88.
40. *Ibid.*, 89.
41. *Ibid.*, 95.
42. *Ibid.*, 100–02.
43. *Ibid.*, 18.

CHAPTER X

For general sources see notes under Chapter IX

1. *Foreign Relations, 1894*, Appendix 2, 106.
2. Meany, Edmund S., *History of the State of Washington*, New York, 1909, 152.
3. *New York Herald*, June 3, 1854, quoted in Alexander, W. D., *The Uncompleted Treaty of Annexation of 1854*, Papers of the Hawaiian Historical Society, no. 9.
4. *Congressional Globe*, 33d Congress, 1st session, Appendix, 55–58.
5. *Foreign Relations, 1894*, Appendix 2, 122–23.
6. *Ibid.*, 124–29. See also Alexander, *The Uncompleted Treaty of Annexation of 1854*, 31–66.
7. Quoted in *Senate Report 227*, 53d Congress, 2d session, 803.
8. *Foreign Relations, 1894*, Appendix 2, 140–43.
9. Letter of July 5, 1868, to Z. S. Spalding, *ibid.*, 144.
10. *Ibid.*, 146.
11. For treaty see *ibid.*, 164–67; Malloy, *Treaties, Conventions, etc.*, I, 915–17.
12. See De Varigny, C., *Quatorze Ans aux Iles Sandwich*, Paris, 1874.
13. For Schofield report see *American Historical Review*, vol. 30, 1924–25, 560–65.
14. *Foreign Relations, 1894*, Appendix 2, 169 and 1160–62.
15. *Ibid.*, 25.
16. Message of Dec. 6, 1886, quoted in Moore, *Digest of International Law*, I, 491.

17. Hopkins, *Hawaii*, 376.
18. See *ibid.*, chap. 24; Simpson, *The Sandwich Islands*, 15–16; Jarves, *History of the Hawaiian or Sandwich Islands*, 366–72, and Elkin, W. B., 'An Inquiry into the Causes of the Decrease of the Hawaiian People,' *American Journal of Sociology*, vol. 8, 1902, 398–411.
19. Official census quoted in Foster, *American Diplomacy in the Orient*, 366.
20. For history see Alexander, *A Brief History of the Hawaiian People*.
21. Kuykendall, *A History of Hawaii*, 269.
22. For her own explanation of her policies see Liliuokalani, *Hawaii's Story*, Boston, 1898.
23. Tyler, Alice Felt, *The Foreign Policy of James G. Blaine*, Minneapolis, 1927, 216–17.
24. *Foreign Relations, 1894*, Appendix 2, 316–17.
25. *Ibid.*, 354.
26. *Ibid.*, 195.
27. *Ibid.*, 209.
28. *Ibid.*, 211.
29. *Ibid.*, 218. See also Alexander, W. D., *History of Later Years of Hawaiian Monarchy*.
30. For treaty see *Foreign Relations, 1894*, Appendix 2, 202–05.
31. *Ibid.*, 244, 411 *passim*.
32. *Ibid.*, 241–42.
33. *Ibid.*, 5.
34. *Ibid.*, 198.

CHAPTER XI

For general sources see notes under Chapter IX

1. *Foreign Relations, 1894*, Appendix 2, 467.
2. Blount Report, *ibid.*, 467–1151. See also *House Report 243*, 53d Congress, 2d session.
3. *House Report 243*, 59.
4. McElroy, Robert, *Grover Cleveland*, II, 59–61.
5. Gresham, Matilda, *Life of Walter Quintin Gresham*, 2 vols., Chicago, 1919, II, 741.
6. *Foreign Relations, 1894*, Appendix 2, 463.
7. *Ibid.*, 464.
8. *Ibid.*, 465.
9. *Ibid.*, 1242.
10. *Ibid.*, 1282.
11. *Ibid.*, 1284.

12. See for example Woolsey, Theodore Salisbury, 'The Law and the Policy for Hawaii,' *Yale Review*, February, 1894, reprinted in *America's Foreign Policy*, New York, 1898.

13. *Foreign Relations, 1894*, Appendix 2, 445–56.

14. For report, February 26, 1894, see *Senate Report 227*, 53d Congress, 2d session.

15. For defense of Cleveland policy see Gillis, *The Hawaiian Incident*; for defense of Stevens see Young, *The Real Hawaii*.

16. *Foreign Relations, 1894*, Appendix 2, 1355.

17. *Boston Herald*, January 30, 1893, quoted in *Senate Report 227*, 171.

18. Mahan, Alfred Thayer, *The Interest of America in Sea Power* (collection of magazine articles), Boston, 1898, 22.

19. *Ibid.*, 48–49.

20. Foster, John W., *Annexation of Hawaii* (pamphlet), Washington, 1897, 14.

21. Quoted in Millis, Walter, *The Martial Spirit*, Boston, 1931, 27, 30. See also such propaganda as Thurston, Lorrin A., *A Handbook on the Annexation of Hawaii*, 1897.

22. For text see *Senate Report 681*, 55th Congress, 2d session, 96–97.

23. *Ibid.*, 65–67.

24. See Bailey, Thomas A., 'Japan's Protest Against the Annexation of Hawaii,' *The Journal of Modern History*, vol. 3, 1931; Dennis, Alfred L. P., *Adventures in American Diplomacy*, New York, 1928, chap. 4.

25. Sherman to Sewell, July 10, 1897, quoted from Department of State Archives in Bailey, *Japan's Protest Against the Annexation of Hawaii*, 50.

26. Hoar, George F., *Autobiography of Seventy Years*, 2 vols., New York, 1905, II, 307–08.

27. *Senate Report 681*, 55th Congress, 2d session.

28. *Ibid.*, 15.

29. *Ibid.*, 27–39.

30. For debates see *Congressional Record*, 55th Congress, 2d session, vol. 31, 1898, 5770, 5973, 6140, 6693 *passim*, but more conveniently Miller, Marion M., *Great Debates in American History*, III, New York, 1913.

31. Miller, III, 207–08.

32. *Ibid.*, 237

33. See Bailey, Thomas A., 'The United States and Hawaii During the Spanish-American War,' *American Historical Review*, vol. 36, 1931.

34. Olcott, Charles S., *The Life of William McKinley*, 2 vols., Boston, 1916, I, 379.
35. See 30 *Statutes at Large*, 750, and for organic act of Hawaiian Territory, 31 *Statutes at Large*, 141.
36. McElroy, *Grover Cleveland*, II, 73.

CHAPTER XII

The basic material for this and the two following chapters is to be found in *Foreign Relations, 1898*; *Message and Documents, 1898–99*, 4 vols., 1899; *Appendix to the Report of the Chief of the Bureau of Navigation, Navy Department*, 1898; *Correspondence Relating to the War with Spain*, 2 vols., Washington, 1902 (affairs in the Philippine Islands, vol. 2); *Report of the Philippine Commission to the President*, 4 vols., Washington, 1900; *Senate Document 62*, 55th Congress, 3d session; *Senate Document 208*, 56th Congress, 1st session; *Senate Document 331*, 57th Congress, 1st session (3 parts). See also Dewey, George, *Autobiography*, New York, 1913; Roosevelt, Theodore, *An Autobiography*, New York, 1919; *Selections from the Correspondence of Theodore Roosevelt and Henry Cabot Lodge*, 2 vols., New York, 1925.

General secondary sources include: Alger, R. A., *The Spanish American War*, New York, 1901; Blount, James H., *The American Occupation of the Philippines*, New York, 1912; Chadwick, French Ensor, *The Relations of the United States and Spain*, 3 vols., New York, 1909–11; Coolidge, Archibald Cary, *The United States as a World Power*, New York, 1908; Elliott, Charles Burke, *The Philippines to the End of the Military Régime*, Indianapolis, 1917; Fernandez, Leandro H., *The Philippine Republic*, Studies in History, Economics and Public Law, Columbia University, vol. 122, New York, 1926; Fish, Carl Russell, *The Path of Empire*, New Haven, 1919; Forbes, W. Cameron, *The Philippine Islands*, 2 vols., Boston, 1928; Kalaw, Teodoro M., *The Philippine Revolution*, Manila, 1925; Latané, John Holladay, *America as a World Power*, New York, 1907; Leroy, James A., *The Americans in the Philippines*, 2 vols., Boston, 1914; Lodge, Henry Cabot, *The War with Spain*, New York, 1899; Long, John D., *The New American Navy*, 2 vols., New York, 1903; Millis, Walter, *The Martial Spirit*, Boston, 1931; Olcott, Charles S., *The Life of William McKinley*, 2 vols., Boston, 1916; Peck, Harry Thurston, *Twenty Years of the Republic*, New York, 1906; Reinsch, Paul S., *World Politics at the End of the Nineteenth Century*, New York, 1916; Rhodes, James Ford, *The McKinley and*

Roosevelt Administrations, New York, 1922; Storey, Moorfield, and Lichanco, Marcial P., *The Conquest of the Philippines by the United States*, New York, 1926; Wilson, H. W., *The Downfall of Spain*, Boston, 1900; Worcester, Dean C., *The Philippines Past and Present*, 2 vols., New York, 1914.

1. King to Gerry, June 4, 1786, Massachusetts Historical Society Proceedings, 1866, 9–12, quoted in Fish, Carl Russell, *American Diplomacy*, New York, 1923, 417.
2. Dennett, *Americans in Eastern Asia*, 33; Morison, *Maritime History of Massachusetts*, 94.
3. Morrell, Capt. Benjamin, Jun., *A Narrative of Four Voyages*, New York, 1853, 383–84.
4. Officer's letter in *National Intelligencer*, Washington, July 29, 1820, quoted in Paullin, *Diplomatic Negotiations of American Naval Officers*, 180–81.
5. Paine, Ralph D., *The Ships and Sailors of Old Salem*, New York, 1909, 411; Peabody, Robert E., *Merchant Venturers of Old Salem*, Boston, 1912, 117.
6. Wilkes, *Narrative of the United States Exploring Expedition*, V, 283–93.
7. Leroy, *The Americans in the Philippines*, I, 32 n.
8. *Ibid.*, 71.
9. See Powers, H. H., *The War as a Suggestion of Manifest Destiny*, Publication of American Academy of Political and Social Science, vol. 235, Philadelphia, 1898.
10. Roosevelt, *An Autobiography*, 231–32; also Bishop, Joseph Bucklin, *Theodore Roosevelt and His Time*, 2 vols., New York, 1920, I, 83.
11. Dewey, *Autobiography*, 145–46.
12. *Ibid.*, 167–69; also, for denial of this account of appointment, Long, *The New American Navy*, I, 177.
13. Dewey, *Autobiography*, 175.
14. *Bureau of Navigation*, 65.
15. *Ibid.*, 67.
16. As quoted in Leroy, *The Americans in the Philippines*, 155.
17. For accounts of battle of Manila Bay see *Bureau of Navigation* reports and Dewey, *Autobiography*, but also Chadwick, *The Relations of the United States and Spain*, and Millis, *The Martial Spirit*, for vivid summaries.
18. *Selections from Correspondence of Roosevelt and Lodge*, I, 299.
19. *Bureau of Navigation*, 97–98; *Correspondence Relating to the*

War with Spain, 635; Alger, *The Spanish-American War*, 326.

20. *Correspondence Relating to the War with Spain*, 676.
21. *Senate Document 62*, 55th Congress, 3d session, 334.
22. *Ibid.*, 341–45.
23. See proclamation, January 5, 1899, in *Senate Document 208*, 56th Congress, 1st session, 104. Able discussion of United States-Filipino relations based upon both American sources and Aguinaldo's *Reseña Verédica* (printed in *Congressional Record*, vol. 35, 1899, Part 8, 440) may be found in Leroy, *The Americans in the Philippines*, 178–88.
24. *Senate Document 331*, 57th Congress, 1st session, 2932.
25. *Ibid.*, 2950–55; Dewey, *Autobiography*, 248.
26. Quoted in Dewey, *Autobiography*, 312.
27. *Senate Document 62*, 55th Congress, 3d session, 341–45.
28. *Ibid.*, 338.
29. *Ibid.*, 328.
30. *Bureau of Navigation*, 100.
31. *Ibid.*, 101.
32. *Ibid.*, 103; *Senate Document 62*, 353.
33. *Bureau of Navigation*, 103; Dewey, *Autobiography*, 312.
34. *Bureau of Navigation*, 109; Dewey, *Autobiography*, 259.
35. Dewey, *Autobiography*, chap. 17. Von Diedrichs's reply in *Marina Rundschau*, March, 1914. See Dennis, *Adventures in American Diplomacy*, 90, who says Dewey's chapter toned down.
36. *Correspondence Relating to the War with Spain*, 713.
37. *Bureau of Navigation*, 152–53. Also eye-witness account in Davis, Oscar King, *Our Conquests in the Pacific*, New York, 1899.
38. *Correspondence Relating to the War with Spain*, 778, 781.
39. Article in the *North American Review*, quoted in *Senate Document 331*, 57th Congress, 1st session, 2978–79.
40. Dewey, *Autobiography*, 248.
41. *Senate Document 208*, 56th Congress, 1st session, 4 ff.
42. *Correspondence Relating to the War with Spain*, 812; *Senate Document 208*, 14.
43. Report of Major General Merritt, *House Document 2*, 55th Congress, 3d session, 48.
44. *Senate Document 331*, 57th Congress, 1st session, 2943 ff. See also Dewey, *Autobiography*.
45. *Correspondence Relating to the War with Spain*, 754; *Bureau of Navigation*, 124.

46. *Senate Document 208,* 56th Congress, 1st session, 22.
47. *Ibid.,* 85.
48. *Foreign Relations, 1898,* 829.

CHAPTER XIII

For general sources see notes under Chapter XII

1. Denby, Charles, Jr., 'America's Opportunity in Asia,' *North American Review,* vol. 166, January, 1898, 36. See also Conant, Charles A., *The United States in the Orient,* Boston, 1901.
2. See Morse, Hosea Ballou, and MacNair, Harley Farnsworth, *Far Eastern International Relations,* Shanghai, 1928, 611–25.
3. Seward, William H., *Works of,* III, 409. For an interpretation of Seward's ideas at end of century see Bancroft, Frederic, 'Seward's Ideas of Territorial Expansion,' *North American Review,* vol. 167, July, 1898.
4. *Correspondence of Roosevelt and Lodge,* I, 300.
5. *Ibid.,* 309–11.
6. Quoted in Miller, *Great Debates in American History,* III, 211.
7. *Literary Digest,* vol. 16, 1898, 573.
8. *North American Review,* June, 1898, quoted in *ibid.,* 697.
9. *Ibid.,* vol. 17, 1898, 91.
10. *Ibid.,* 92.
11. Bülow to Holleben, *Die Grosse Politik,* XV, 44–45, quoted in Townsend, *The Rise and Fall of Germany's Colonial Empire,* 194.
12. For German intrigues, etc., see Shippee, Lester Burrell, 'Germany and the Spanish American War,' *American Historical Review,* vol. 30, 1925, 764–77; Townsend, *The Rise and Fall of Germany's Colonial Empire,* 192–95; Keim, *Forty Years of German-American Political Relations,* 221 ff.; White, Andrew D., *Autobiography,* 2 vols., 1905; and especially, because based upon State Department Archives and the Hay Papers as well as German and other sources, Dennis, *Adventures in American Diplomacy,* 76–86.
13. Hay to Lodge, Hay Papers, *ibid.,* 98.
14. Hay to Day, *ibid.,* 100.
15. *Die Grosse Politik,* XV, 75–77, in Townsend, *The Rise and Fall of Germany's Colonial Empire,* 195.
16. In *New York Times,* October 20, 1900, quoted in Reyes,

José S., *Legislative History of America's Economic Policy Toward the Philippines*, Studies in History, Economics and Public Law, Columbia University, vol. 106, no. 2, New York, 1923, 68.

17. Annual Message of 1897.
18. For foreign opinion see Viallate, Achille, 'Les Préliminaires de la Guerre Hispano-Américain,' *Revue Historique*, 1903, 281.
19. *Correspondence Relating to the War with Spain*, 635; Alger, *The Spanish-American War*, 326.
20. Day to Hay, June 3, 1898, Hay Papers, in Dennis, *Adventures in American Diplomacy*, 99.
21. Day to Hay, June 14, *ibid.*, 99.
22. *Correspondence of Roosevelt and Lodge*, I, 311.
23. *Ibid.*, 323.
24. *Ibid.*, 330.
25. Olcott, *The Life of William McKinley*, II, 62.
26. *New York Times*, July 31, 1898, quoted in Reyes, *Legislative History of America's Economic Policy Toward the Philippines*, 38.
27. Olcott, II, 63.
28. *Foreign Relations, 1898*, 821.
29. For protocol, *ibid.*, 829.
30. Olcott, II, 63.
31. *Bureau of Navigation*, 123.
32. *Correspondence of Roosevelt and Lodge*, I, 313.
33. Quoted in *Literary Digest*, vol. 17, August 27, 1898, 242.
34. *Ibid.*, September 10, 307–08.
35. See Mahan, Alfred Thayer, *Lessons of the War with Spain*, Boston, 1899.
36. *Correspondence of Roosevelt and Lodge*, I, 337.
37. *Century*, August, 1898, quoted in *Senate Document 62*, 55th Congress, 3d session, 563–71.
38. *Literary Digest*, August 27, 242.
39. *Senate Document 62*, 330.
40. *Ibid.*, 331–32.
41. Dodsworth, W., *Our Industrial Position and our Policy in the Pacific*, New York, 1898, 13.
42. *Literary Digest*, September 3, 1898, 290.
43. Cortissoz, Royal, *The Life of Whitelaw Reid*, 2 vols., New York, 1921, II, 224.
44. *Foreign Relations, 1898*, 907–08.
45. *Ibid.*, 920–21, 928; *Senate Document 62*, 477–87.

46. *Foreign Relations, 1898*, 932–33.
47. *Ibid.*, 934.
48. *Ibid.*, 935.
49. Quoted in *Literary Digest*, October 22, 1898, 509.
50. Olcott, II, 108.
51. *Foreign Relations, 1898*, 935.
52. Quoted from *Christian Advocate*, January 22, 1903, in Olcott, II, 108.
53. Moon, Parker T., *Imperialism and World Politics*, 394–95.
54. Olcott, II, 165.
55. *Foreign Relations, 1898*, 937–38.
56. *Ibid.*, 831–40.

CHAPTER XIV

For general sources see under Chapter XII

1. The literature on the issue of imperialism is voluminous. Among the more important anti-imperialist pamphlets are: Sumner, William G., *The Conquest of the United States by Spain*; Schurz, Carl, *American Imperialism*; Adams, Charles Francis, '*Imperialism' and 'The Tracks of Our Forefathers'*; Schurz, Carl, *The Policy of Imperialism*; Hoar, George F., *Cuba and the Philippines*; Boutwell, George S., *The President's Policy*; Storey, Moorfield, *Is It Right?* For two contrasting points of view see Pettigrew, R. F., *The Course of Empire*, New York, 1920, and Reid, Whitelaw, *Problems of Expansion*, New York, 1900.
2. Quoted in *Literary Digest*, vol. 17, 1898, 3.
3. Congressional debates on Philippine question are scattered throughout pages of *Congressional Record*, 55th Congress, 1st session, 1898–99, but abstracts are more conveniently found in Miller, *Great Debates in American History*, vol. 3. For quotation noted see Miller, III, 260.
4. *Ibid.*, 318.
5. Carnegie, Andrew, *The Autobiography of*, Boston, 1920, 364.
6. *Literary Digest*, vol. 17, 1898, 739–40.
7. *Correspondence Relating to the War with Spain*, 859; *Senate Document 208*, 56th Congress, 1st session, 82.
8. See analysis of votes in Reyes, *Legislative History of America's Economic Policy toward the Philippines*, 12–45. See also Hibben, Paxton, *The Peerless Leader*, New York, 1929, 221–22.
9. See *Correspondence of Roosevelt and Lodge*.

10. See *Senate Document 182*, 57th Congress, 1st session.
11. *Correspondence Relating to the War with Spain*, 836.
12. Dewey, *Autobiography*, 284.
13. *Correspondence Relating to the War with Spain*, 859 ff.
14. *Ibid.*, 873.
15. *Senate Document 208*, 56th Congress, 1st session, 102–04
16. *Correspondence Relating to the War with Spain*, 893.
17. *Senate Document 208*, 106.
18. *Correspondence Relating to the War with Spain*, 898, 978.
19. *Ibid.*, 898–1351.
20. *Senate Document 208*, 151–52; also see *Report of the Philippine Commission to the President.*
21. Olcott, II, 175.
22. Bancroft, Frederic, *Life of Schurz*, III, 446, quoted in Elliott, *The Philippines to the End of the Military Régime*, 460.
23. See Sullivan, Mark, *Our Times, I, The Turn of the Century*, New York, 1926, 4–7.
24. *Correspondence Relating to the War with Spain*; Funston, Frederick, *Memories of Two Wars*, New York, 1911.
25. *Congressional Record*, 56th Congress, 1st session, vol. 33; 1900, 704.
26. *Ibid.*, 712.

INDEX

71
72
74
75
76
77
79
81
83
85
88